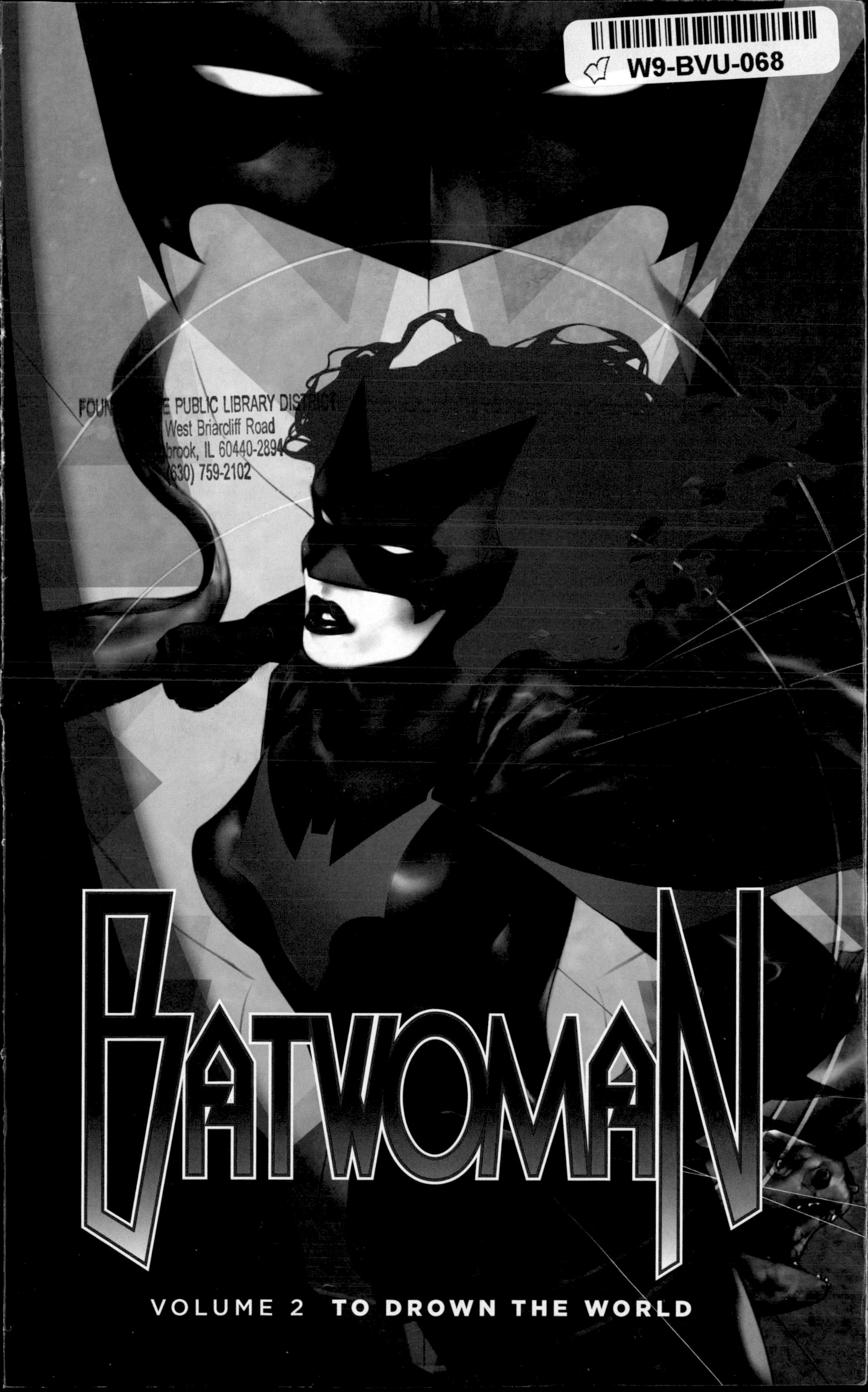
BATWOMAN
VOLUME 2 TO DROWN THE WORLD

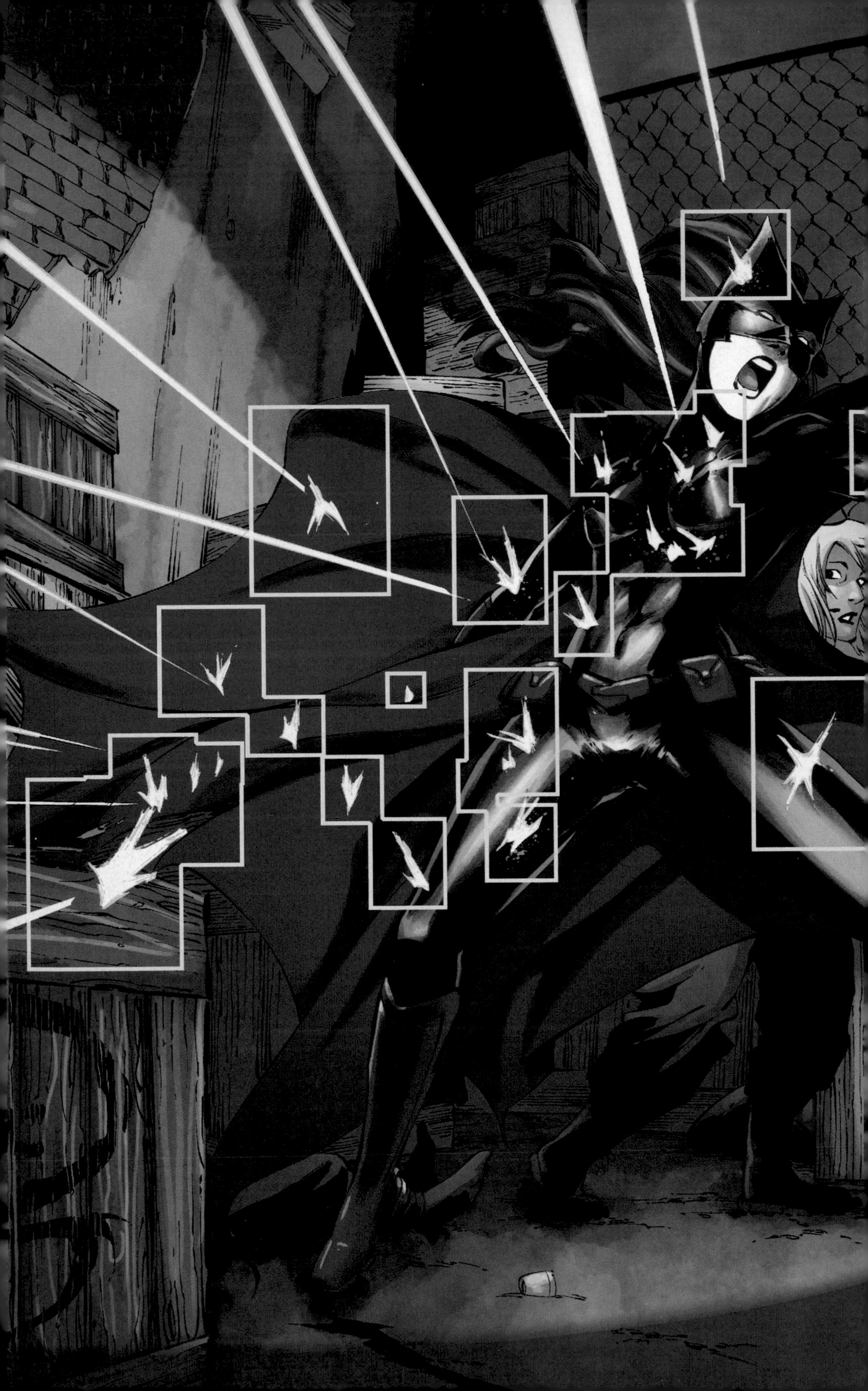

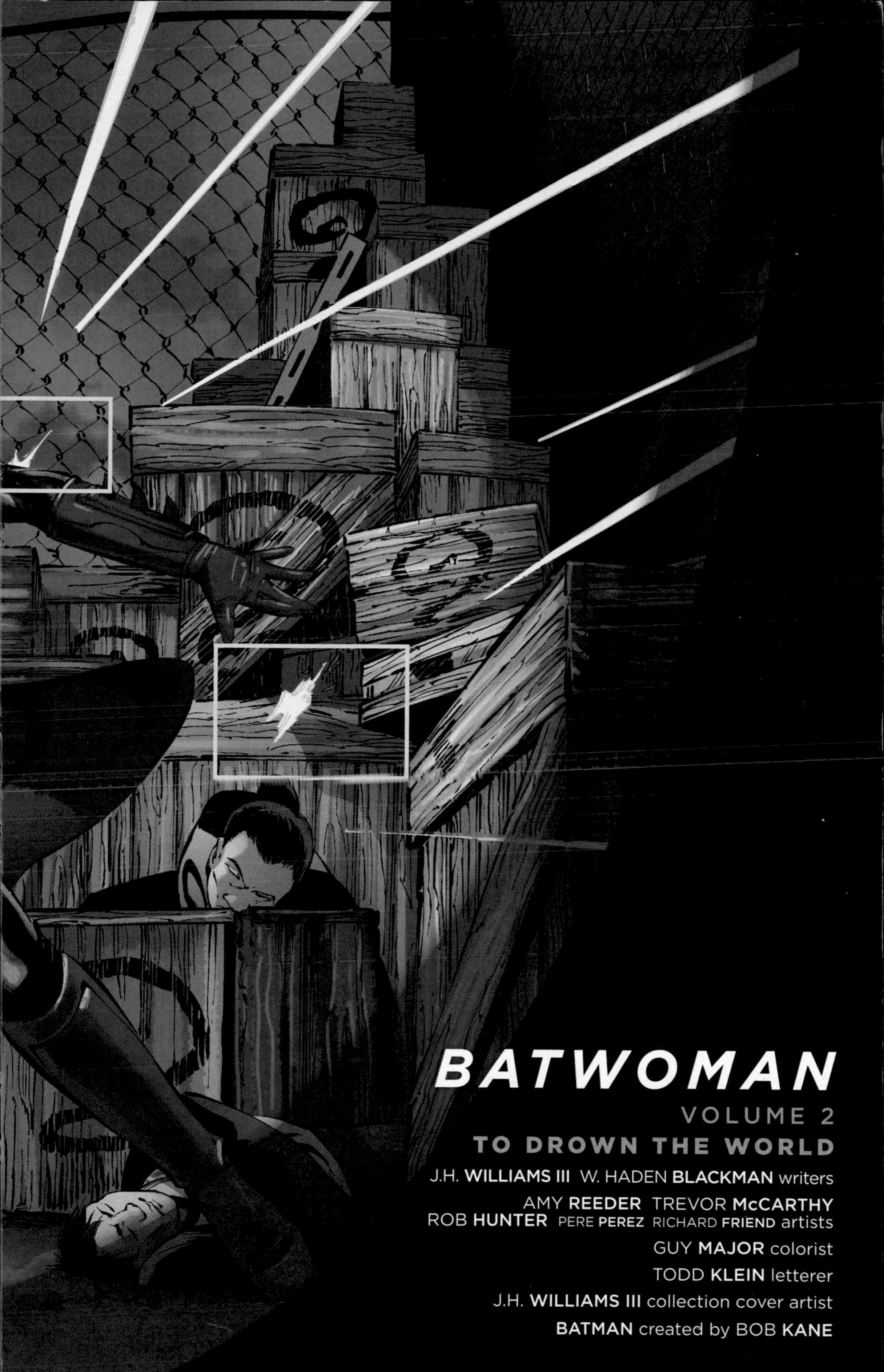

BATWOMAN

VOLUME 2

TO DROWN THE WORLD

J.H. **WILLIAMS III** W. HADEN **BLACKMAN** writers

AMY **REEDER** TREVOR **McCARTHY**
ROB **HUNTER** PERE **PEREZ** RICHARD **FRIEND** artists

GUY **MAJOR** colorist

TODD **KLEIN** letterer

J.H. **WILLIAMS III** collection cover artist

BATMAN created by BOB **KANE**

MIKE MARTS Editor – Original Series HARVEY RICHARDS Associate Editor – Original Series
RICKEY PURDIN Assistant Editor– Original Series PETER HAMBOUSSI Editor
ROBBIN BRÖSTERMAN Design Director – Books ROBBIE BIEDERMAN Pubication Design

BOB HARRAS Senior VP – Editor-in-Chief, DC Comics

DIANE NELSON President DAN DIDIO and JIM LEE Co-Publishers
GEOFF JOHNS Chief Creative Officer AMIT DESAI Senior VP – Marketing & Franchise Management
AMY GENKINS Senior VP – Business & Legal Affairs NAIRI GARDINER Senior VP – Finance
JEFF BOISON VP – Publishing Planning MARK CHIARELLO VP – Art Direction & Design
JOHN CUNNINGHAM VP – Marketing TERRI CUNNINGHAM VP – Editorial Administration
LARRY GANEM VP – Talent Relations & Services ALISON GILL Senior VP – Manufacturing & Operations
HANK KANALZ Senior VP – Vertigo & Integrated Publishing JAY KOGAN VP – Business & Legal Affairs, Publishing
JACK MAHAN VP – Business Affairs, Talent NICK NAPOLITANO VP – Manufacturing Administration
SUE POHJA VP – Book Sales FRED RUIZ VP – Manufacturing Operations
COURTNEY SIMMONS Senior VP – Publicity BOB WAYNE Senior VP – Sales

BATWOMAN VOLUME TWO: TO DROWN THE WORLD

DC Comics, 1700 Broadway, New York, NY 10019
A Warner Bros. Entertainment Company.
Printed by RR Donnelley, Salem, VA, USA. 9/19/14. Second Printing.

HC ISBN: 978-1-4012-3790-5
SC ISBN: 978-1-4012-3792-9

SUSTAINABLE FORESTRY INITIATIVE
Certified Chain of Custody
20% Certified Forest Content,
80% Certified Sourcing
www.sfiprogram.org
SFI-01042
APPLIES TO TEXT STOCK ONLY

Library of Congress Cataloging-in-Publication Data

Williams, J. H., III.
Batwoman. Volume 2, To drown the world / J.H. Williams III, W. Haden Blackman, Amy Reeder, Trevor McCarthy.
p. cm.
"Originally published in single magazine form in Batwoman 6-11."
ISBN 978-1-4012-3792-9
1. Graphic novels. I. Blackman, W. Haden. II. Hadley, Amy Reeder, 1980- III. McCarthy, Trevor. IV. Title. V. Title: To drown the world.
PN6728.B365W56 2012
741.5'973—dc23
2012032148

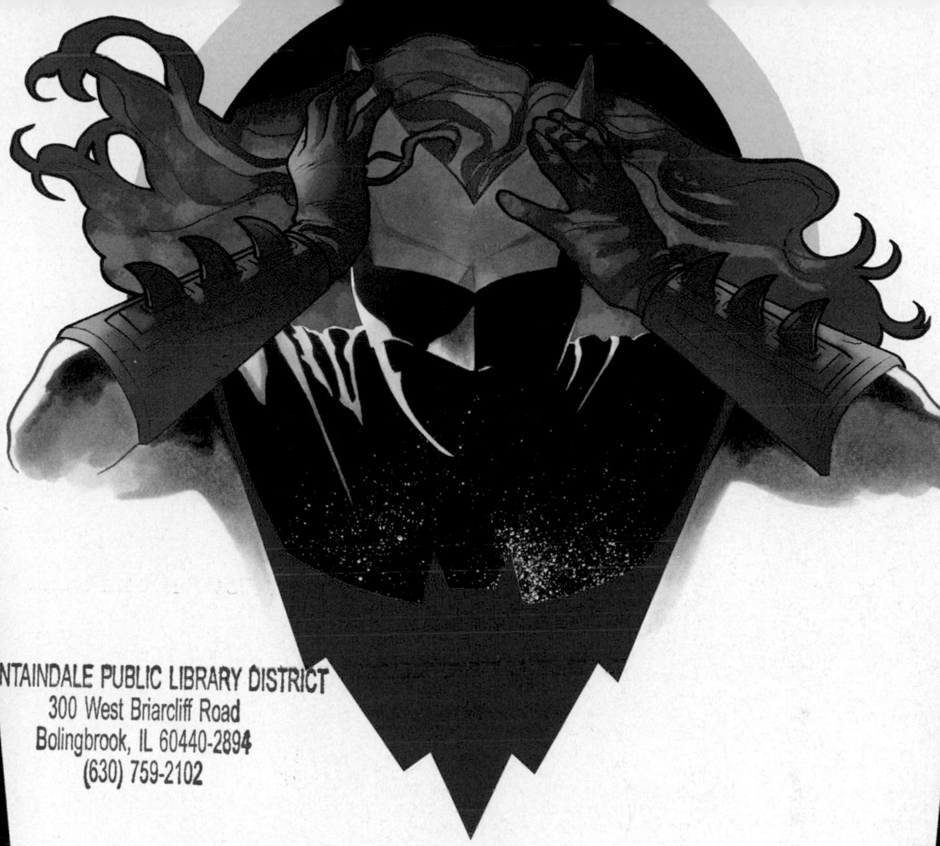

STORY SO FAR

Kate Kane survived a brutal kidnapping by terrorists that left her mother dead and her twin sister lost.

Following in her father's footsteps, she vowed to serve her country and attended West Point until she was expelled under "Don't Ask, Don't Tell."

Now she is many things: estranged daughter, grieving sister, proud lesbian, brave soldier, determined hero.

She is BATWOMAN.

And she is alone.

Batwoman shut her father out of her life when she learned he'd hidden the truth about her sister, Beth, believed dead for years—who'd instead had been brainwashed by the fanatical Religion of Crime, returning to Gotham as a psychotic killer now called Alice.

She has lost her young cousin, protégé and partner, Bette Kane, a.k.a. Flamebird, to a monstrous, hook-handed killer. The teen hero now clings to life in a hospital bed.

She has rejected the Batman's offer to join his international crimefighting organization, Batman, Incorporated—and been blackmailed by Director Bones of the U.S. Department of Extranormal Operations into becoming the D.E.O.'s agent in Gotham.

She has earned the love of Gotham City Police Detective Maggie Sawyer—but this by-the-book cop wants Kate Kane's vigilante alter ego taken down.

And though she has defeated La Llorona—the seemingly supernatural Weeping Woman responsible for a rash of kidnappings and murders across Gotham—she has not rescued the children from her watery embrace.

She is left with only one clue: MEDUSA, an international crime conspiracy with monsters in its service and Gotham City in its crosshairs...

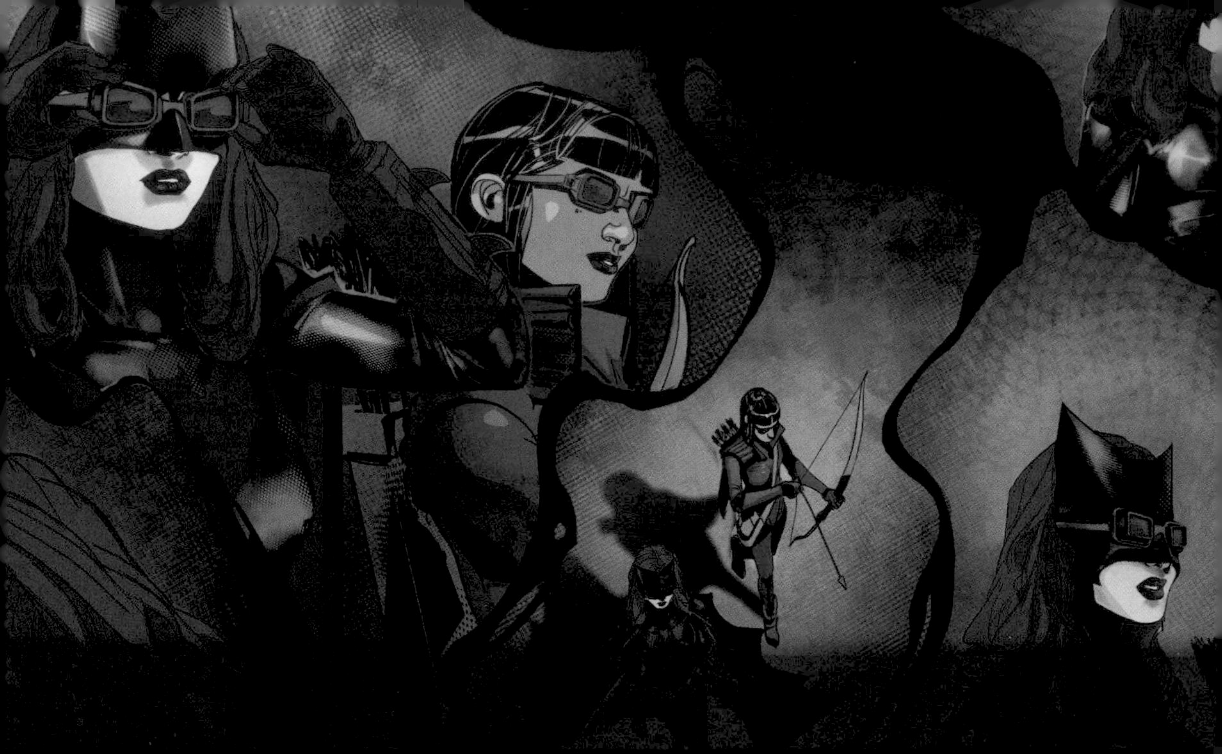

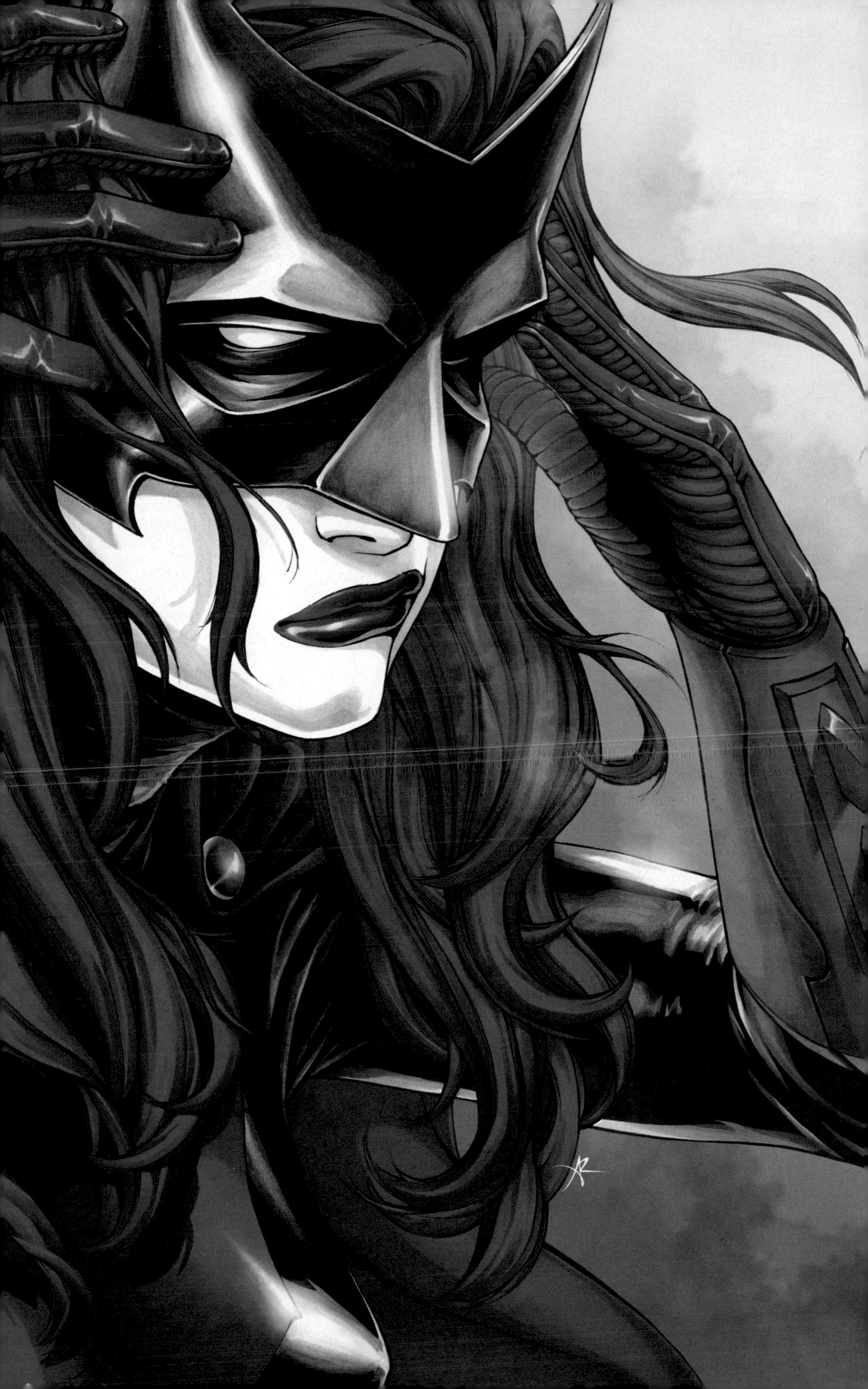

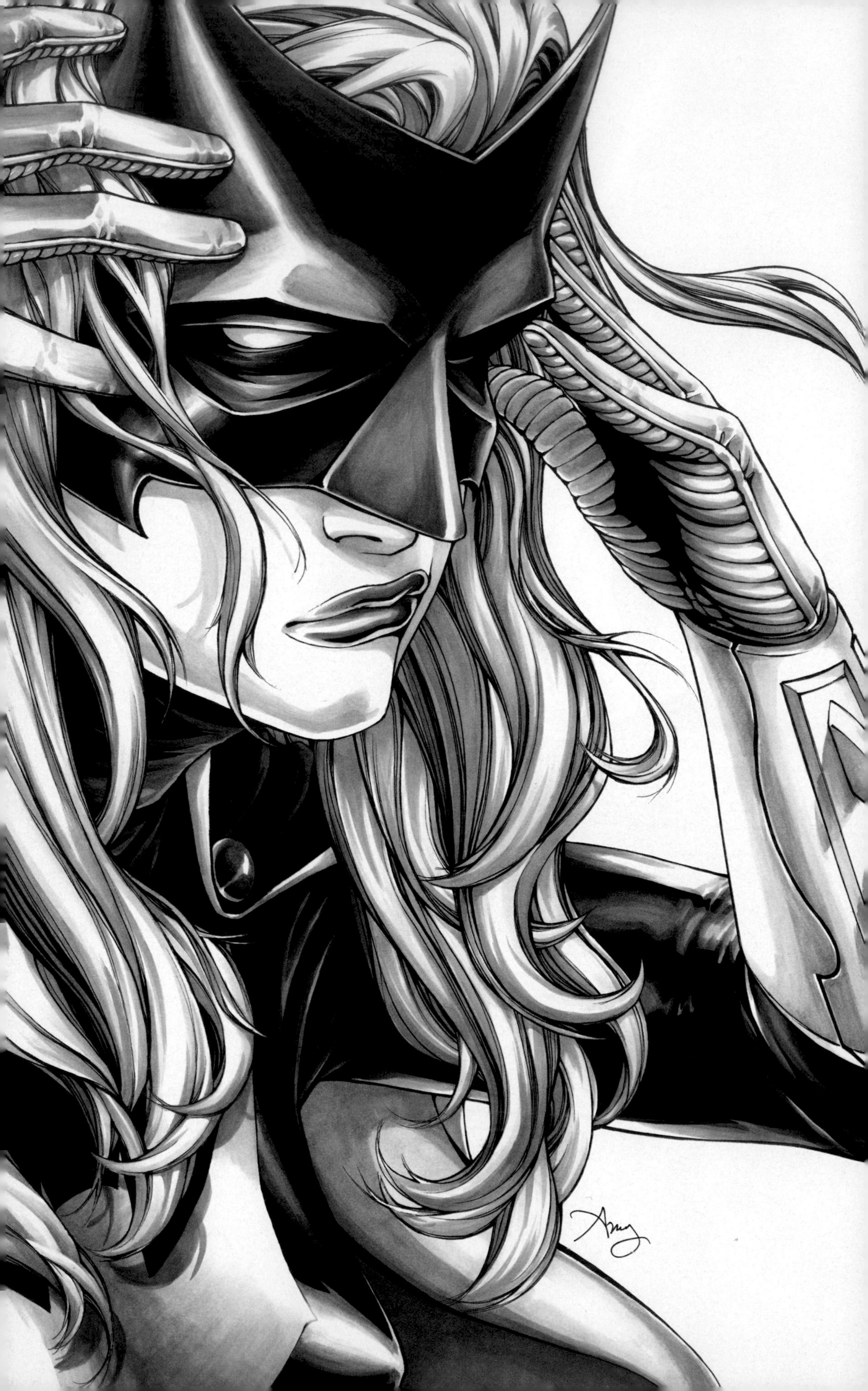

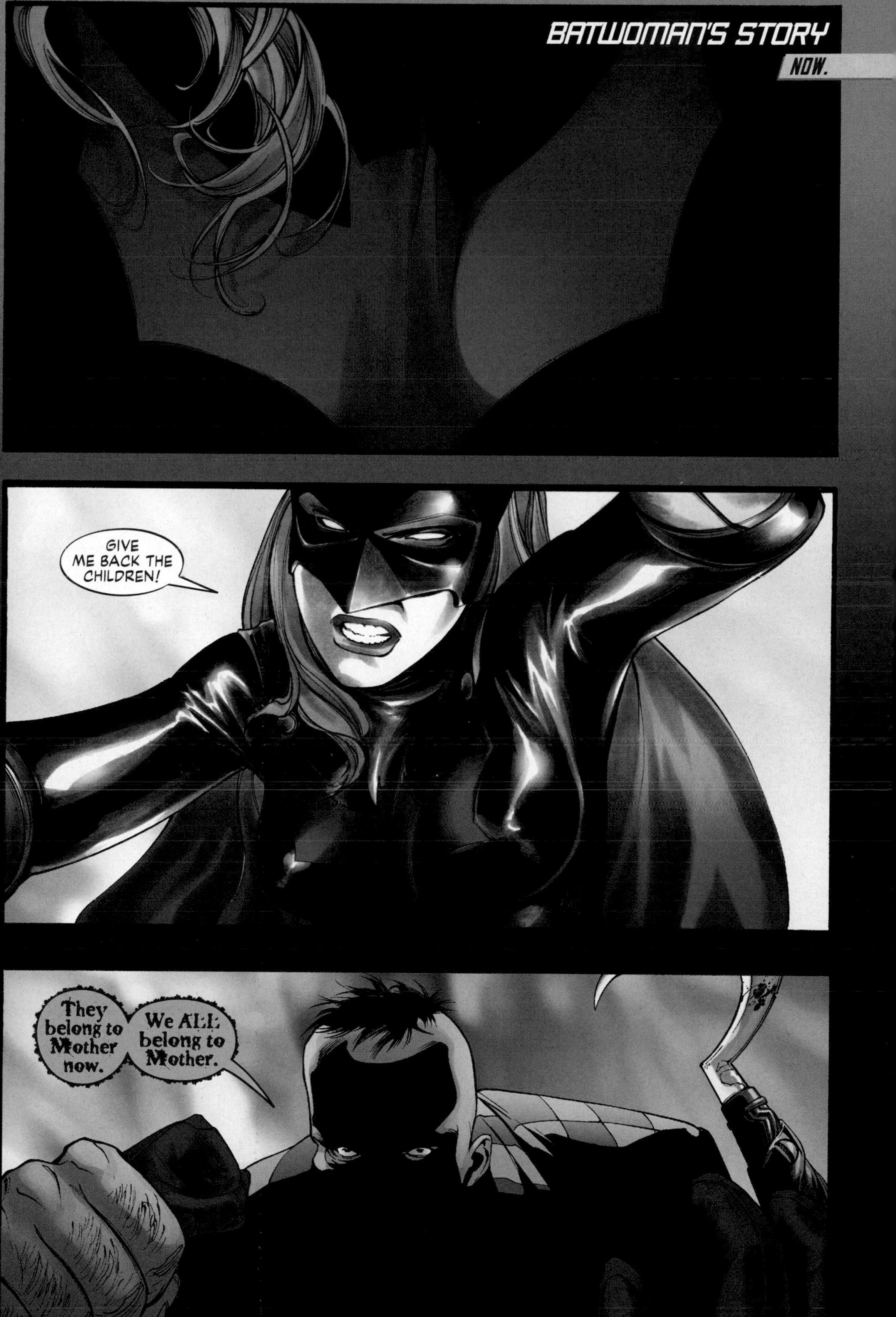
BATWOMAN'S STORY
NOW.
GIVE ME BACK THE CHILDREN!
They belong to Mother now.
We ALL belong to Mother.

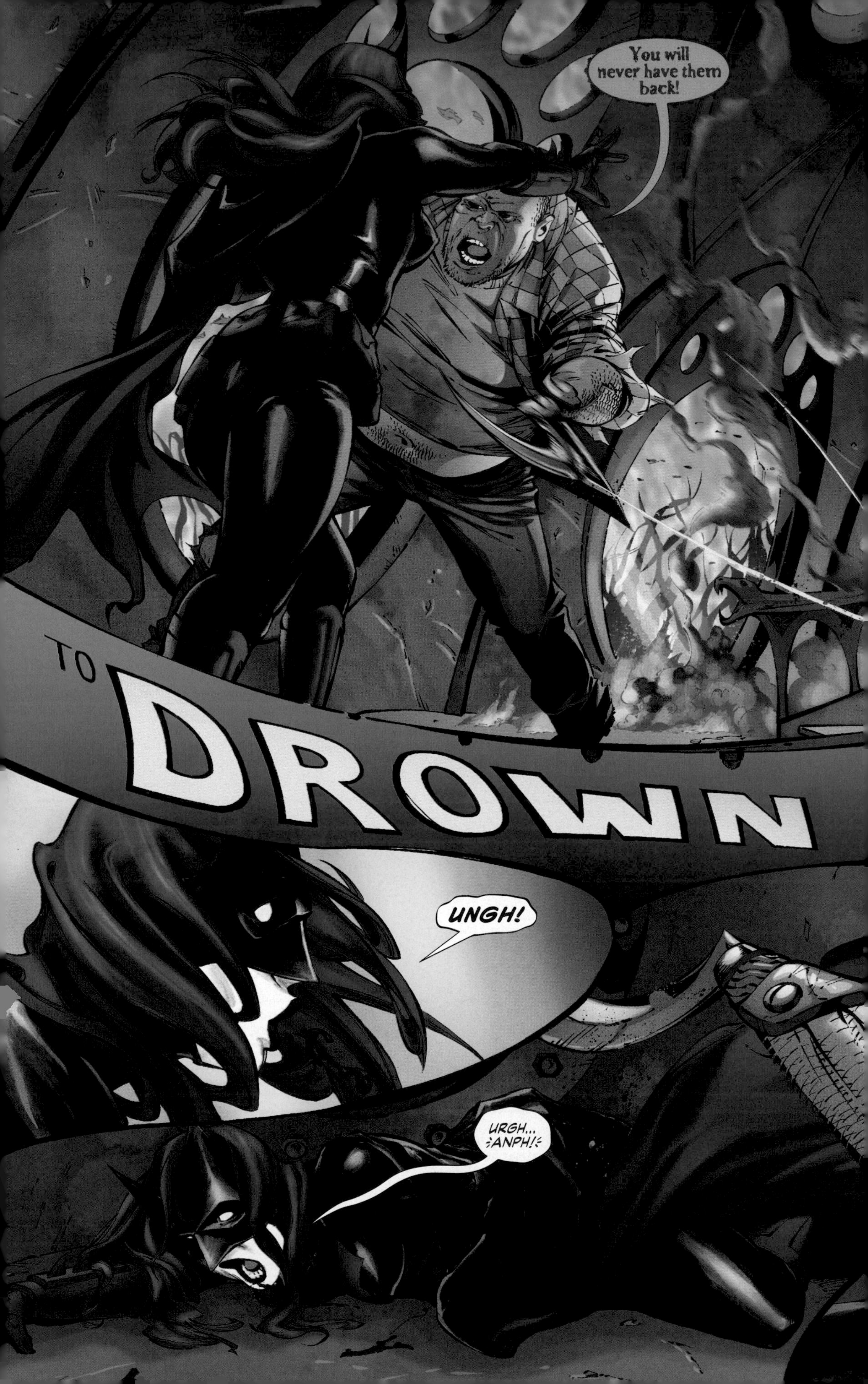
You will never have them back!
TO DROWN
UNGH!
URGH... ANPH!

J.H. WILLIAMS III &
W. HADEN BLACKMAN
writers

AMY
REEDER
penciller & cover

ROB HUNTER &
RICHARD FRIEND
inkers

GUY
MAJOR
colorist

TODD
KLEIN
letterer

HARVEY RICHARDS
associate editor

RICKEY PURDIN
asst. editor

MIKE MARTS
editor

THE WORLD

PART ONE

Let's see
what you've got
inside.

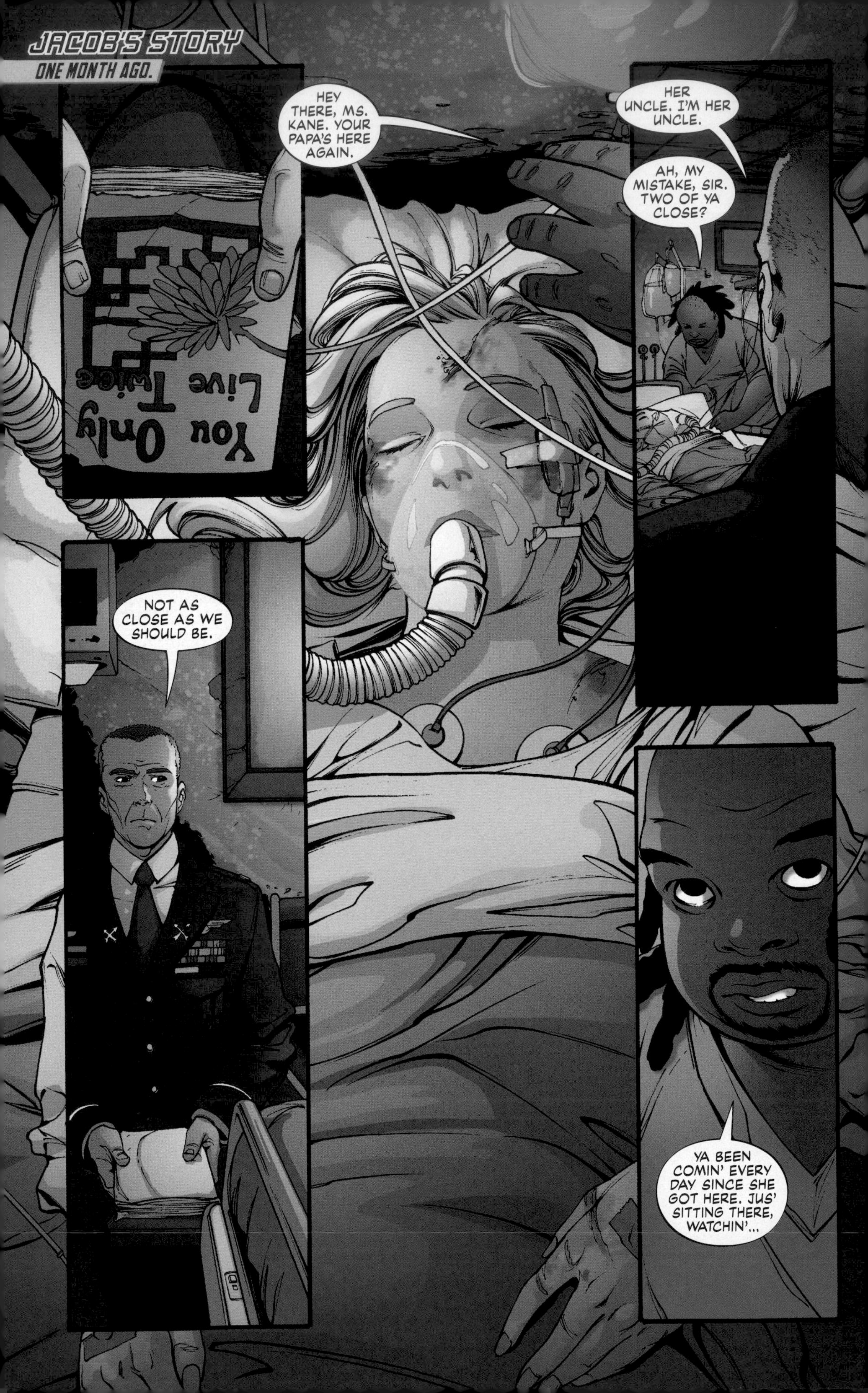
JACOB'S STORY
ONE MONTH AGO.
You Only Live Twice
HEY THERE, MS. KANE. YOUR PAPA'S HERE AGAIN.
HER UNCLE. I'M HER UNCLE.
AH, MY MISTAKE, SIR. TWO OF YA CLOSE?
NOT AS CLOSE AS WE SHOULD BE.
YA BEEN COMIN' EVERY DAY SINCE SHE GOT HERE. JUS' SITTING THERE, WATCHIN'...

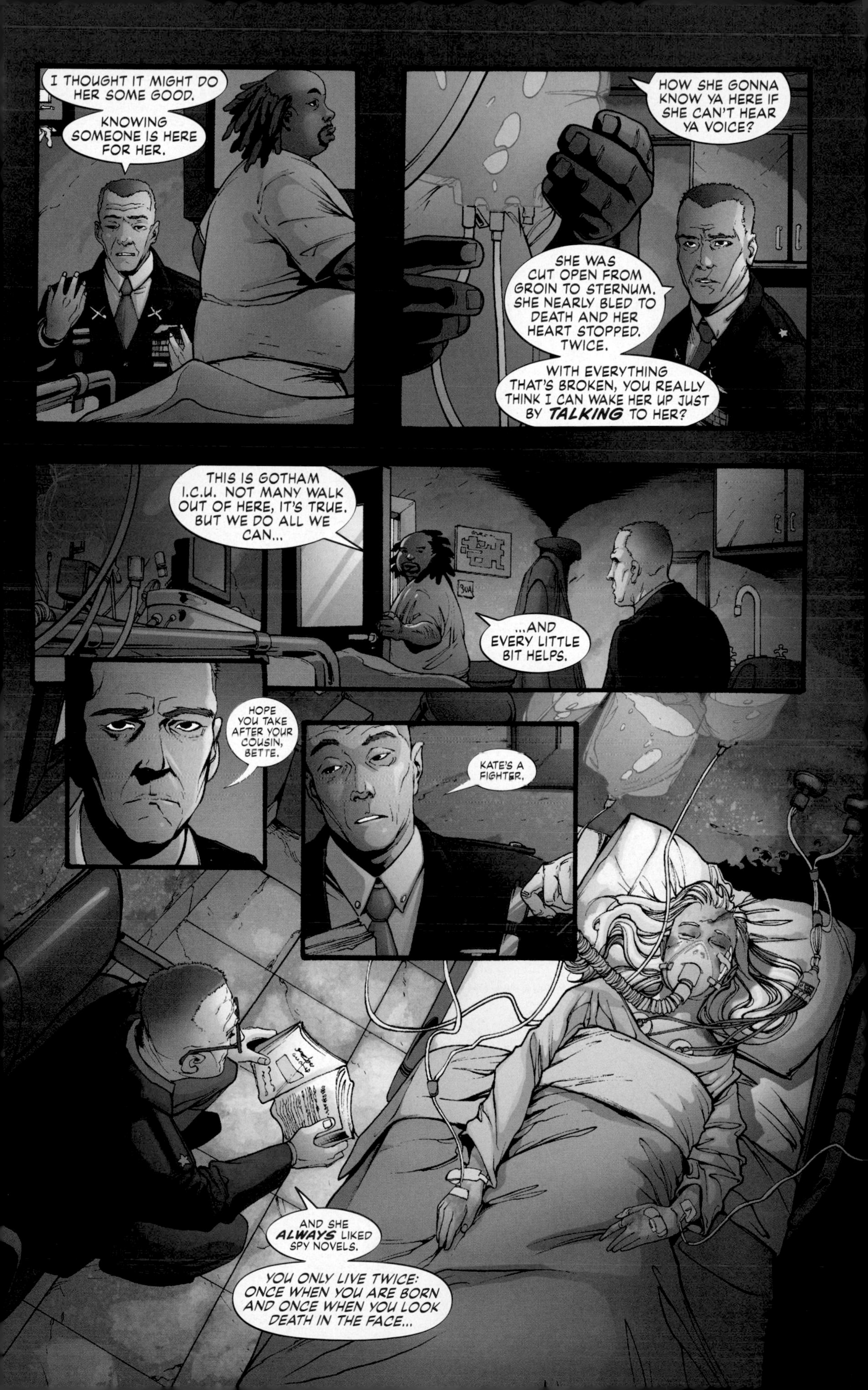
I THOUGHT IT MIGHT DO HER SOME GOOD.
KNOWING SOMEONE IS HERE FOR HER.
HOW SHE GONNA KNOW YA HERE IF SHE CAN'T HEAR YA VOICE?
SHE WAS CUT OPEN FROM GROIN TO STERNUM. SHE NEARLY BLED TO DEATH AND HER HEART STOPPED. TWICE.
WITH EVERYTHING THAT'S BROKEN, YOU REALLY THINK I CAN WAKE HER UP JUST BY TALKING TO HER?
THIS IS GOTHAM I.C.U. NOT MANY WALK OUT OF HERE, IT'S TRUE. BUT WE DO ALL WE CAN...
...AND EVERY LITTLE BIT HELPS.
HOPE YOU TAKE AFTER YOUR COUSIN, BETTE.
KATE'S A FIGHTER.
AND SHE ALWAYS LIKED SPY NOVELS.
YOU ONLY LIVE TWICE: ONCE WHEN YOU ARE BORN AND ONCE WHEN YOU LOOK DEATH IN THE FACE...

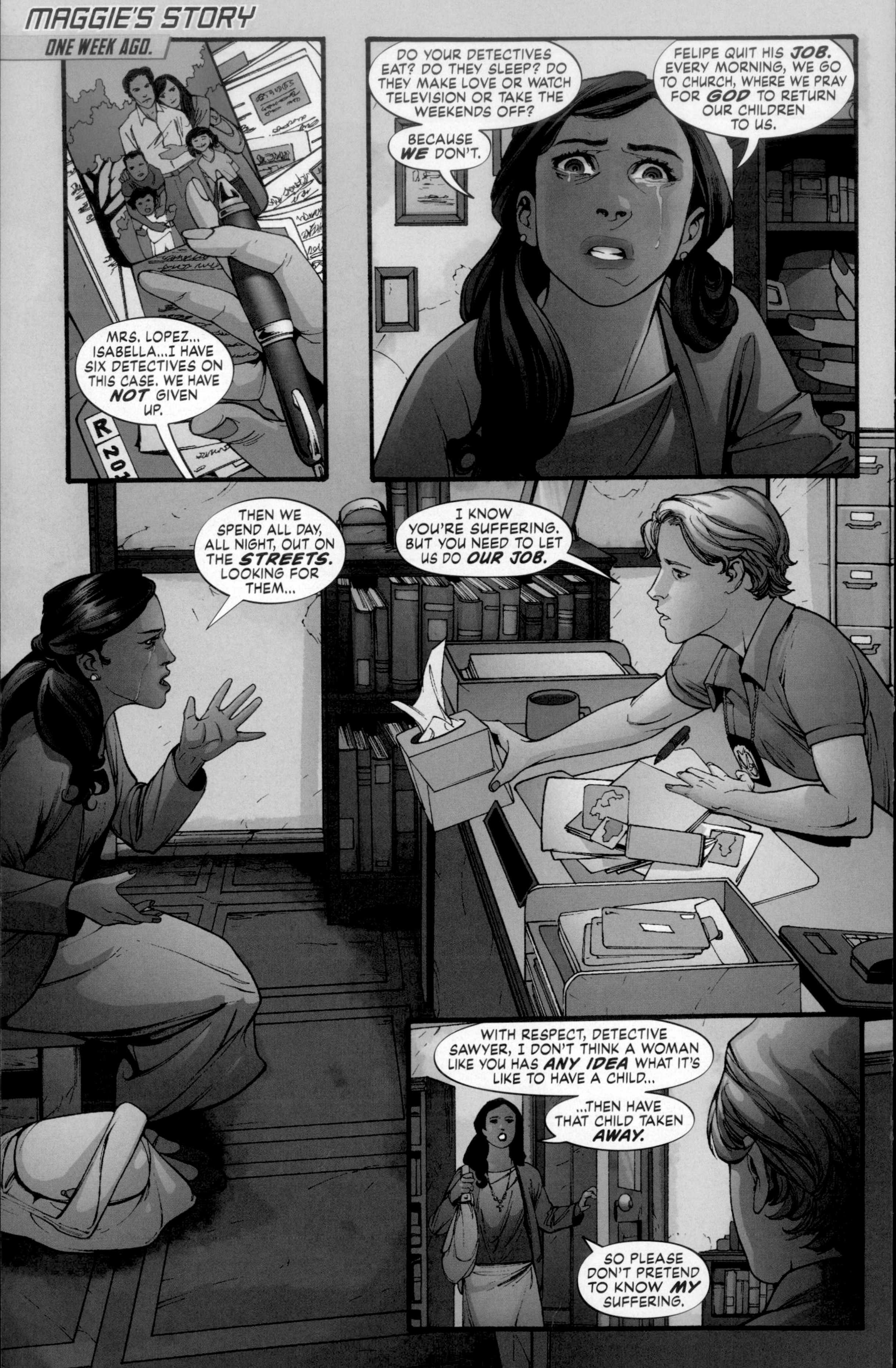
MAGGIE'S STORY
ONE WEEK AGO.
MRS. LOPEZ... ISABELLA...I HAVE SIX DETECTIVES ON THIS CASE. WE HAVE NOT GIVEN UP.
DO YOUR DETECTIVES EAT? DO THEY SLEEP? DO THEY MAKE LOVE OR WATCH TELEVISION OR TAKE THE WEEKENDS OFF?
BECAUSE WE DON'T.
FELIPE QUIT HIS JOB. EVERY MORNING, WE GO TO CHURCH, WHERE WE PRAY FOR GOD TO RETURN OUR CHILDREN TO US.
THEN WE SPEND ALL DAY, ALL NIGHT, OUT ON THE STREETS. LOOKING FOR THEM...
I KNOW YOU'RE SUFFERING. BUT YOU NEED TO LET US DO OUR JOB.
WITH RESPECT, DETECTIVE SAWYER, I DON'T THINK A WOMAN LIKE YOU HAS ANY IDEA WHAT IT'S LIKE TO HAVE A CHILD...
...THEN HAVE THAT CHILD TAKEN AWAY.
SO PLEASE DON'T PRETEND TO KNOW MY SUFFERING.

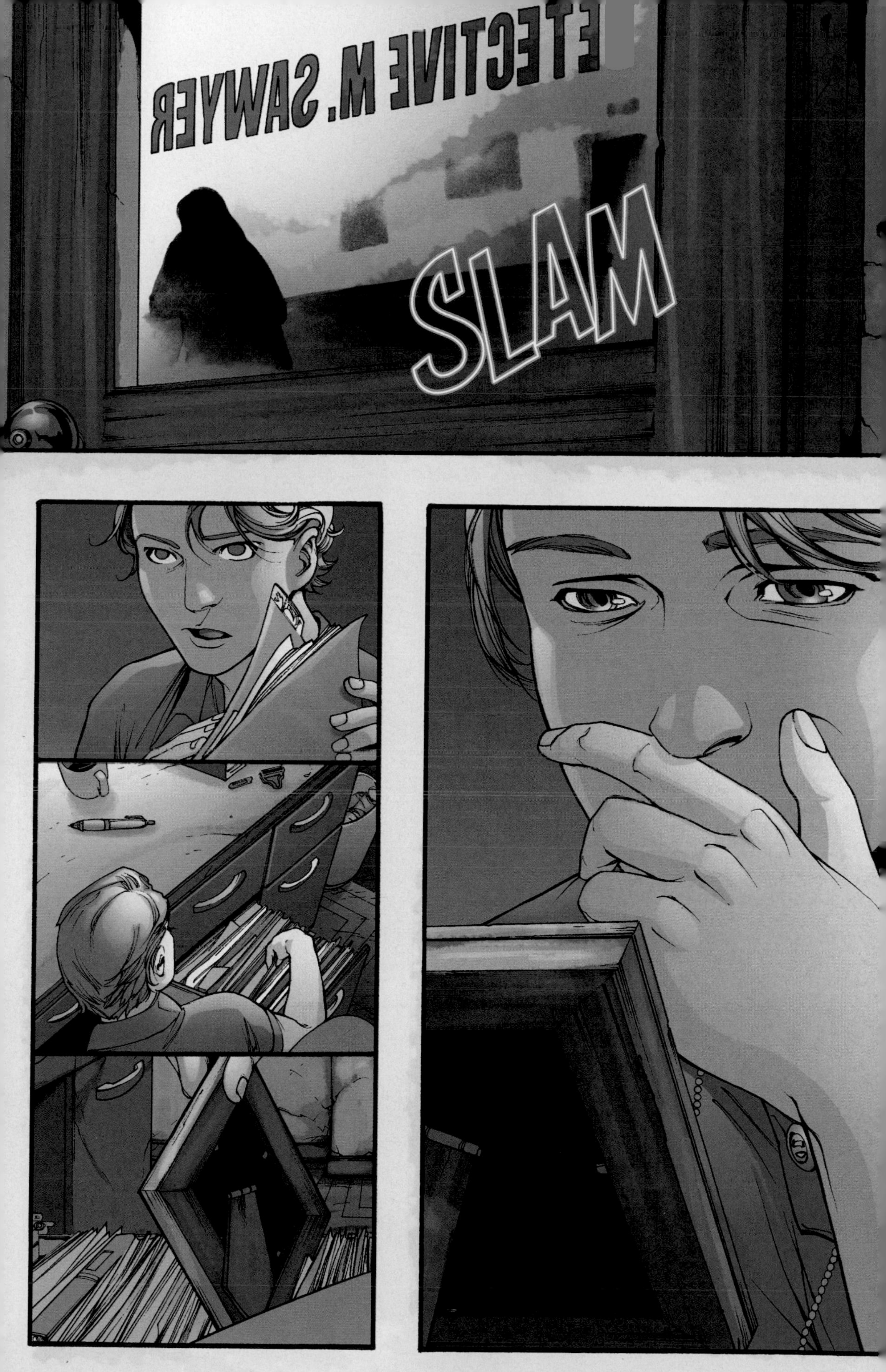
ETECTIVE M. SAWYER
SLAM

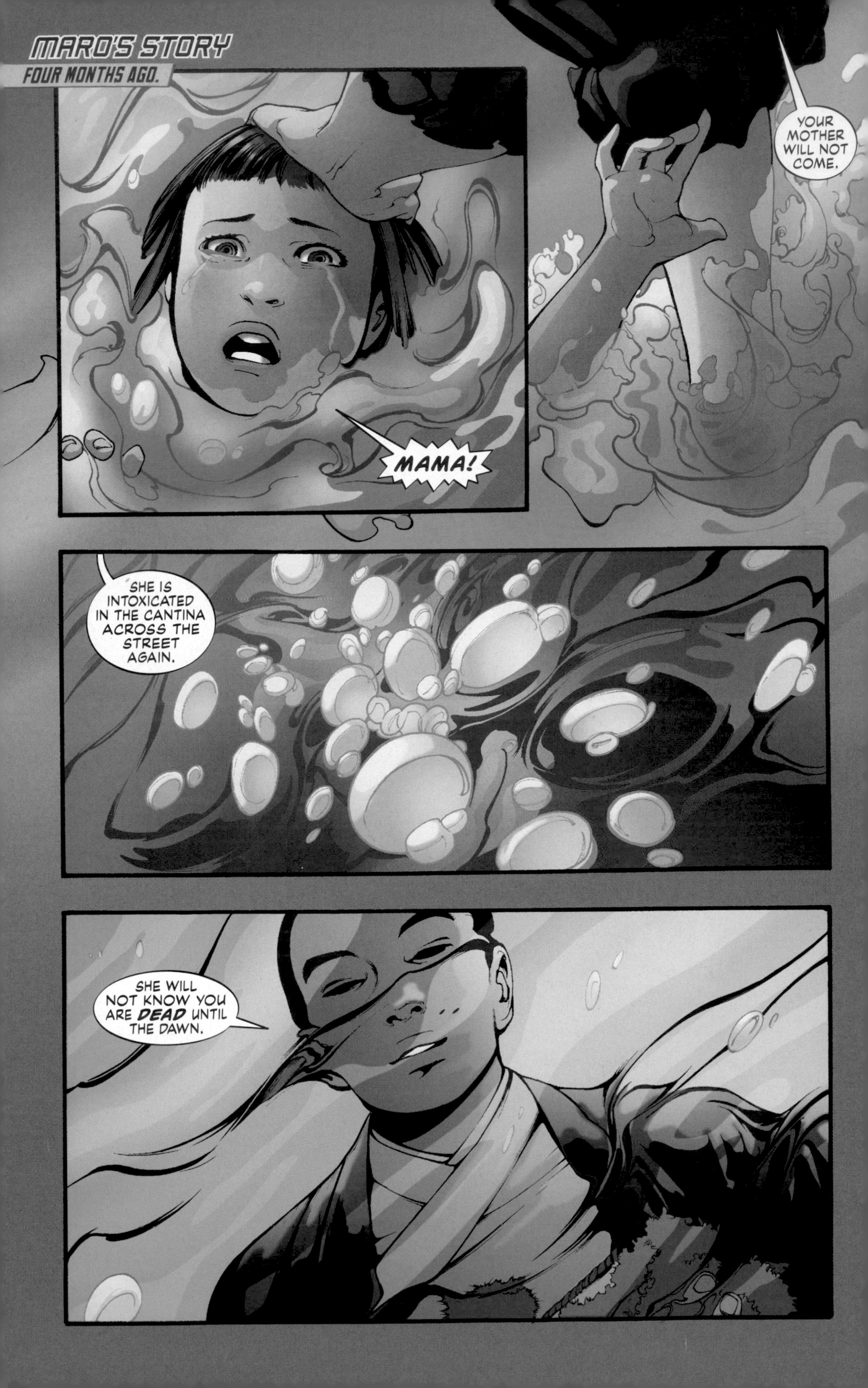
MARO'S STORY
FOUR MONTHS AGO.
MAMA!
YOUR MOTHER WILL NOT COME.
SHE IS INTOXICATED IN THE CANTINA ACROSS THE STREET AGAIN.
SHE WILL NOT KNOW YOU ARE DEAD UNTIL THE DAWN.

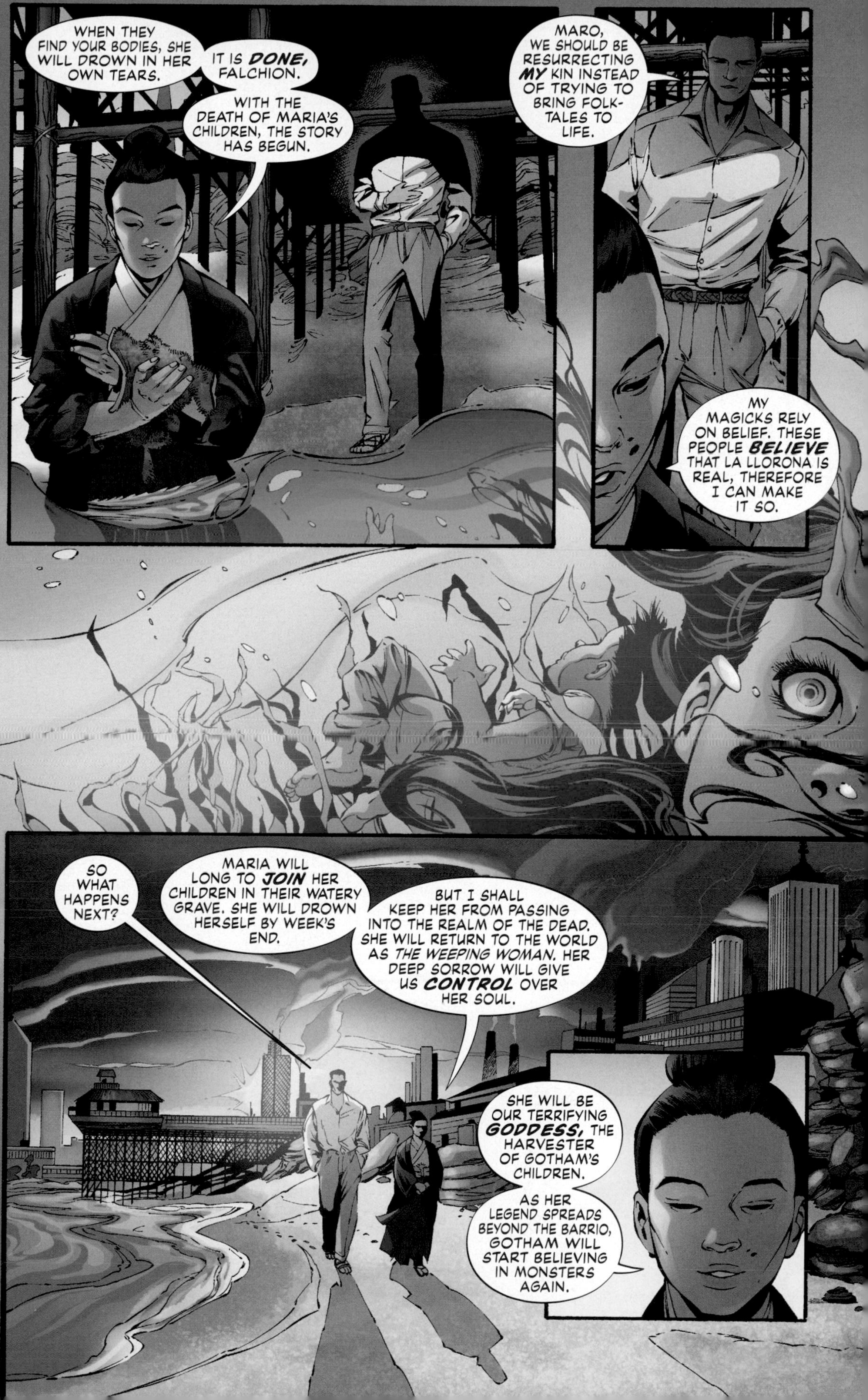
WHEN THEY FIND YOUR BODIES, SHE WILL DROWN IN HER OWN TEARS.
IT IS DONE, FALCHION.
WITH THE DEATH OF MARIA'S CHILDREN, THE STORY HAS BEGUN.
MARO, WE SHOULD BE RESURRECTING MY KIN INSTEAD OF TRYING TO BRING FOLK-TALES TO LIFE.
MY MAGICKS RELY ON BELIEF. THESE PEOPLE BELIEVE THAT LA LLORONA IS REAL, THEREFORE I CAN MAKE IT SO.
SO WHAT HAPPENS NEXT?
MARIA WILL LONG TO JOIN HER CHILDREN IN THEIR WATERY GRAVE. SHE WILL DROWN HERSELF BY WEEK'S END.
BUT I SHALL KEEP HER FROM PASSING INTO THE REALM OF THE DEAD. SHE WILL RETURN TO THE WORLD AS THE WEEPING WOMAN. HER DEEP SORROW WILL GIVE US CONTROL OVER HER SOUL.
SHE WILL BE OUR TERRIFYING GODDESS, THE HARVESTER OF GOTHAM'S CHILDREN.
AS HER LEGEND SPREADS BEYOND THE BARRIO, GOTHAM WILL START BELIEVING IN MONSTERS AGAIN.

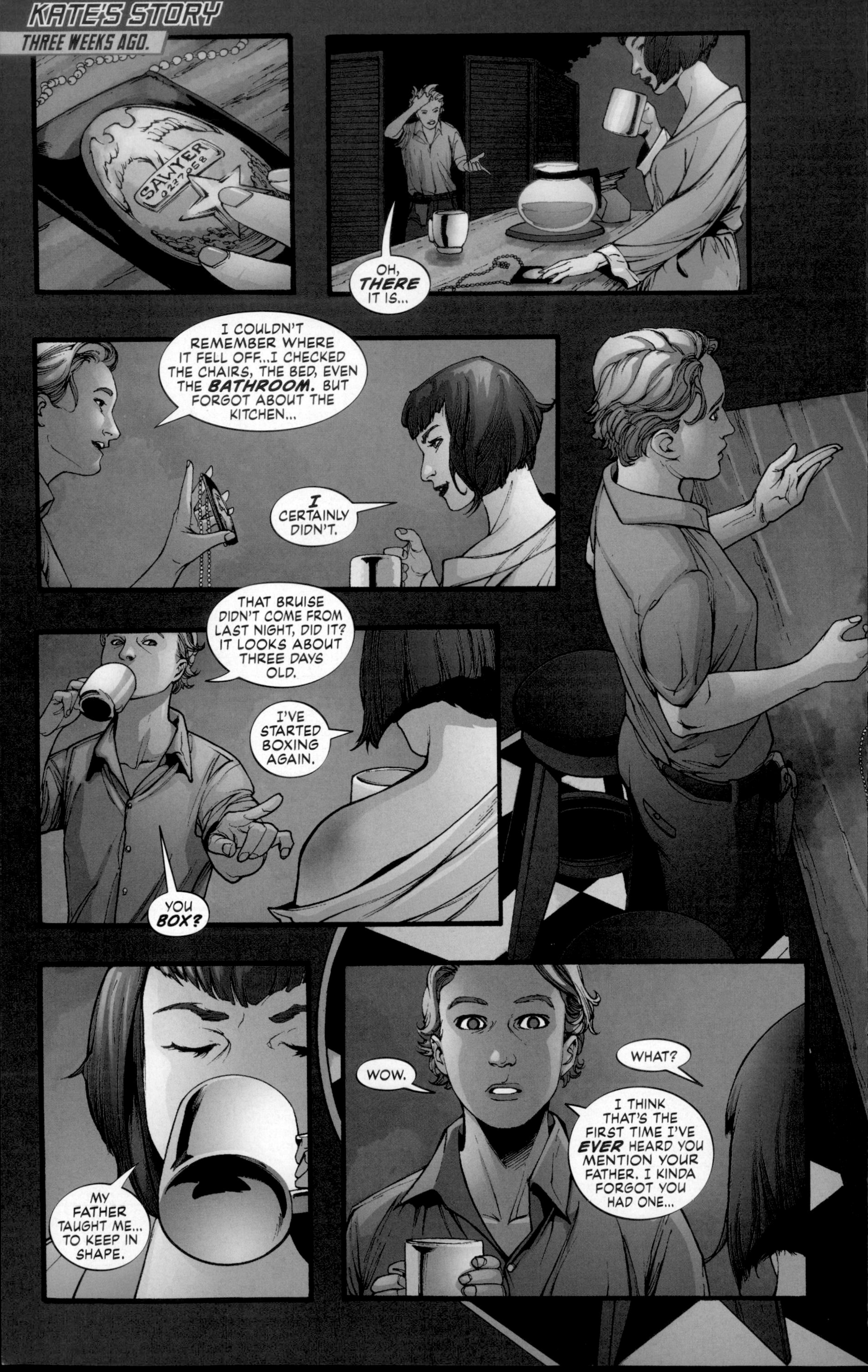
KATE'S STORY
THREE WEEKS AGO.
SAWYER 0237058
OH, THERE IT IS...
I COULDN'T REMEMBER WHERE IT FELL OFF...I CHECKED THE CHAIRS, THE BED, EVEN THE BATHROOM. BUT FORGOT ABOUT THE KITCHEN...
I CERTAINLY DIDN'T.
THAT BRUISE DIDN'T COME FROM LAST NIGHT, DID IT? IT LOOKS ABOUT THREE DAYS OLD.
I'VE STARTED BOXING AGAIN.
YOU BOX?
MY FATHER TAUGHT ME... TO KEEP IN SHAPE.
WOW.
WHAT?
I THINK THAT'S THE FIRST TIME I'VE EVER HEARD YOU MENTION YOUR FATHER. I KINDA FORGOT YOU HAD ONE...

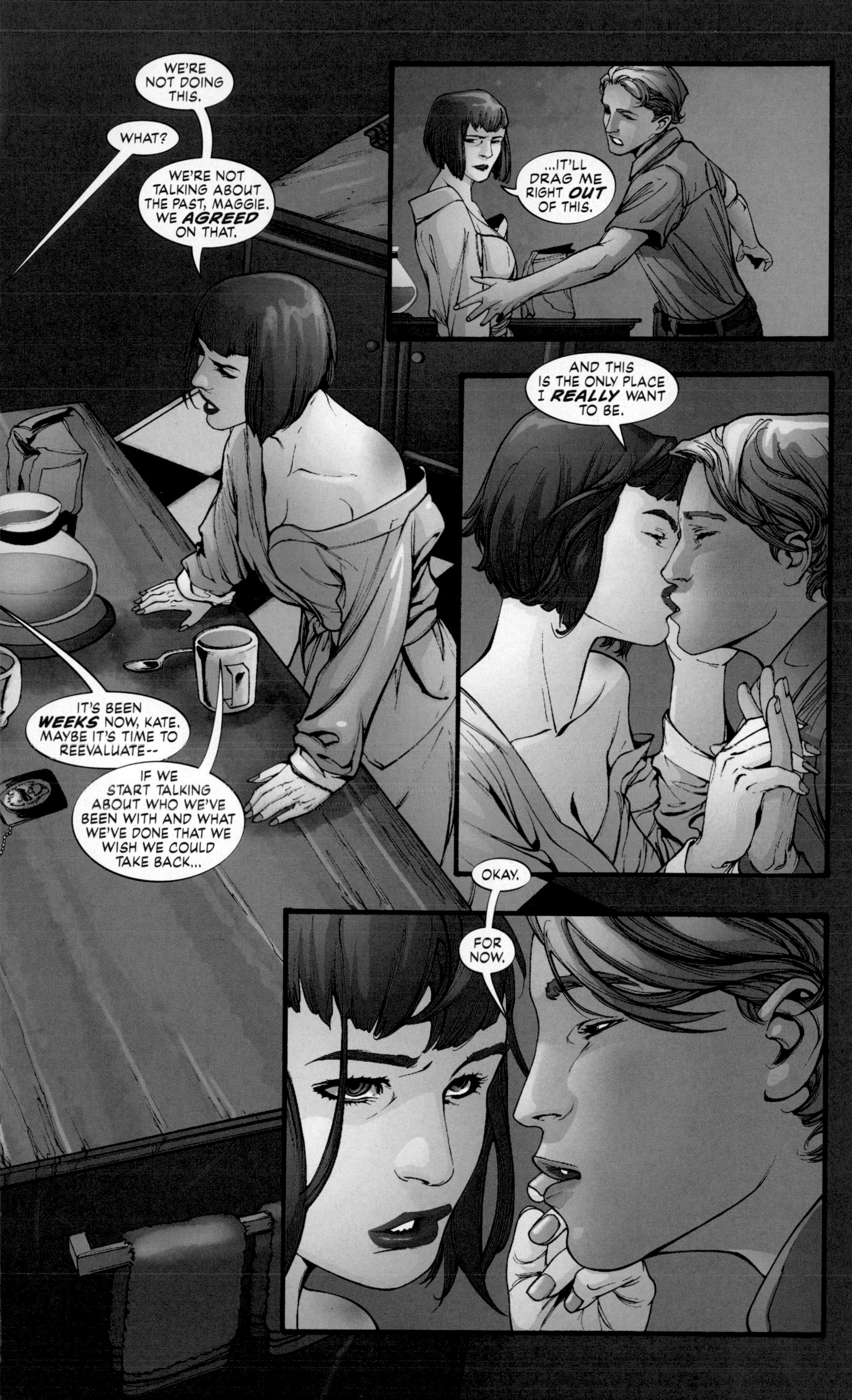
WE'RE NOT DOING THIS.
WHAT?
WE'RE NOT TALKING ABOUT THE PAST, MAGGIE. WE AGREED ON THAT.
...IT'LL DRAG ME RIGHT OUT OF THIS.
AND THIS IS THE ONLY PLACE I REALLY WANT TO BE.
IT'S BEEN WEEKS NOW, KATE. MAYBE IT'S TIME TO REEVALUATE--
IF WE START TALKING ABOUT WHO WE'VE BEEN WITH AND WHAT WE'VE DONE THAT WE WISH WE COULD TAKE BACK...
OKAY.
FOR NOW.

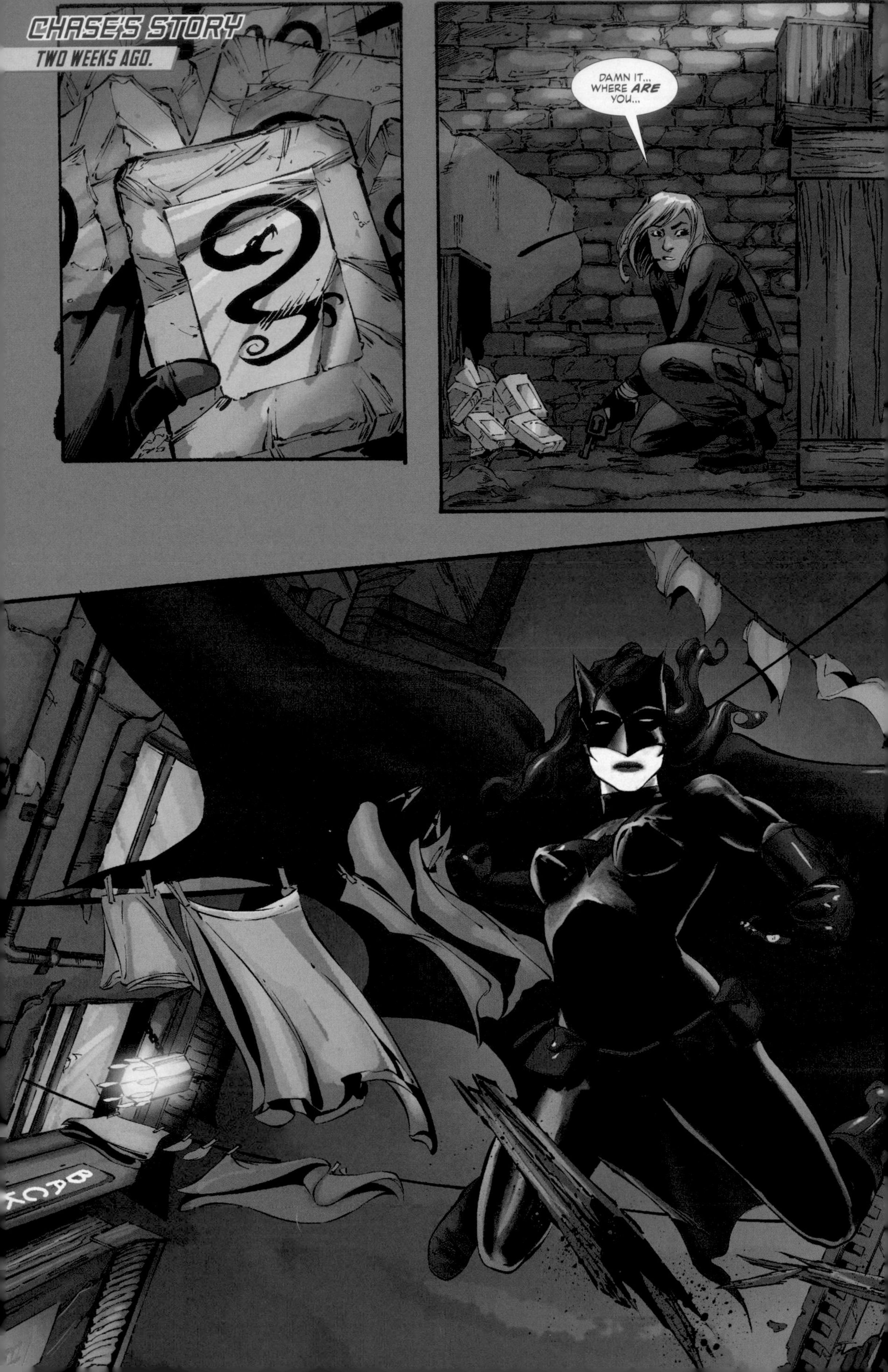
CHASE'S STORY
TWO WEEKS AGO.
DAMN IT... WHERE ARE YOU...
BACK

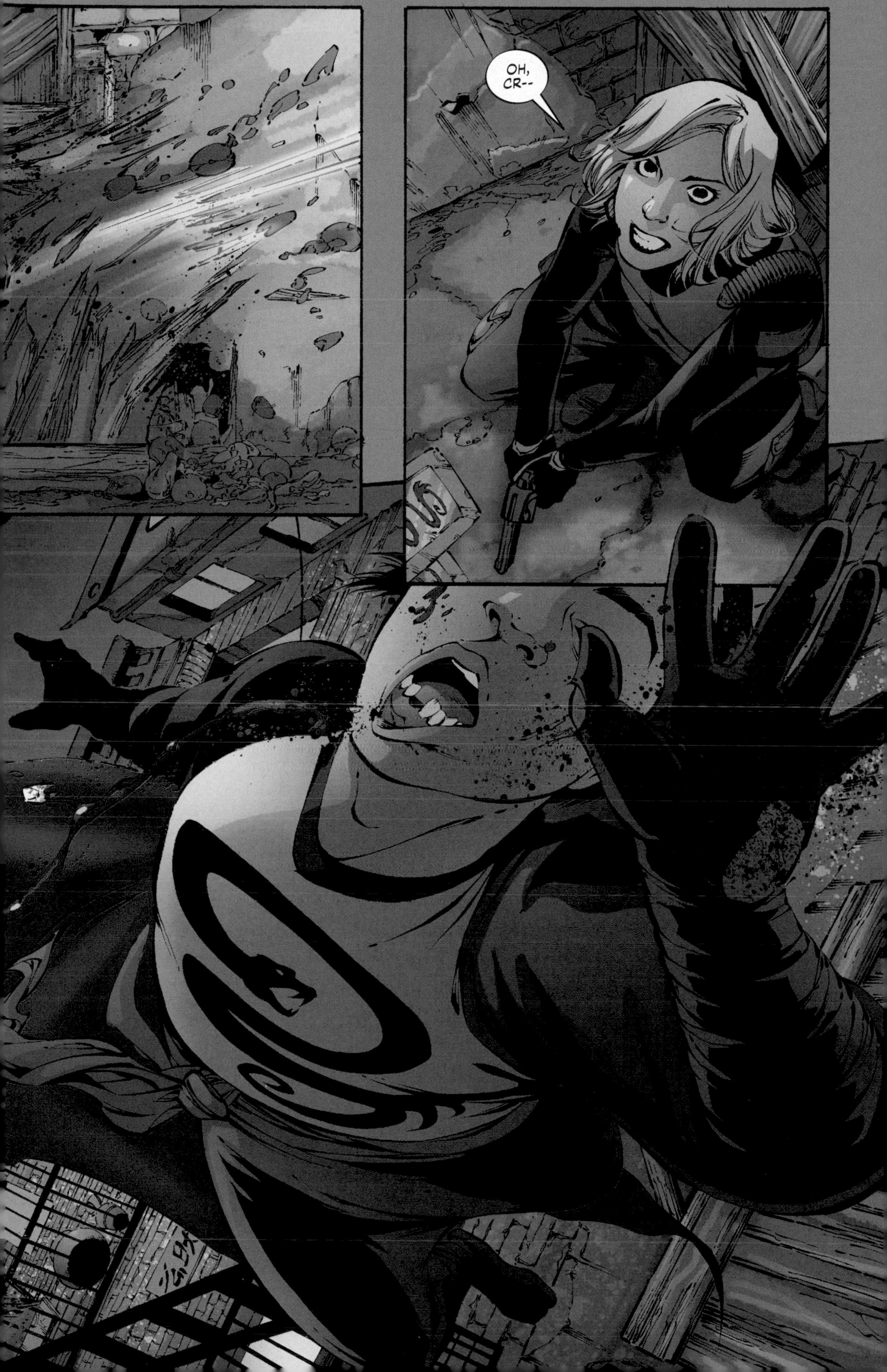
OH, CR--

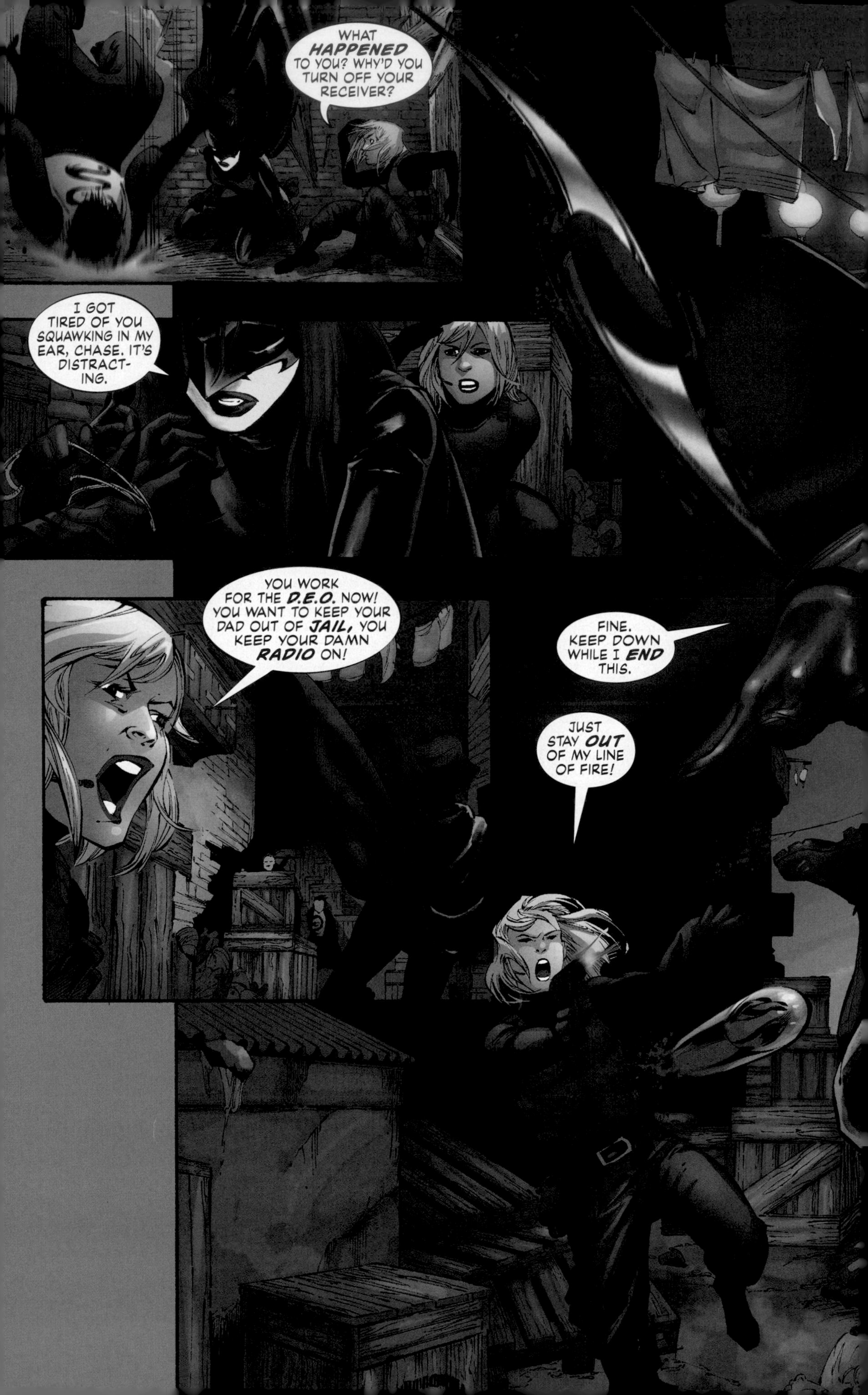
WHAT HAPPENED TO YOU? WHY'D YOU TURN OFF YOUR RECEIVER?
I GOT TIRED OF YOU SQUAWKING IN MY EAR, CHASE. IT'S DISTRACTING.
YOU WORK FOR THE D.E.O. NOW! YOU WANT TO KEEP YOUR DAD OUT OF JAIL, YOU KEEP YOUR DAMN RADIO ON!
FINE. KEEP DOWN WHILE I END THIS.
JUST STAY OUT OF MY LINE OF FIRE!

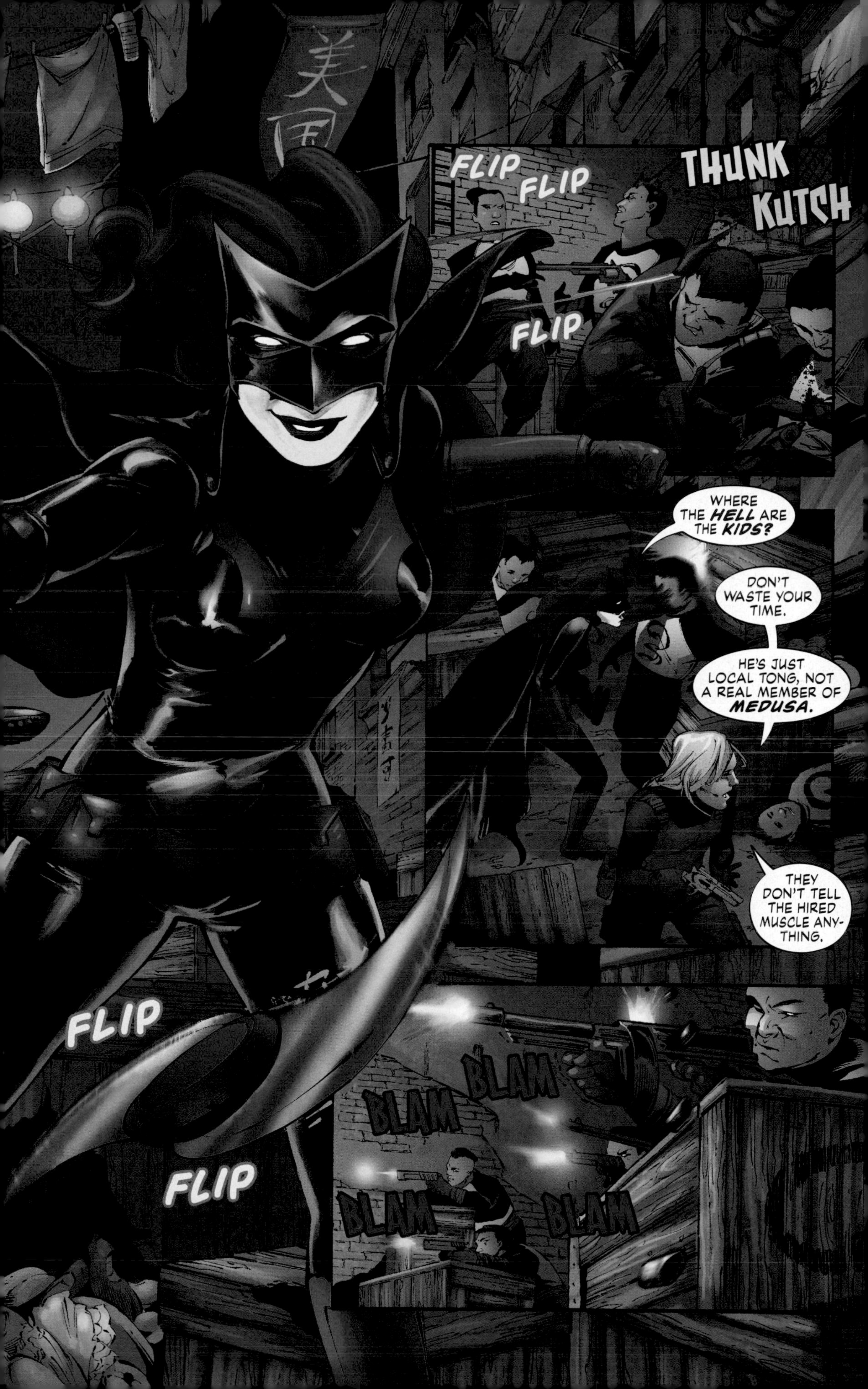
FLIP
FLIP
THUNK
KUTCH
FLIP
WHERE THE HELL ARE THE KIDS?
DON'T WASTE YOUR TIME.
HE'S JUST LOCAL TONG, NOT A REAL MEMBER OF MEDUSA.
THEY DON'T TELL THE HIRED MUSCLE ANY-THING.
FLIP
BLAM
BLAM
BLAM
BLAM
FLIP

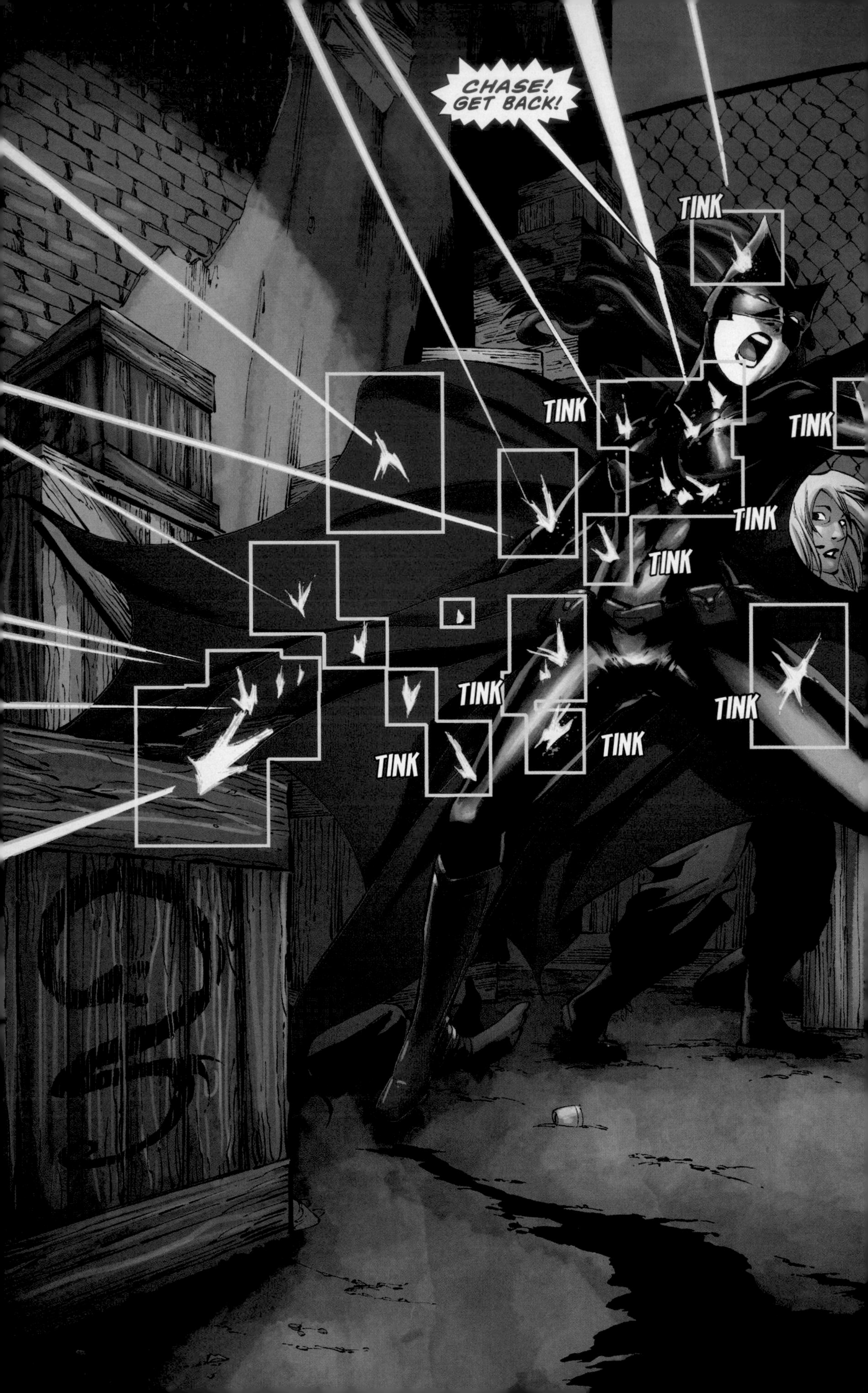
CHASE! GET BACK!
TINK
TINK
TINK
TINK
TINK
TINK
TINK
TINK
TINK
TINK

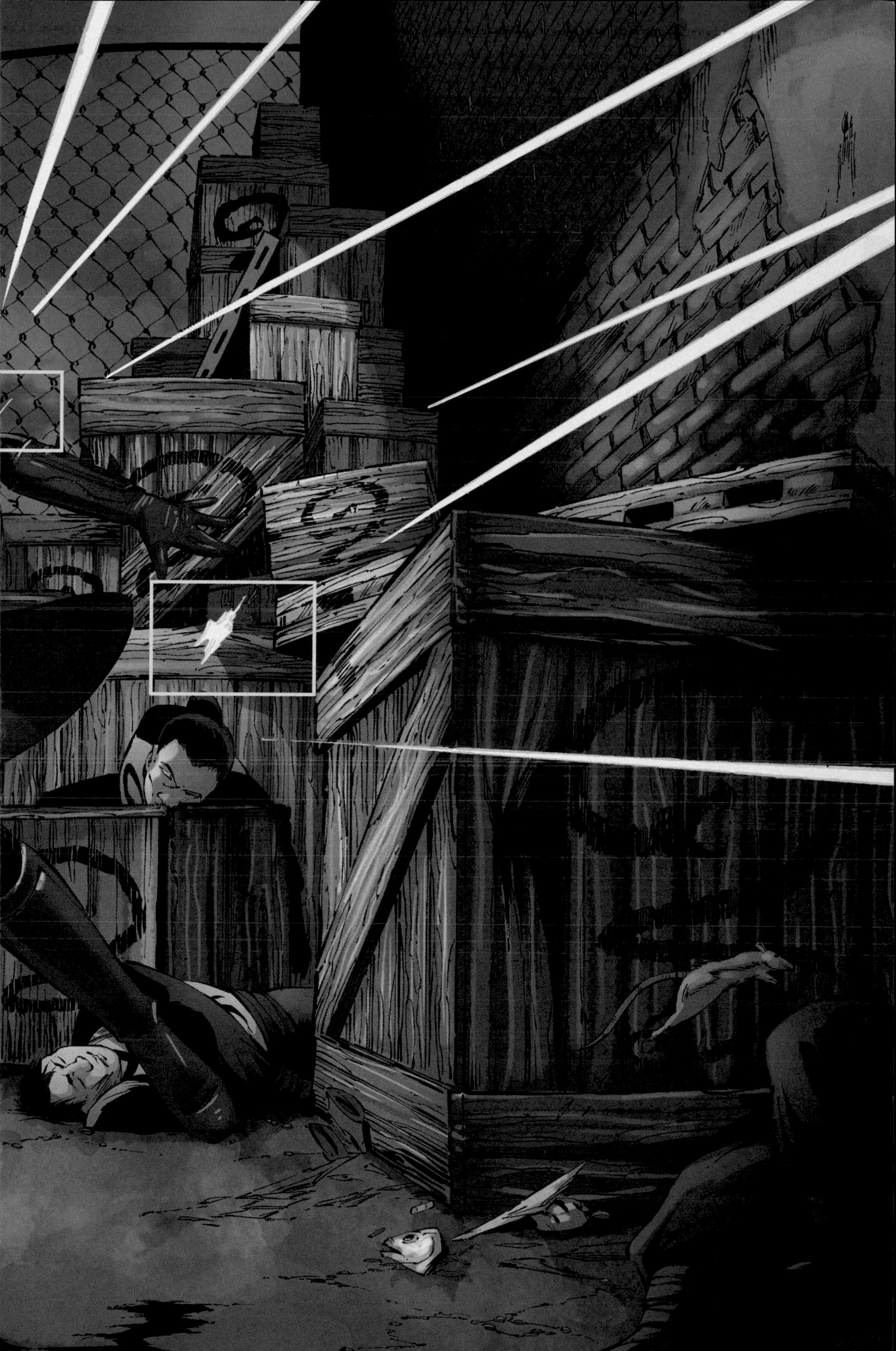

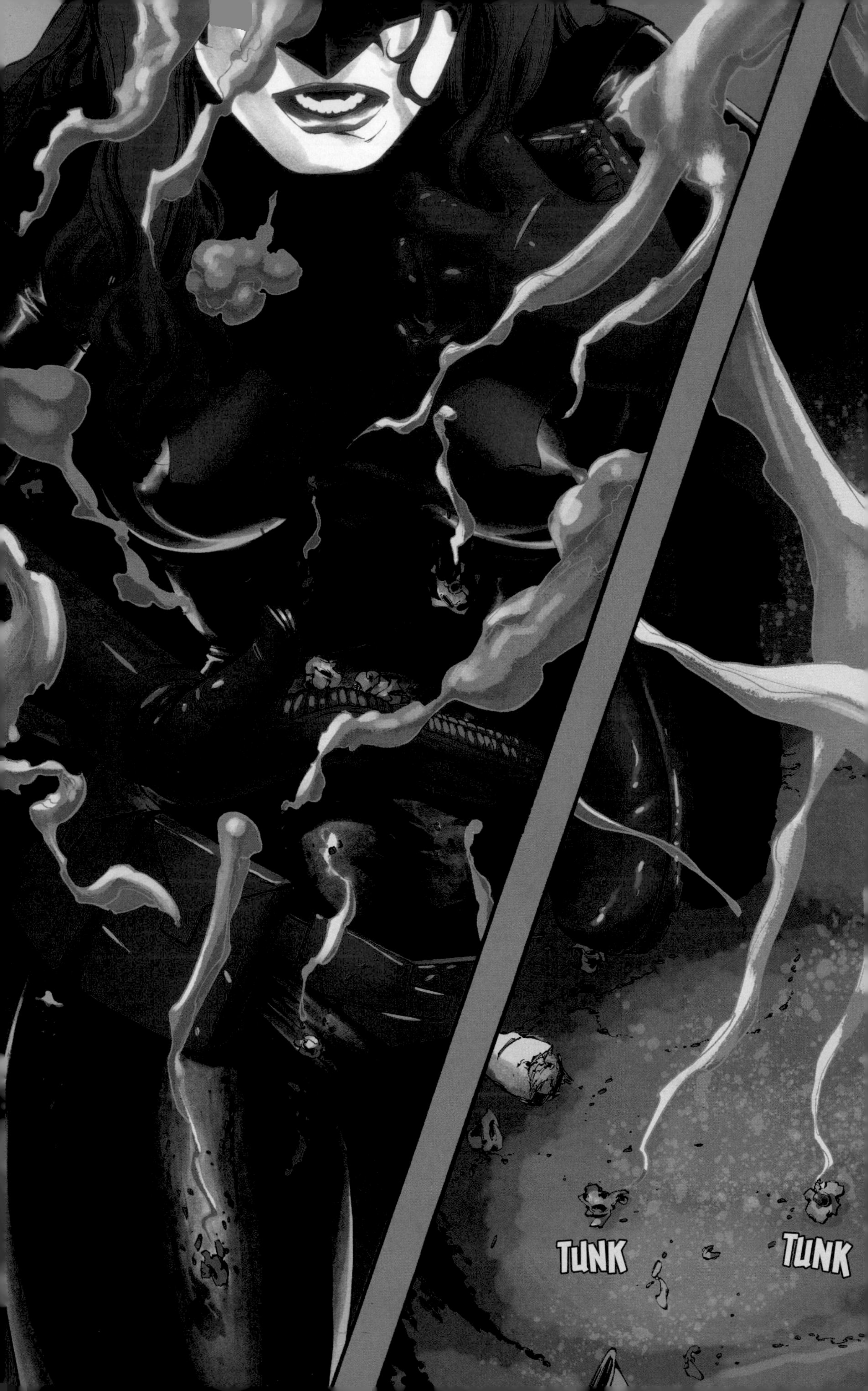
TUNK
TUNK

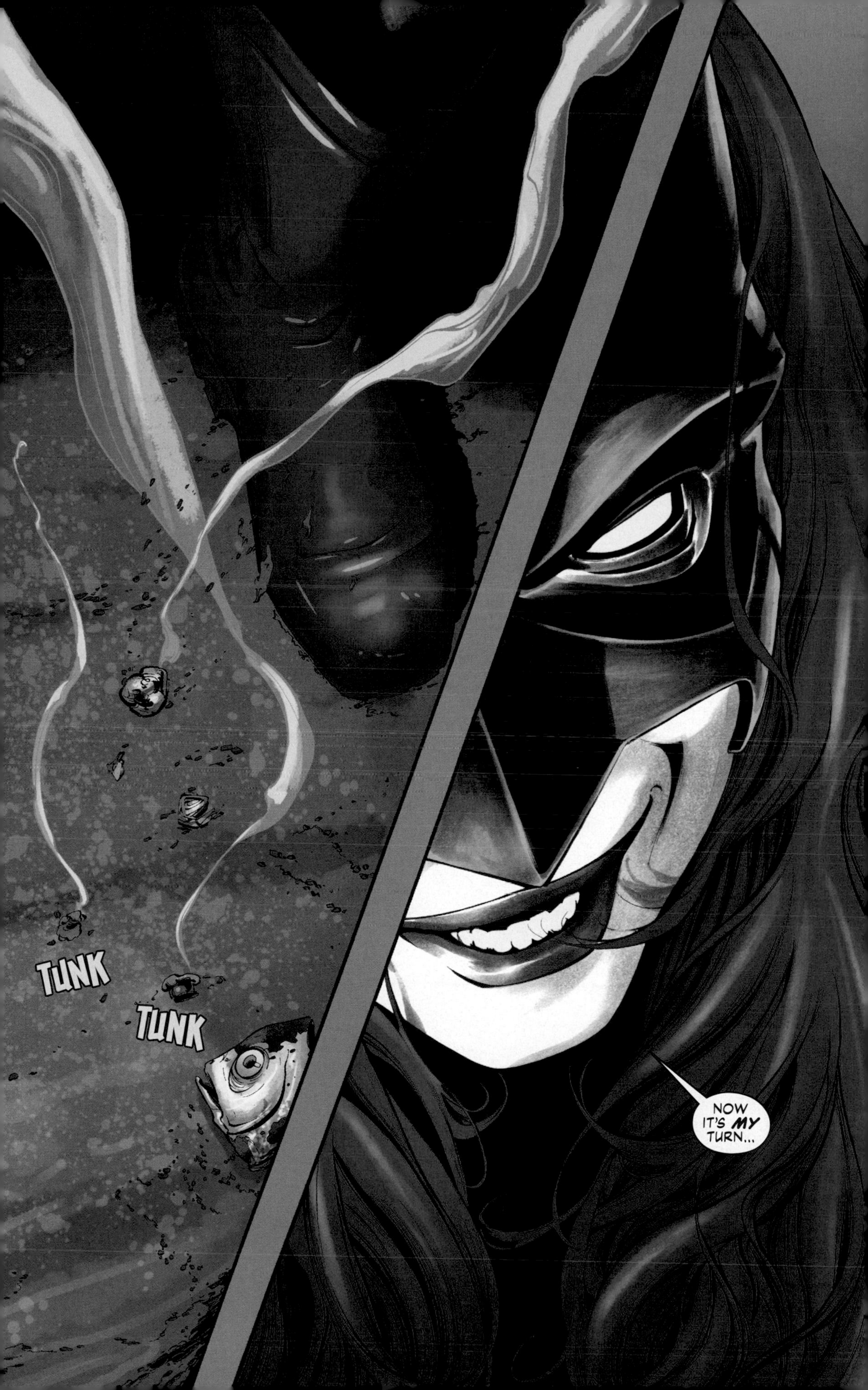
TUNK
TUNK
NOW IT'S MY TURN...

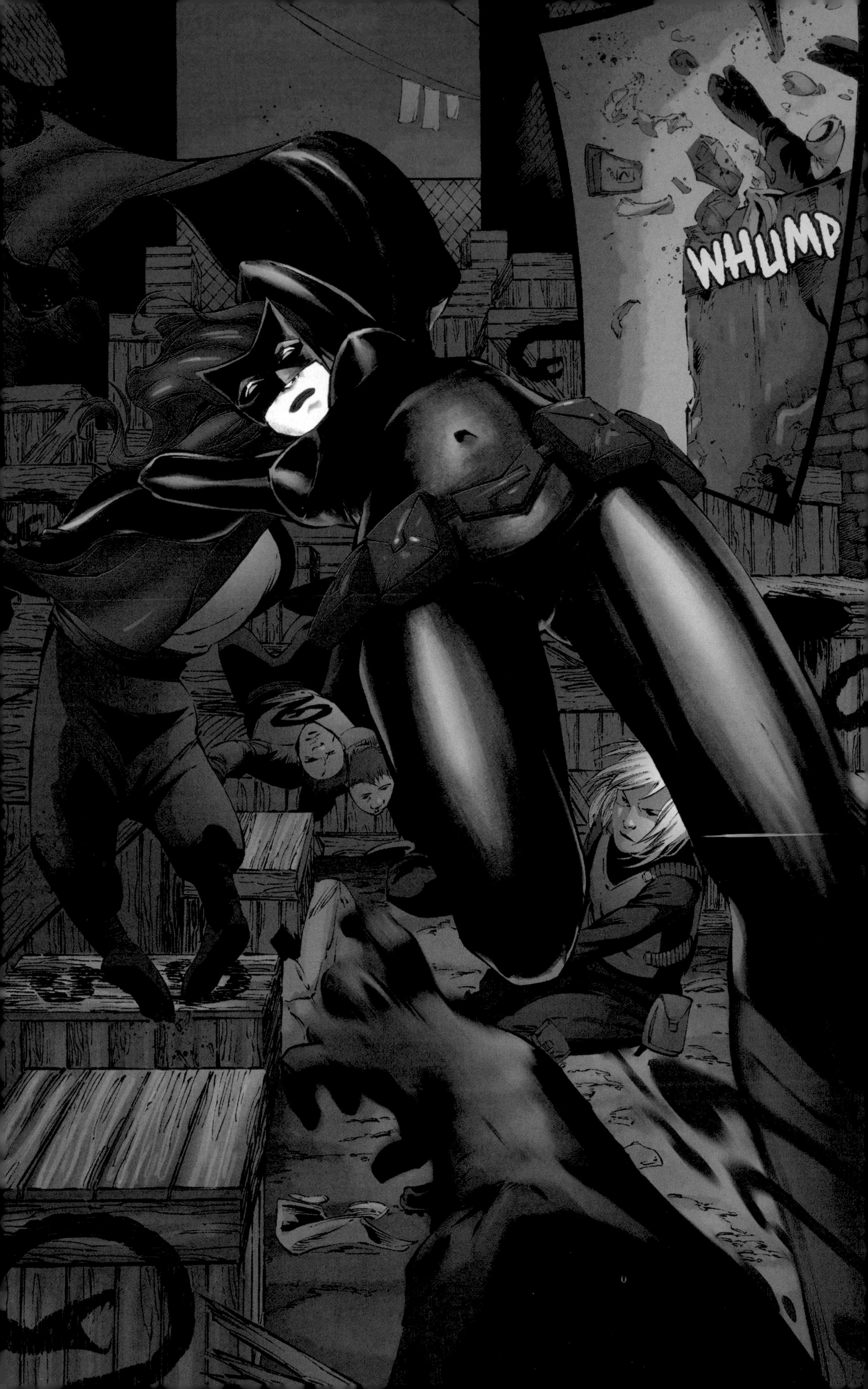
WHUMP

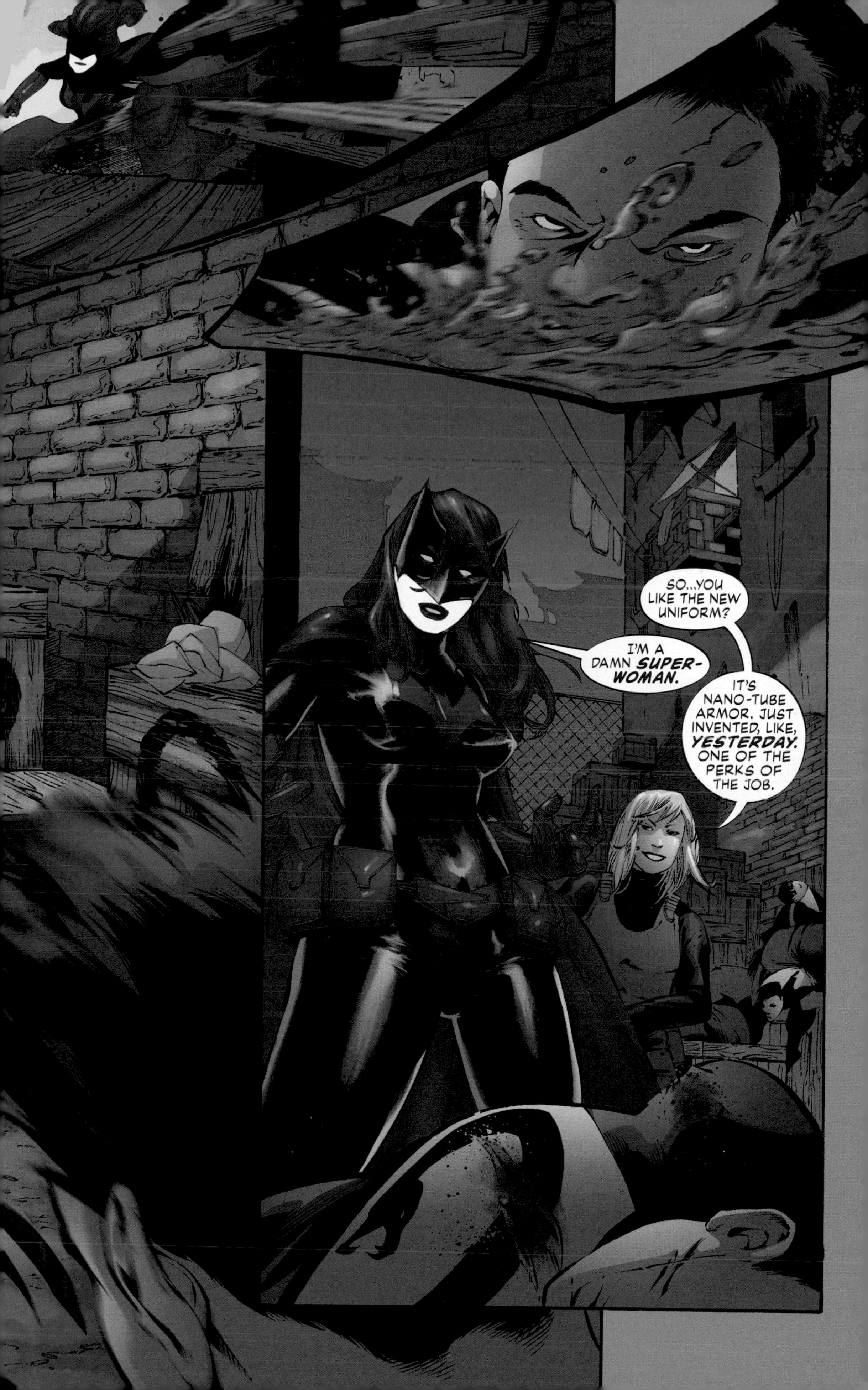
SO...YOU LIKE THE NEW UNIFORM?
I'M A DAMN SUPER-WOMAN.
IT'S NANO-TUBE ARMOR. JUST INVENTED, LIKE, YESTERDAY. ONE OF THE PERKS OF THE JOB.

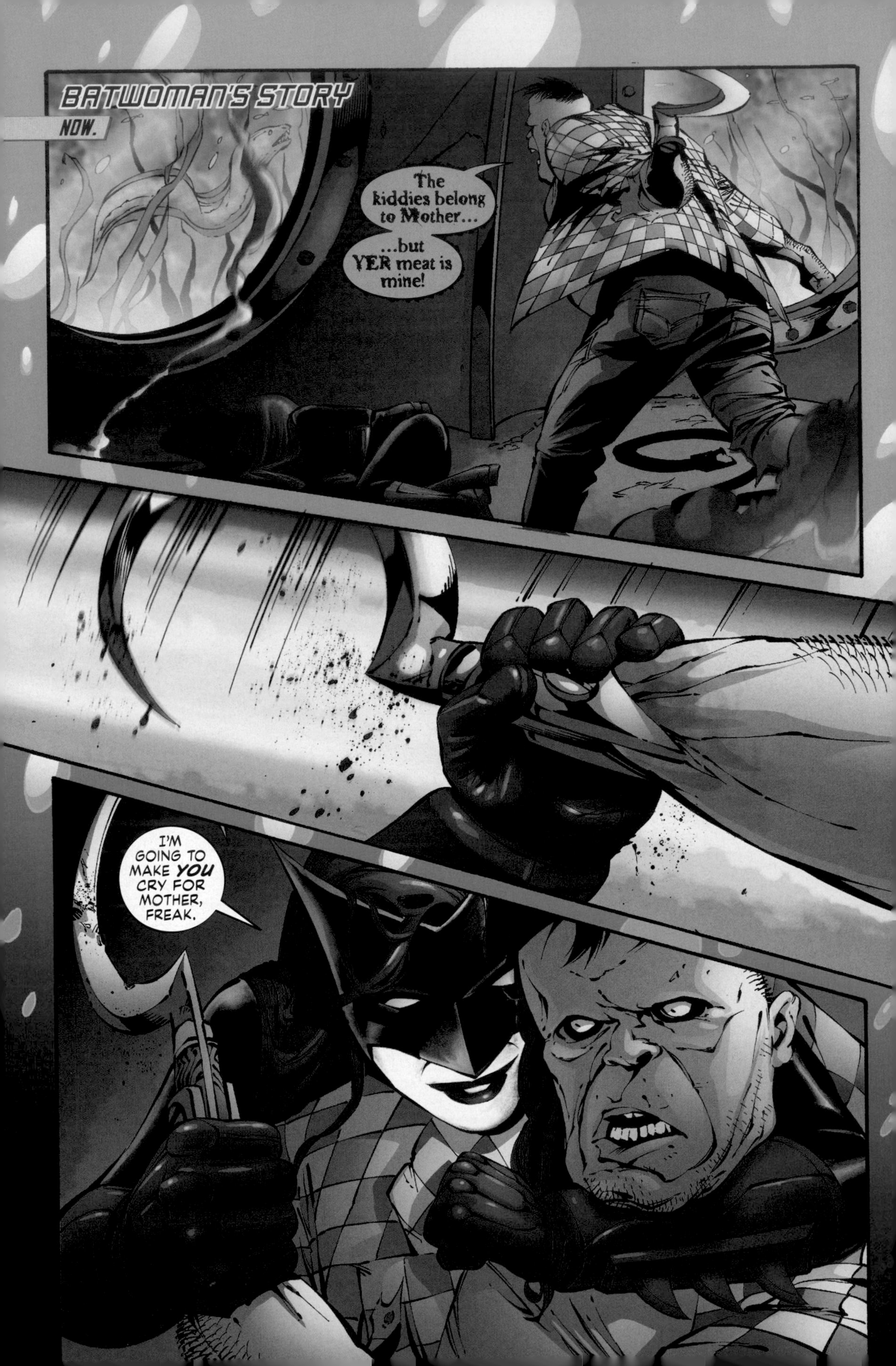
BATWOMAN'S STORY
NOW.
The kiddies belong to Mother...
...but YER meat is mine!
I'M GOING TO MAKE YOU CRY FOR MOTHER, FREAK.

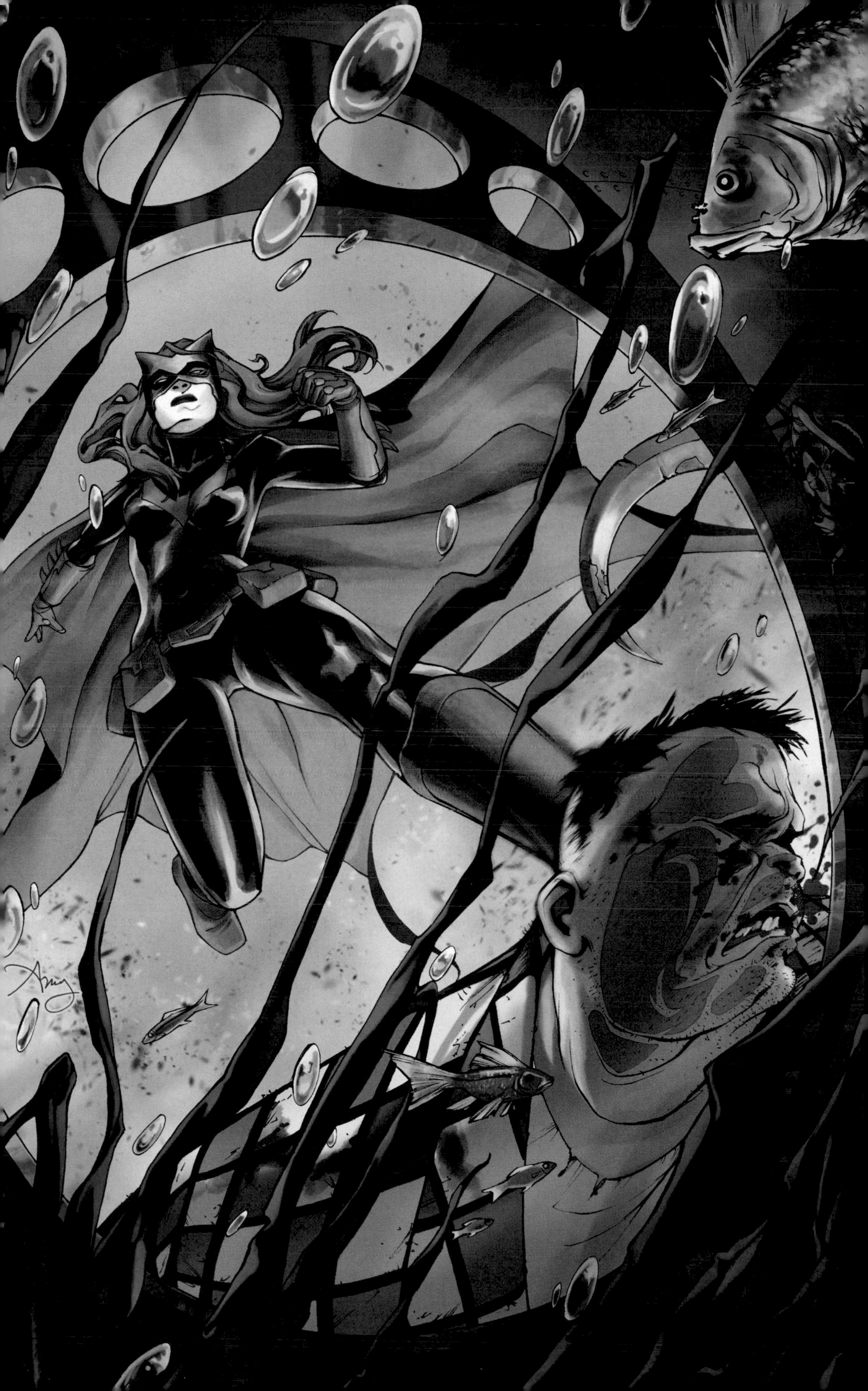

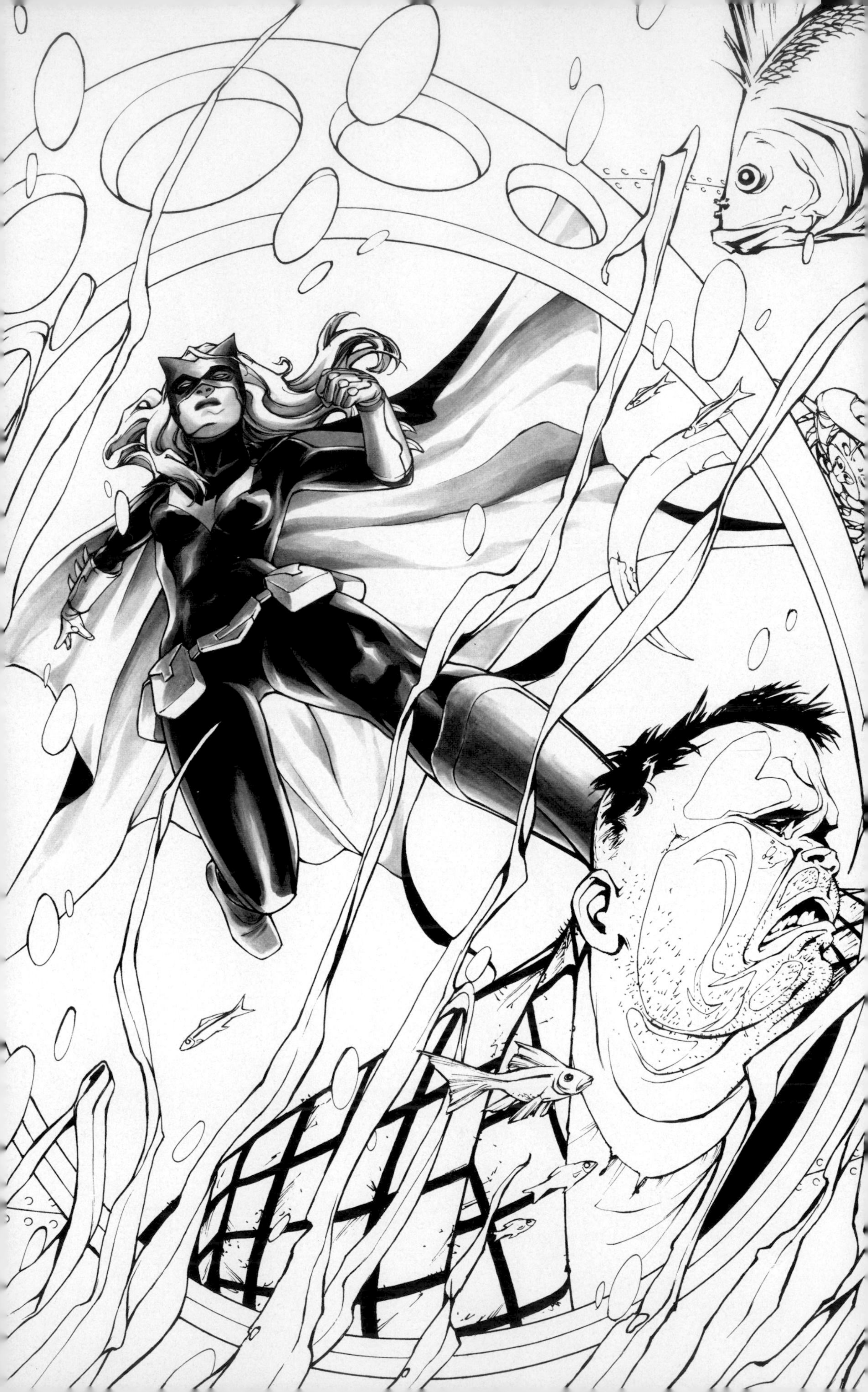

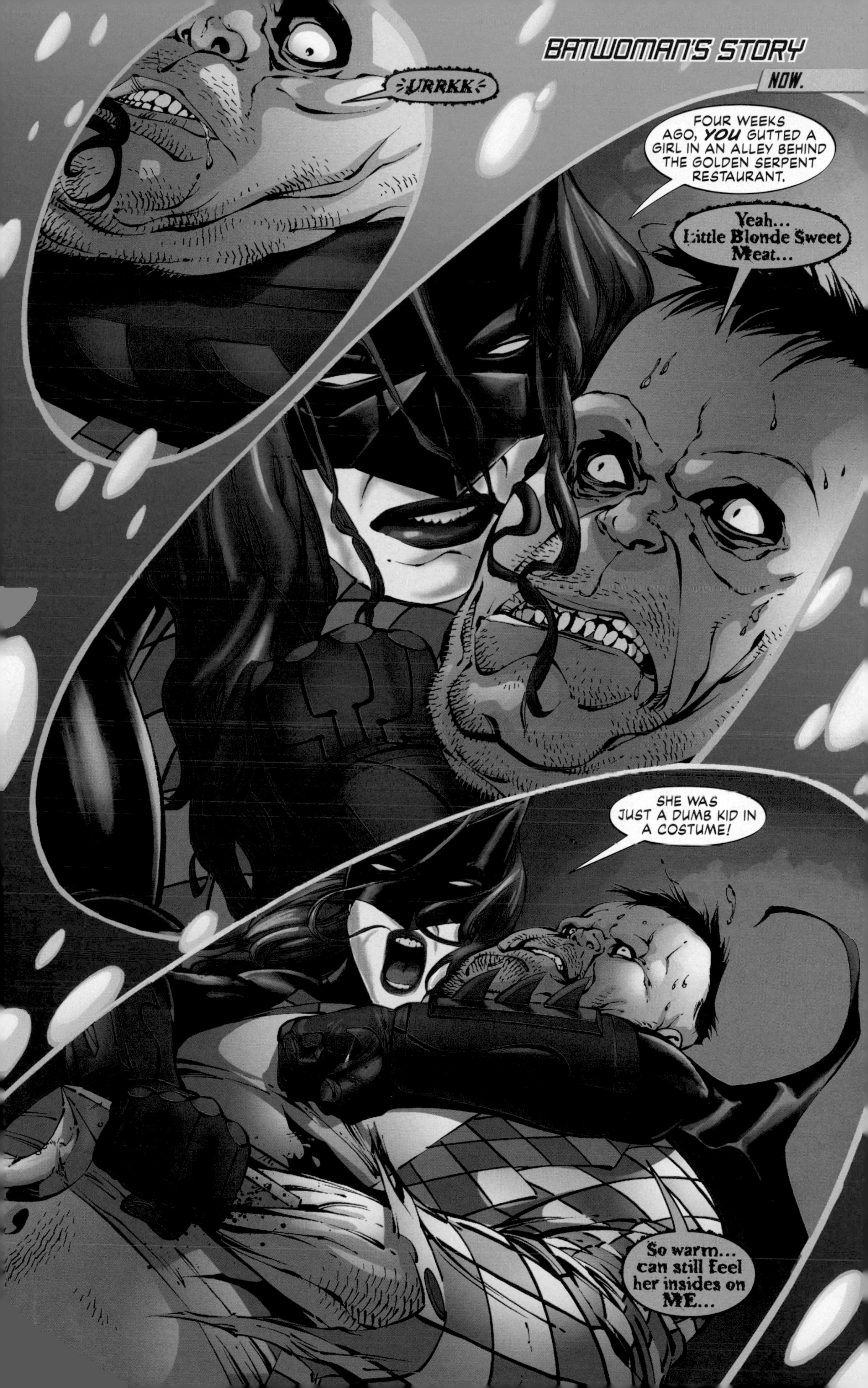
BATWOMAN'S STORY
NOW.
URRKK
FOUR WEEKS AGO, YOU GUTTED A GIRL IN AN ALLEY BEHIND THE GOLDEN SERPENT RESTAURANT.
Yeah... Little Blonde Sweet Meat...
SHE WAS JUST A DUMB KID IN A COSTUME!
So warm... can still feel her insides on ME...

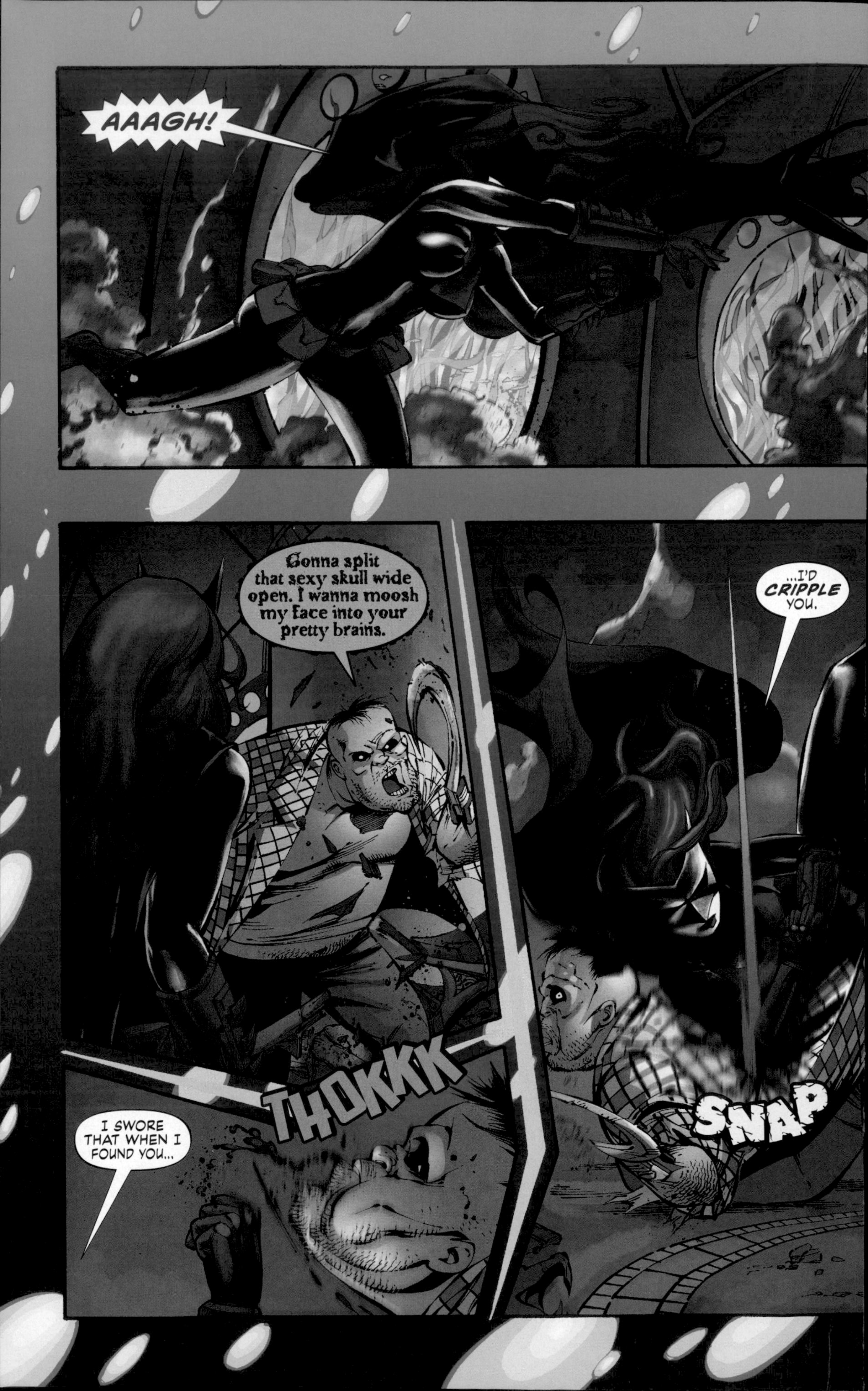
AAAGH!
Gonna split that sexy skull wide open. I wanna moosh my face into your pretty brains.
THOKKK
I SWORE THAT WHEN I FOUND YOU...
...I'D CRIPPLE YOU.
SNAP

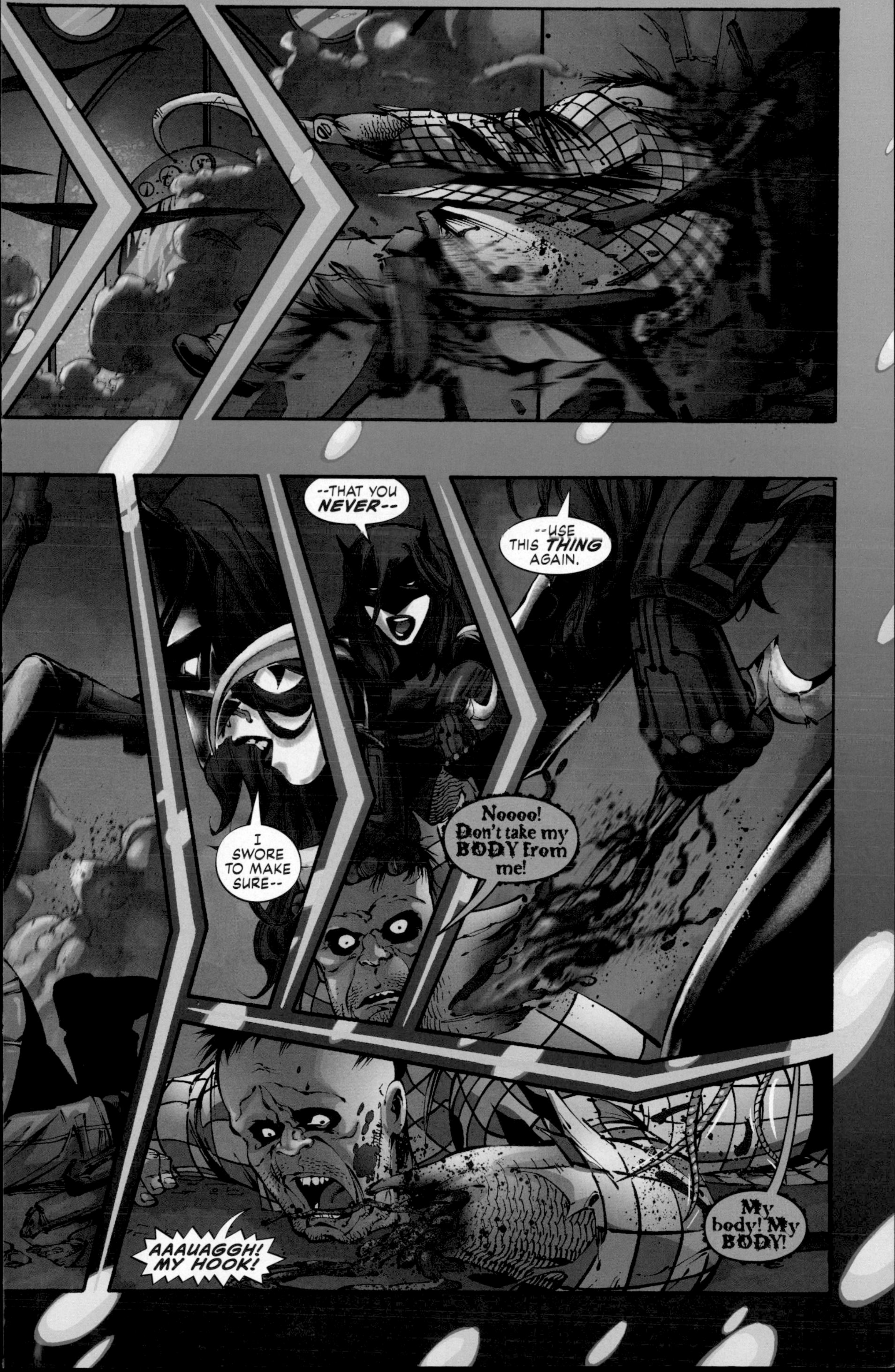

I SWORE TO MAKE SURE--
--THAT YOU NEVER--
--USE THIS THING AGAIN.
Noooo! Don't take my BODY from me!
AAAUAGGH! MY HOOK!
My body! My BODY!

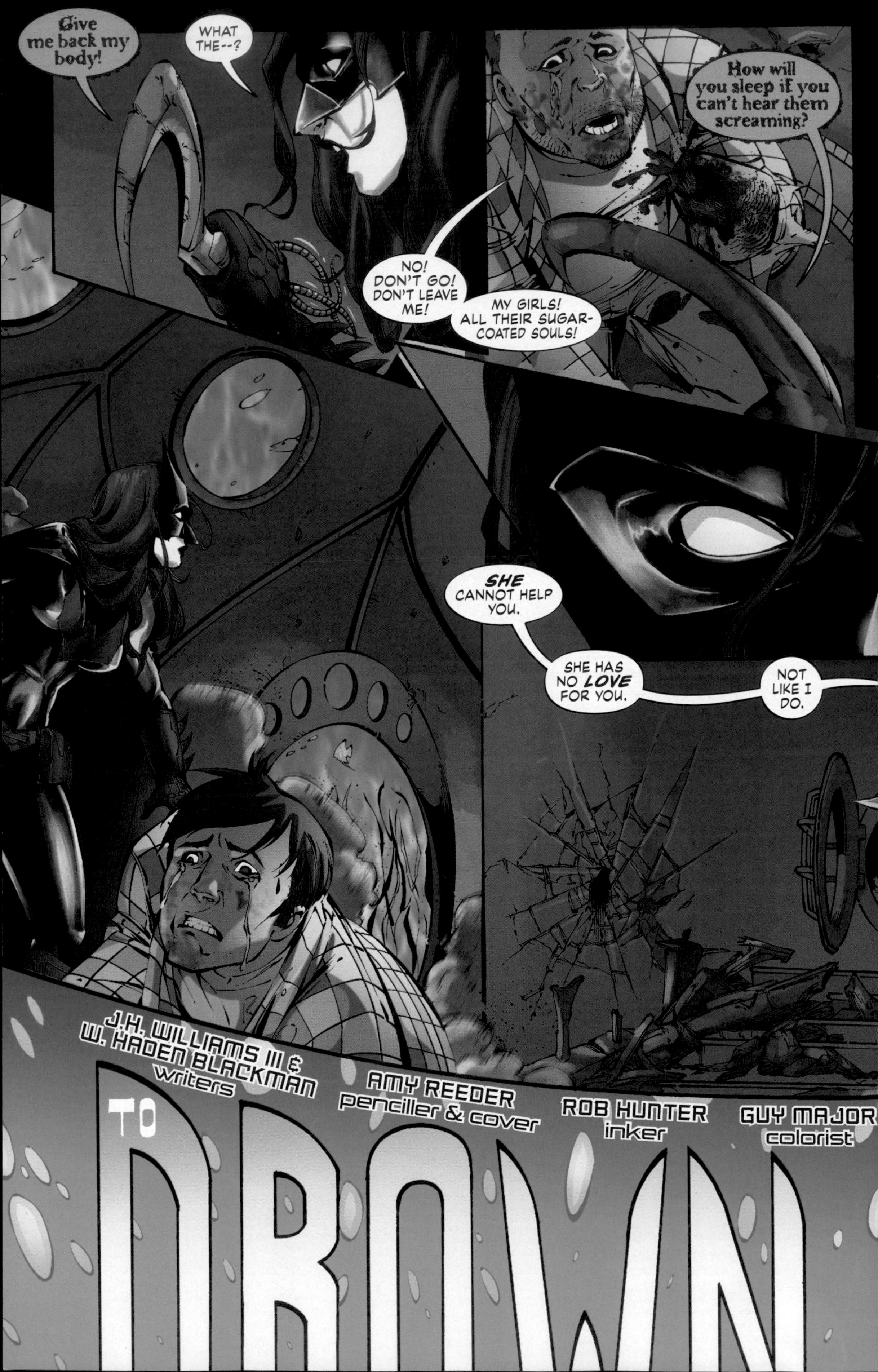
Give me back my body!
WHAT THE--?
How will you sleep if you can't hear them screaming?
NO! DON'T GO! DON'T LEAVE ME!
MY GIRLS! ALL THEIR SUGAR-COATED SOULS!
SHE CANNOT HELP YOU.
SHE HAS NO LOVE FOR YOU.
NOT LIKE I DO.
J.H. WILLIAMS III & W. HADEN BLACKMAN writers
AMY REEDER penciller & cover
ROB HUNTER inker
GUY MAJOR colorist
TO DROWN

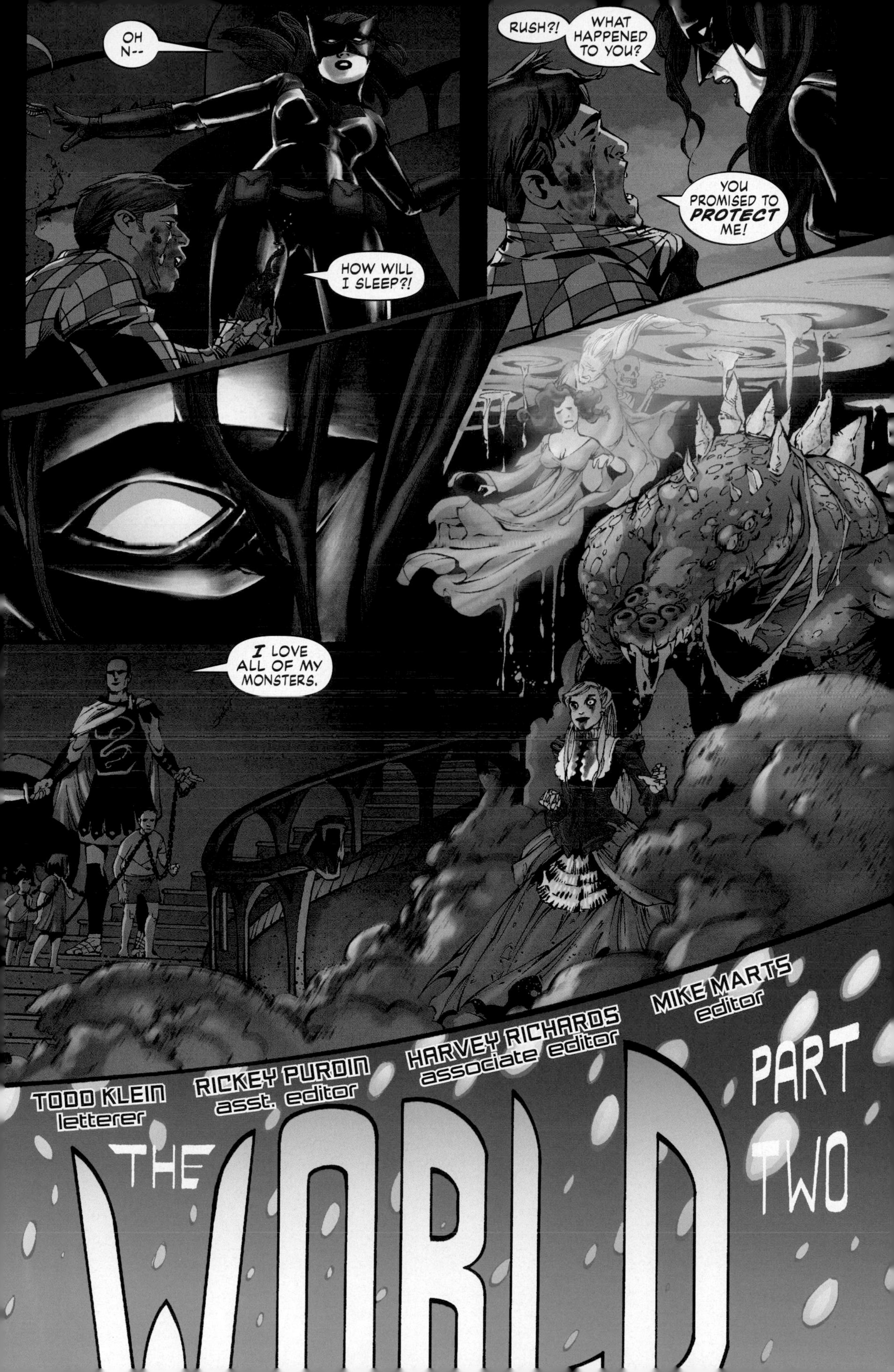

OH N--
HOW WILL I SLEEP?!
RUSH?!
WHAT HAPPENED TO YOU?
YOU PROMISED TO PROTECT ME!
I LOVE ALL OF MY MONSTERS.
TODD KLEIN letterer
RICKEY PURDIN asst. editor
HARVEY RICHARDS associate editor
MIKE MARTS editor
THE WORLD
PART TWO

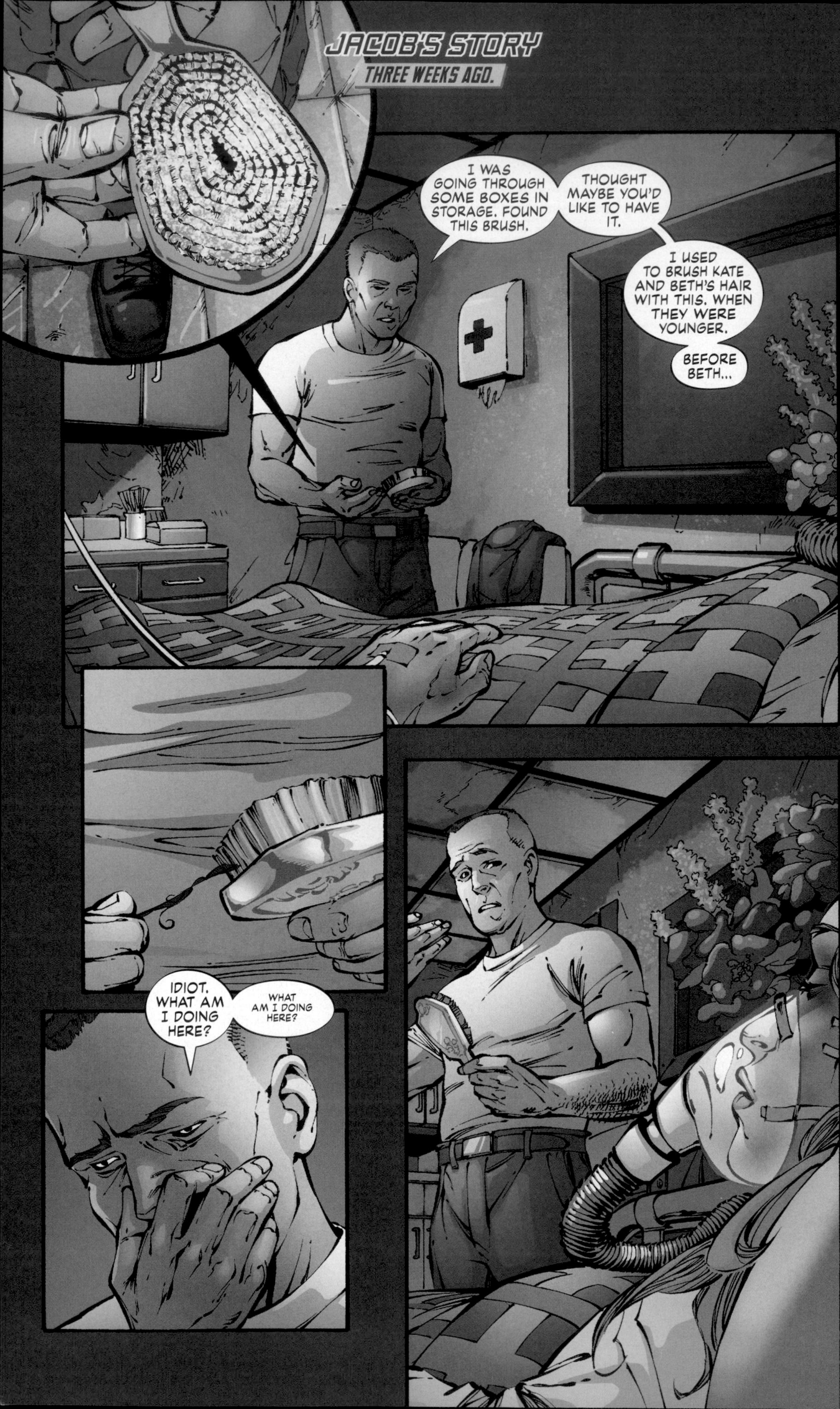
JACOB'S STORY
THREE WEEKS AGO.
I WAS GOING THROUGH SOME BOXES IN STORAGE. FOUND THIS BRUSH.
THOUGHT MAYBE YOU'D LIKE TO HAVE IT.
I USED TO BRUSH KATE AND BETH'S HAIR WITH THIS. WHEN THEY WERE YOUNGER.
BEFORE BETH...
IDIOT. WHAT AM I DOING HERE?
WHAT AM I DOING HERE?

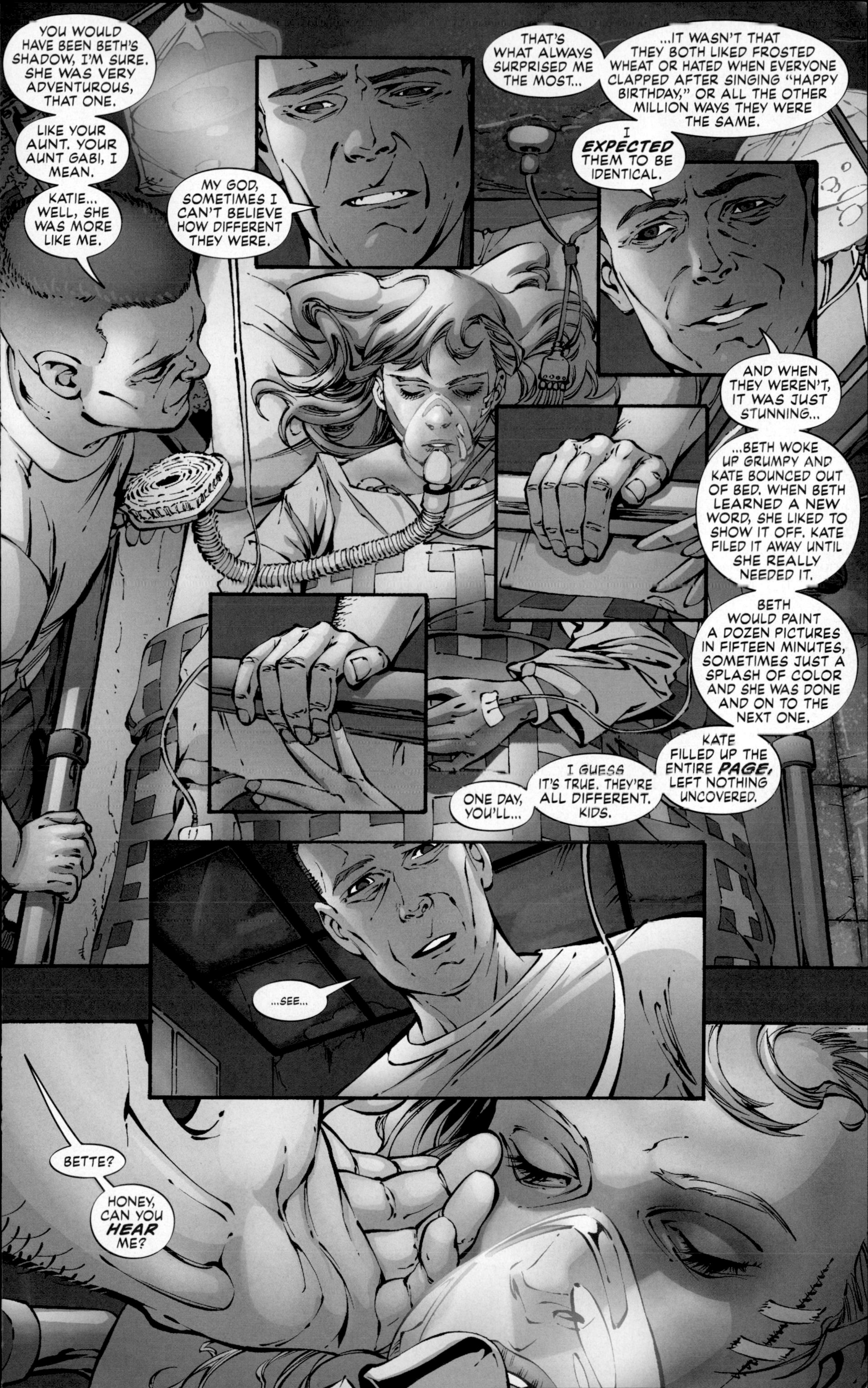
YOU WOULD HAVE BEEN BETH'S SHADOW, I'M SURE. SHE WAS VERY ADVENTUROUS, THAT ONE.
LIKE YOUR AUNT. YOUR AUNT GABI, I MEAN.
KATIE... WELL, SHE WAS MORE LIKE ME.
MY GOD, SOMETIMES I CAN'T BELIEVE HOW DIFFERENT THEY WERE.
THAT'S WHAT ALWAYS SURPRISED ME THE MOST...
...IT WASN'T THAT THEY BOTH LIKED FROSTED WHEAT OR HATED WHEN EVERYONE CLAPPED AFTER SINGING "HAPPY BIRTHDAY," OR ALL THE OTHER MILLION WAYS THEY WERE THE SAME.
I *EXPECTED* THEM TO BE IDENTICAL.
AND WHEN THEY WEREN'T, IT WAS JUST STUNNING...
...BETH WOKE UP GRUMPY AND KATE BOUNCED OUT OF BED. WHEN BETH LEARNED A NEW WORD, SHE LIKED TO SHOW IT OFF. KATE FILED IT AWAY UNTIL SHE REALLY NEEDED IT.
BETH WOULD PAINT A DOZEN PICTURES IN FIFTEEN MINUTES, SOMETIMES JUST A SPLASH OF COLOR AND SHE WAS DONE AND ON TO THE NEXT ONE.
KATE FILLED UP THE ENTIRE *PAGE*, LEFT NOTHING UNCOVERED.
I GUESS IT'S TRUE. THEY'RE ALL DIFFERENT. KIDS.
ONE DAY, YOU'LL...
...SEE...
BETTE?
HONEY, CAN YOU *HEAR* ME?

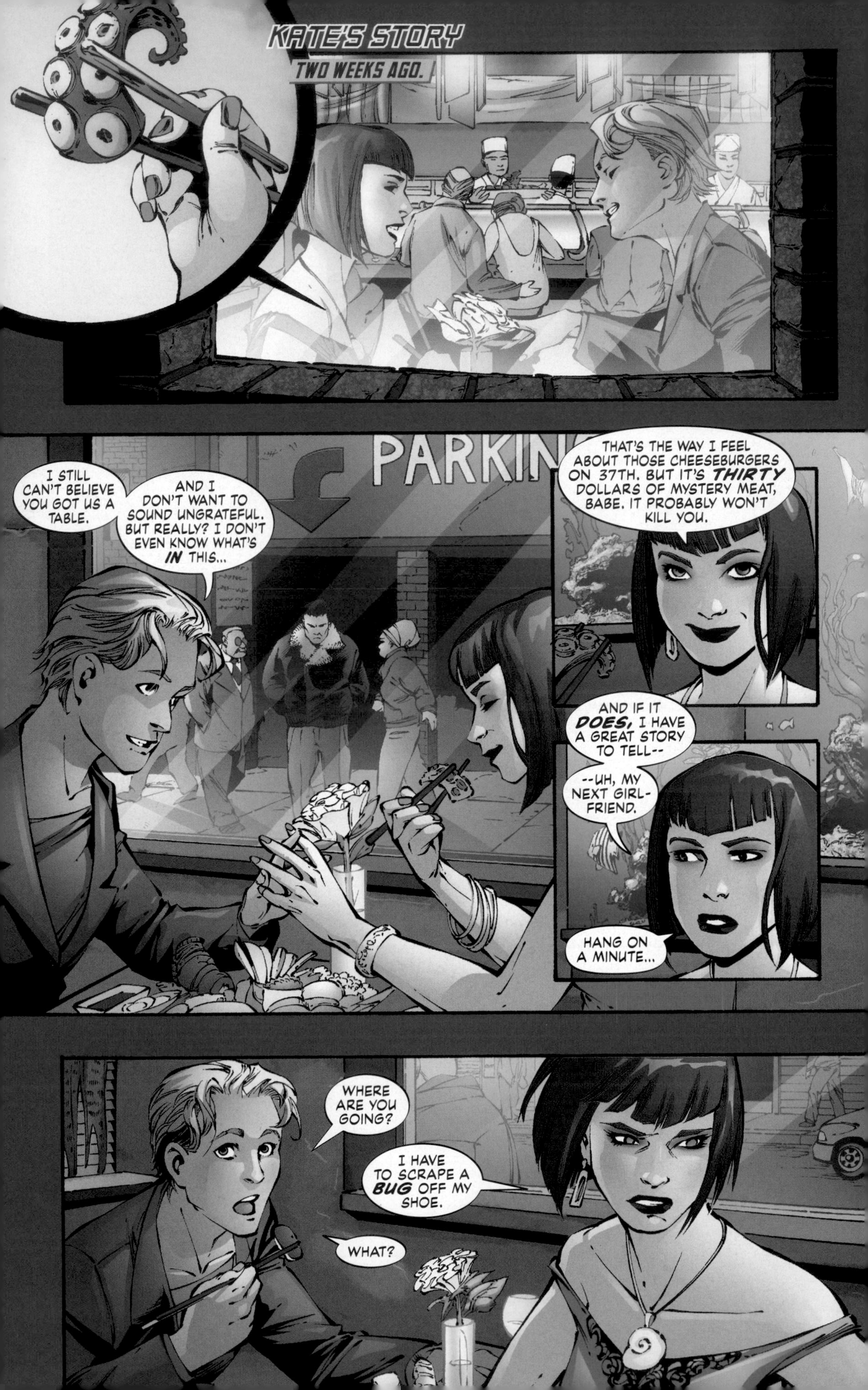
KATE'S STORY
TWO WEEKS AGO.
PARKING
I STILL CAN'T BELIEVE YOU GOT US A TABLE.
AND I DON'T WANT TO SOUND UNGRATEFUL. BUT REALLY? I DON'T EVEN KNOW WHAT'S IN THIS...
THAT'S THE WAY I FEEL ABOUT THOSE CHEESEBURGERS ON 37TH. BUT IT'S THIRTY DOLLARS OF MYSTERY MEAT, BABE. IT PROBABLY WON'T KILL YOU.
AND IF IT DOES, I HAVE A GREAT STORY TO TELL--
--UH, MY NEXT GIRL-FRIEND.
HANG ON A MINUTE...
WHERE ARE YOU GOING?
I HAVE TO SCRAPE A BUG OFF MY SHOE.
WHAT?

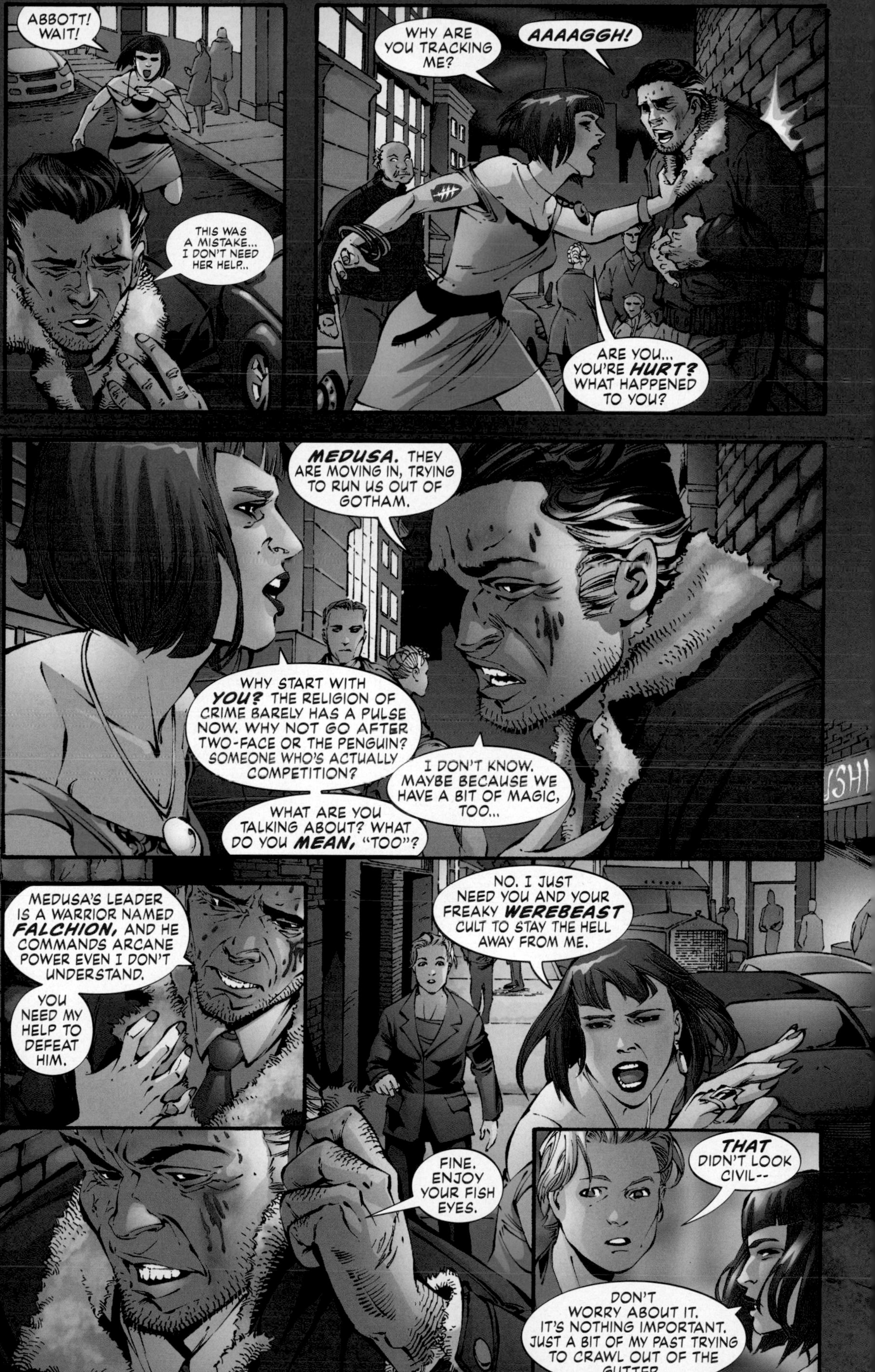
ABBOTT! WAIT!
THIS WAS A MISTAKE... I DON'T NEED HER HELP...
WHY ARE YOU TRACKING ME?
AAAAGGH!
ARE YOU... YOU'RE HURT? WHAT HAPPENED TO YOU?
MEDUSA. THEY ARE MOVING IN, TRYING TO RUN US OUT OF GOTHAM.
WHY START WITH YOU? THE RELIGION OF CRIME BARELY HAS A PULSE NOW. WHY NOT GO AFTER TWO-FACE OR THE PENGUIN? SOMEONE WHO'S ACTUALLY COMPETITION?
I DON'T KNOW. MAYBE BECAUSE WE HAVE A BIT OF MAGIC, TOO...
WHAT ARE YOU TALKING ABOUT? WHAT DO YOU MEAN, "TOO"?
MEDUSA'S LEADER IS A WARRIOR NAMED FALCHION, AND HE COMMANDS ARCANE POWER EVEN I DON'T UNDERSTAND.
YOU NEED MY HELP TO DEFEAT HIM.
NO. I JUST NEED YOU AND YOUR FREAKY WEREBEAST CULT TO STAY THE HELL AWAY FROM ME.
FINE. ENJOY YOUR FISH EYES.
THAT DIDN'T LOOK CIVIL--
DON'T WORRY ABOUT IT. IT'S NOTHING IMPORTANT. JUST A BIT OF MY PAST TRYING TO CRAWL OUT OF THE GUTTER.

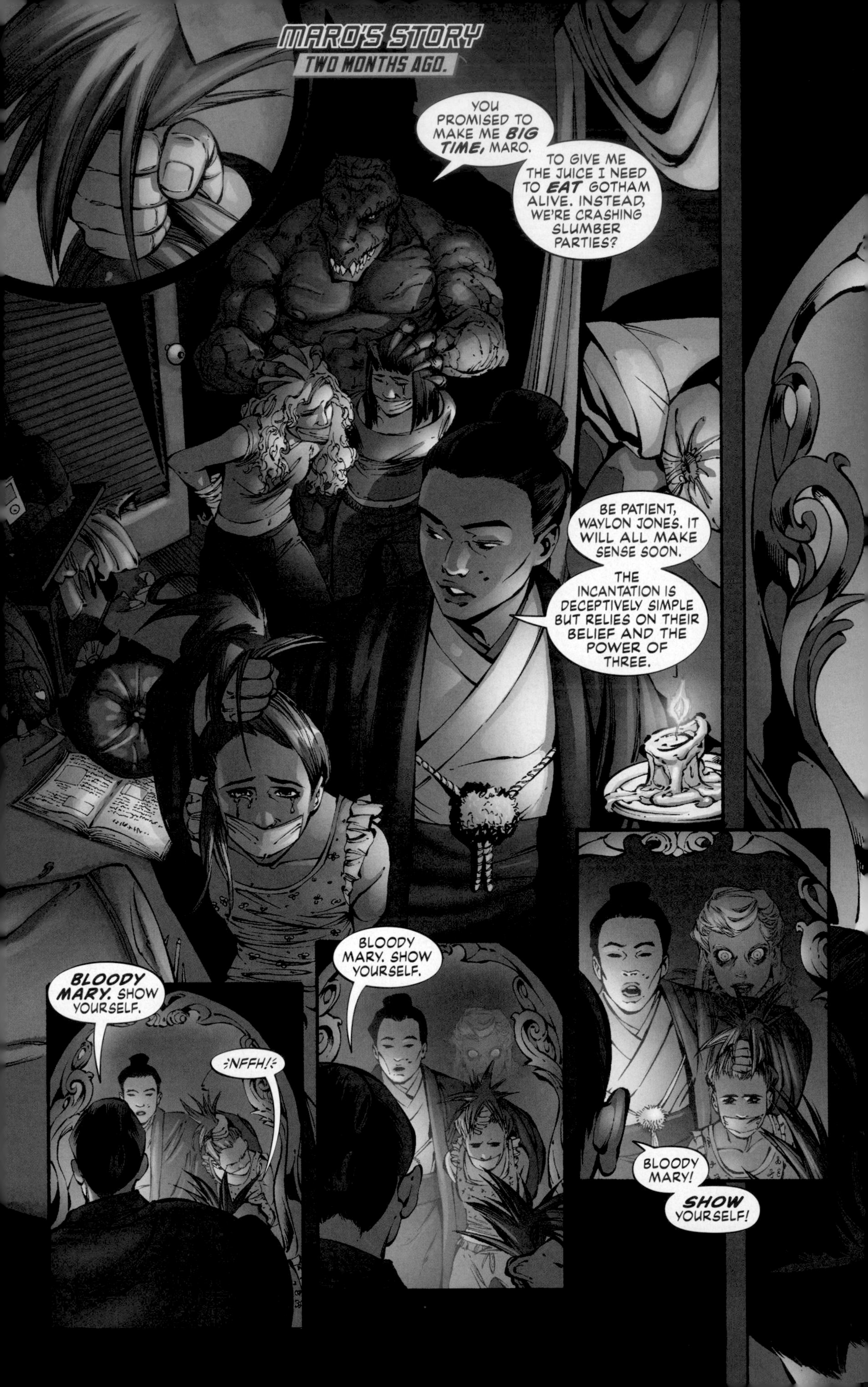
MARO'S STORY
TWO MONTHS AGO.
YOU PROMISED TO MAKE ME BIG TIME, MARO.
TO GIVE ME THE JUICE I NEED TO EAT GOTHAM ALIVE. INSTEAD, WE'RE CRASHING SLUMBER PARTIES?
BE PATIENT, WAYLON JONES. IT WILL ALL MAKE SENSE SOON.
THE INCANTATION IS DECEPTIVELY SIMPLE BUT RELIES ON THEIR BELIEF AND THE POWER OF THREE.
BLOODY MARY. SHOW YOURSELF.
NFFH!
BLOODY MARY. SHOW YOURSELF.
BLOODY MARY!
SHOW YOURSELF!

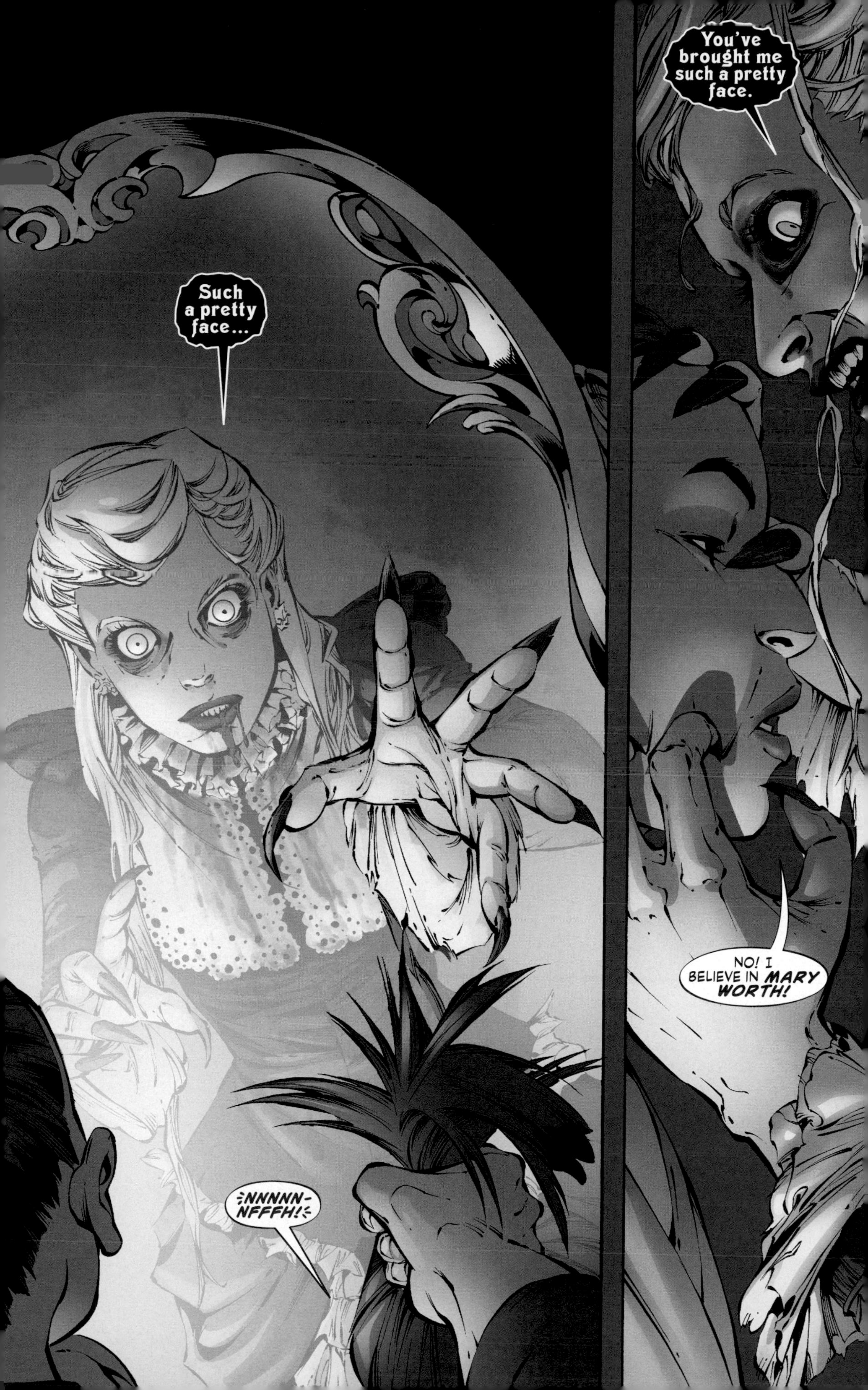
Such a pretty face...
NNNNN-NFFFH!
You've brought me such a pretty face.
NO! I BELIEVE IN MARY WORTH!

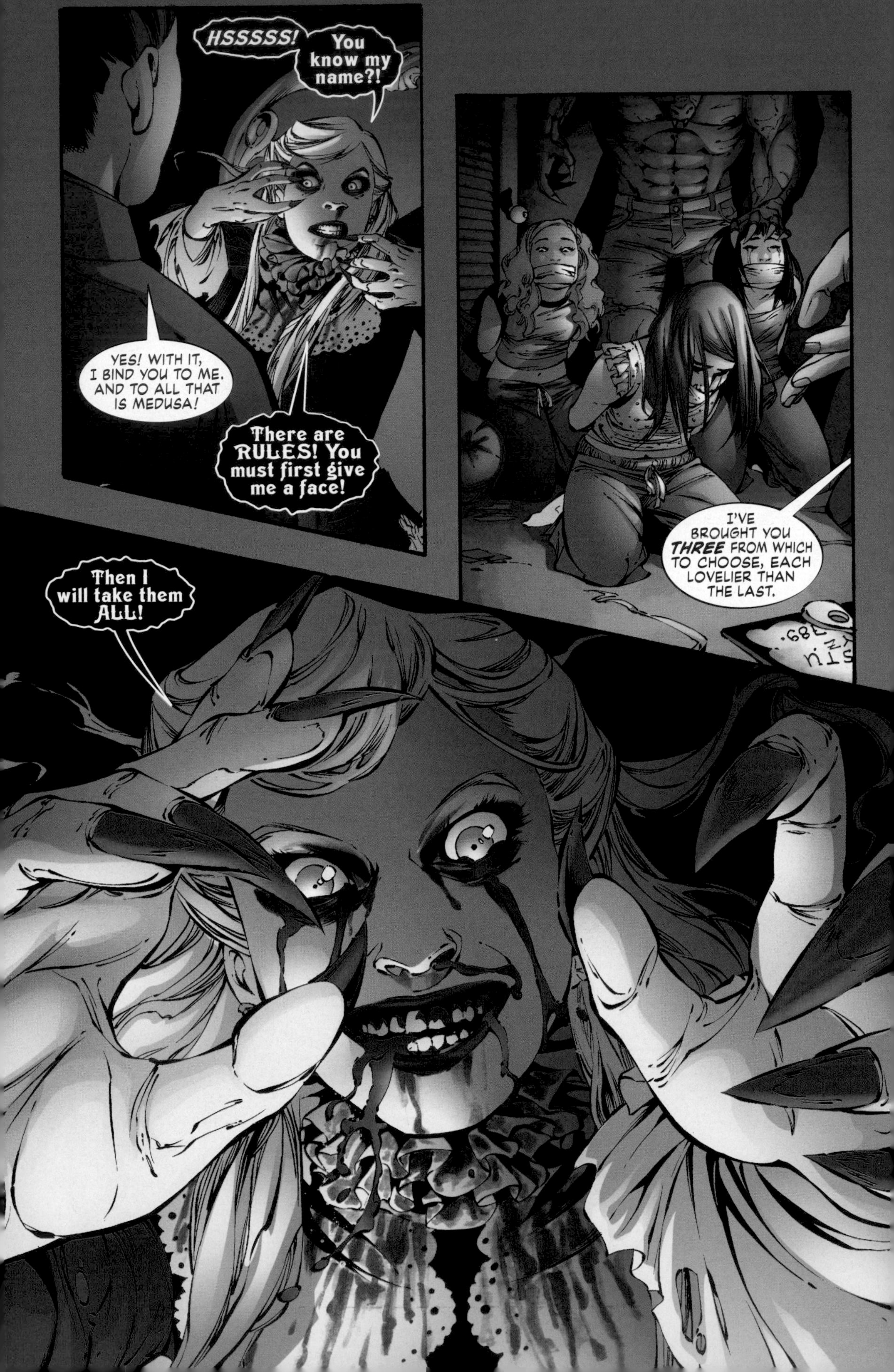
HSSSSS!
You know my name?!
YES! WITH IT, I BIND YOU TO ME. AND TO ALL THAT IS MEDUSA!
There are RULES! You must first give me a face!
I'VE BROUGHT YOU THREE FROM WHICH TO CHOOSE, EACH LOVELIER THAN THE LAST.
Then I will take them ALL!

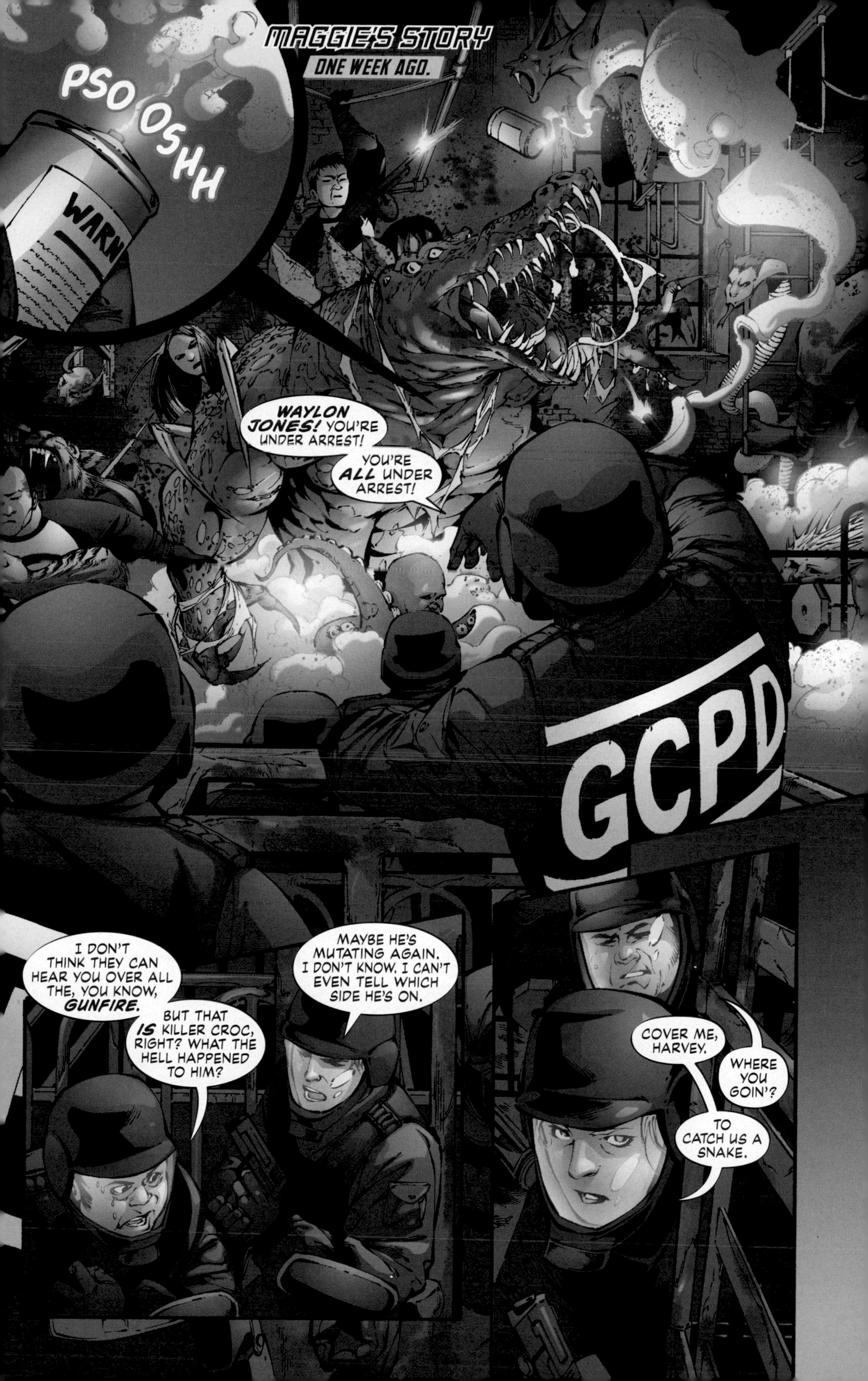
MAGGIE'S STORY
ONE WEEK AGO.
PSOOOSHH
WARN
WAYLON JONES! YOU'RE UNDER ARREST!
YOU'RE ALL UNDER ARREST!
GCPD
I DON'T THINK THEY CAN HEAR YOU OVER ALL THE, YOU KNOW, GUNFIRE.
BUT THAT IS KILLER CROC, RIGHT? WHAT THE HELL HAPPENED TO HIM?
MAYBE HE'S MUTATING AGAIN. I DON'T KNOW. I CAN'T EVEN TELL WHICH SIDE HE'S ON.
COVER ME, HARVEY.
WHERE YOU GOIN'?
TO CATCH US A SNAKE.

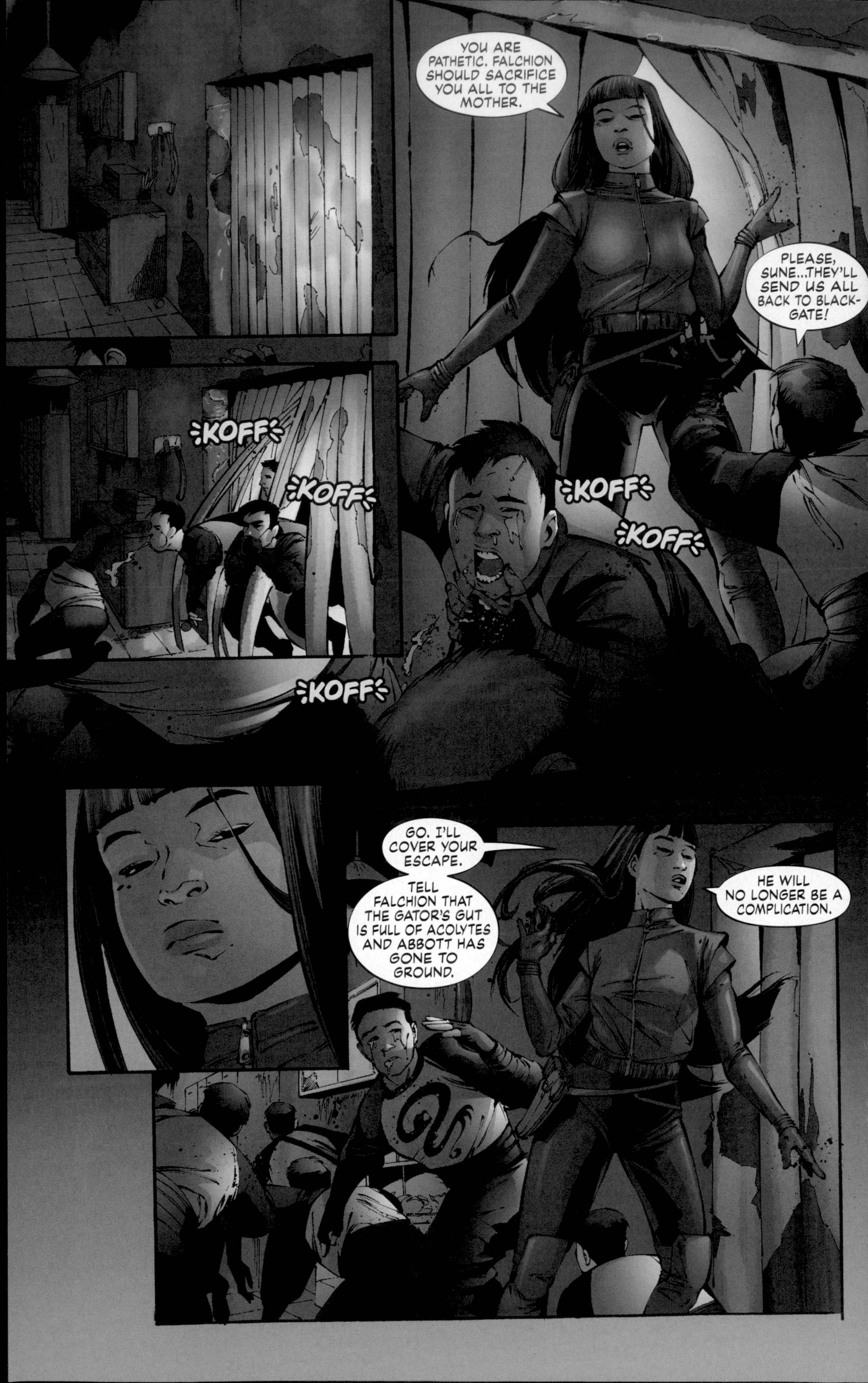
YOU ARE PATHETIC. FALCHION SHOULD SACRIFICE YOU ALL TO THE MOTHER.
PLEASE, SUNE...THEY'LL SEND US ALL BACK TO BLACK-GATE!
KOFF
KOFF
KOFF
KOFF
KOFF
GO. I'LL COVER YOUR ESCAPE.
TELL FALCHION THAT THE GATOR'S GUT IS FULL OF ACOLYTES AND ABBOTT HAS GONE TO GROUND.
HE WILL NO LONGER BE A COMPLICATION.

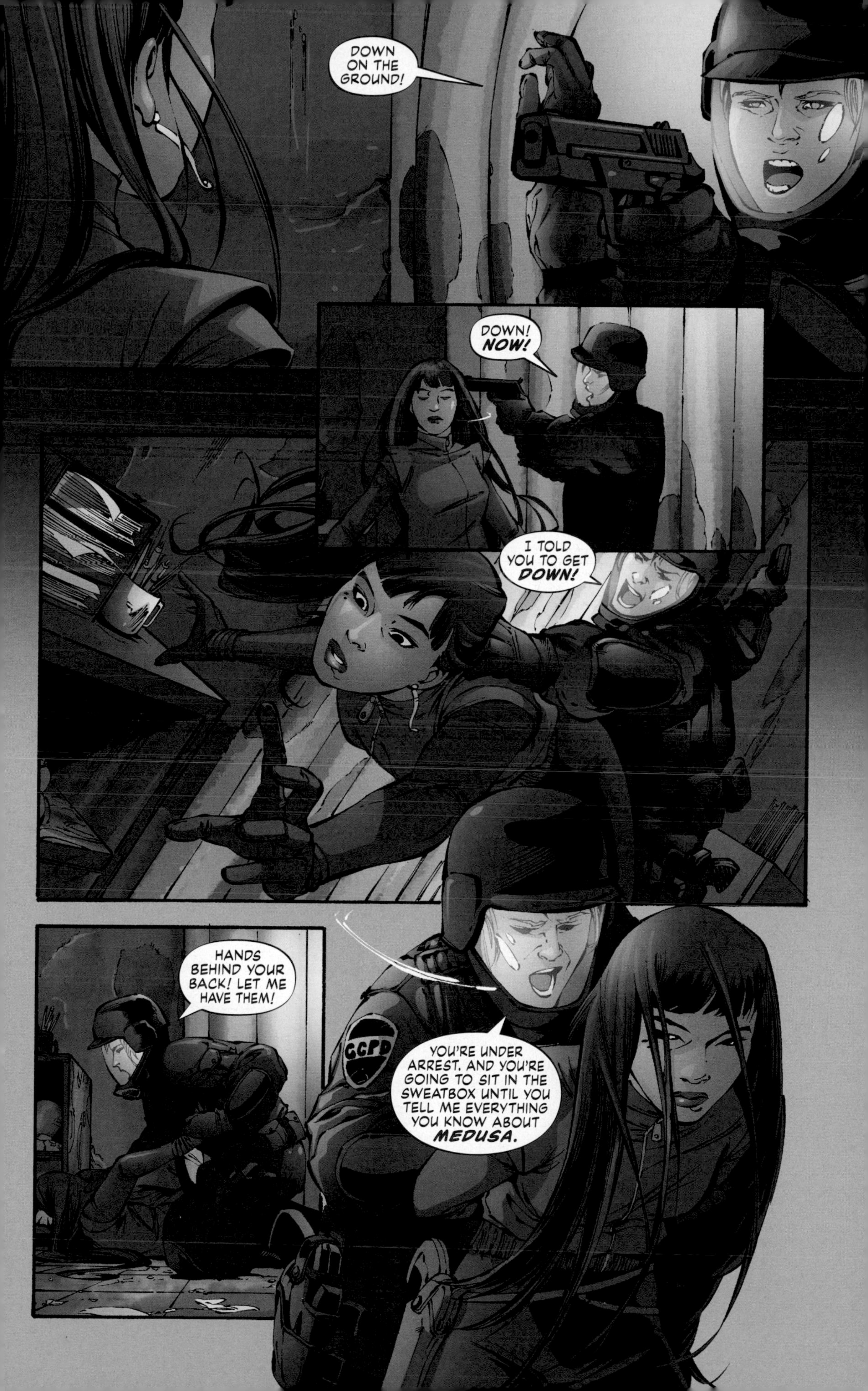

DOWN ON THE GROUND!
DOWN! **NOW!**
I TOLD YOU TO GET **DOWN!**
HANDS BEHIND YOUR BACK! LET ME HAVE THEM!
GCPD
YOU'RE UNDER ARREST. AND YOU'RE GOING TO SIT IN THE SWEATBOX UNTIL YOU TELL ME EVERYTHING YOU KNOW ABOUT **MEDUSA**.

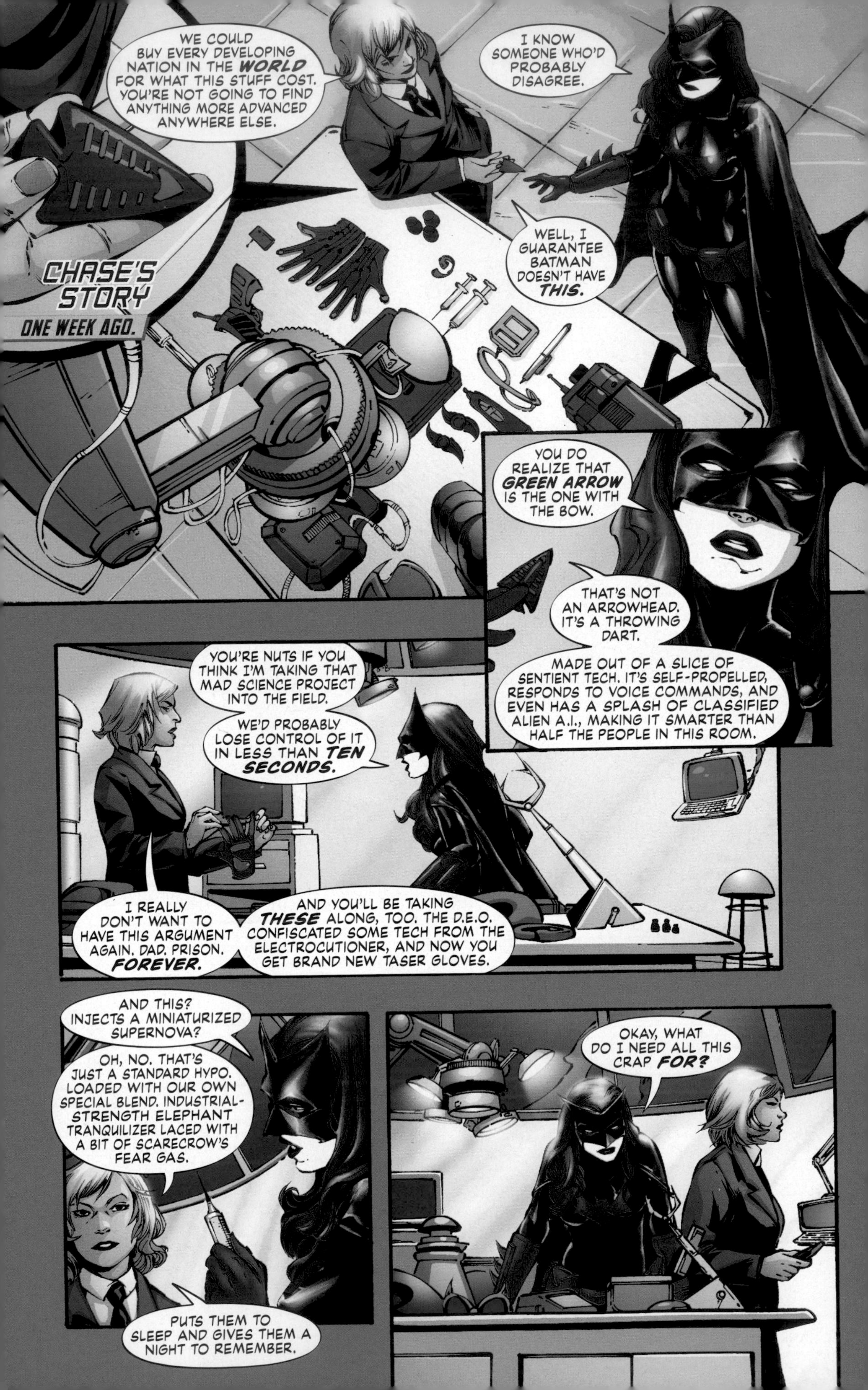
WE COULD BUY EVERY DEVELOPING NATION IN THE WORLD FOR WHAT THIS STUFF COST. YOU'RE NOT GOING TO FIND ANYTHING MORE ADVANCED ANYWHERE ELSE.
I KNOW SOMEONE WHO'D PROBABLY DISAGREE.
CHASE'S STORY
ONE WEEK AGO.
WELL, I GUARANTEE BATMAN DOESN'T HAVE THIS.
YOU DO REALIZE THAT GREEN ARROW IS THE ONE WITH THE BOW.
THAT'S NOT AN ARROWHEAD. IT'S A THROWING DART.
MADE OUT OF A SLICE OF SENTIENT TECH. IT'S SELF-PROPELLED, RESPONDS TO VOICE COMMANDS, AND EVEN HAS A SPLASH OF CLASSIFIED ALIEN A.I., MAKING IT SMARTER THAN HALF THE PEOPLE IN THIS ROOM.
YOU'RE NUTS IF YOU THINK I'M TAKING THAT MAD SCIENCE PROJECT INTO THE FIELD.
WE'D PROBABLY LOSE CONTROL OF IT IN LESS THAN TEN SECONDS.
I REALLY DON'T WANT TO HAVE THIS ARGUMENT AGAIN. DAD. PRISON. FOREVER.
AND YOU'LL BE TAKING THESE ALONG, TOO. THE D.E.O. CONFISCATED SOME TECH FROM THE ELECTROCUTIONER, AND NOW YOU GET BRAND NEW TASER GLOVES.
AND THIS? INJECTS A MINIATURIZED SUPERNOVA?
OH, NO. THAT'S JUST A STANDARD HYPO. LOADED WITH OUR OWN SPECIAL BLEND. INDUSTRIAL-STRENGTH ELEPHANT TRANQUILIZER LACED WITH A BIT OF SCARECROW'S FEAR GAS.
PUTS THEM TO SLEEP AND GIVES THEM A NIGHT TO REMEMBER.
OKAY, WHAT DO I NEED ALL THIS CRAP FOR?

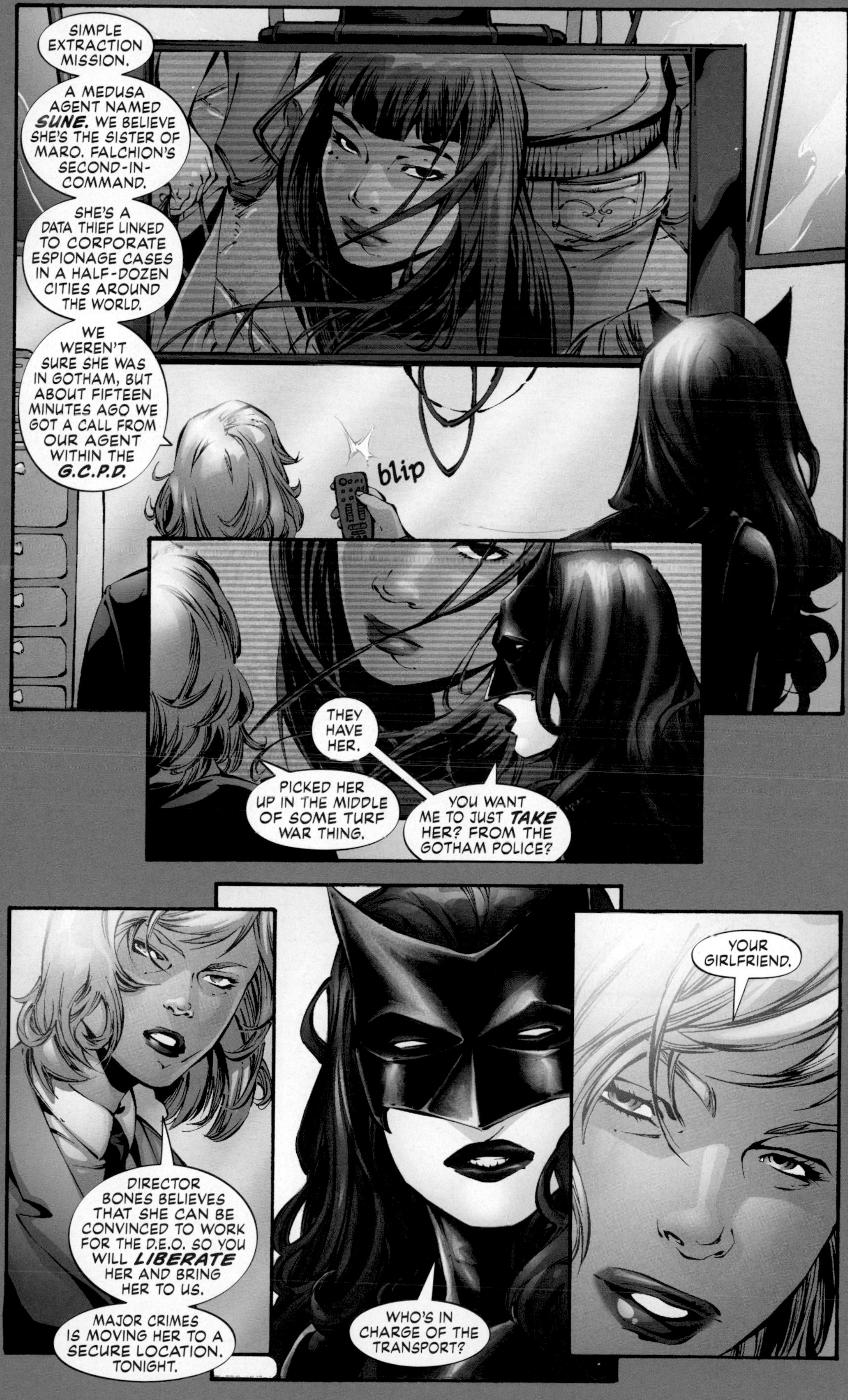
SIMPLE EXTRACTION MISSION.
A MEDUSA AGENT NAMED SUNE. WE BELIEVE SHE'S THE SISTER OF MARO. FALCHION'S SECOND-IN-COMMAND.
SHE'S A DATA THIEF LINKED TO CORPORATE ESPIONAGE CASES IN A HALF-DOZEN CITIES AROUND THE WORLD.
WE WEREN'T SURE SHE WAS IN GOTHAM, BUT ABOUT FIFTEEN MINUTES AGO WE GOT A CALL FROM OUR AGENT WITHIN THE G.C.P.D.
blip
THEY HAVE HER.
PICKED HER UP IN THE MIDDLE OF SOME TURF WAR THING.
YOU WANT ME TO JUST TAKE HER? FROM THE GOTHAM POLICE?
DIRECTOR BONES BELIEVES THAT SHE CAN BE CONVINCED TO WORK FOR THE D.E.O. SO YOU WILL LIBERATE HER AND BRING HER TO US.
MAJOR CRIMES IS MOVING HER TO A SECURE LOCATION. TONIGHT.
WHO'S IN CHARGE OF THE TRANSPORT?
YOUR GIRLFRIEND.

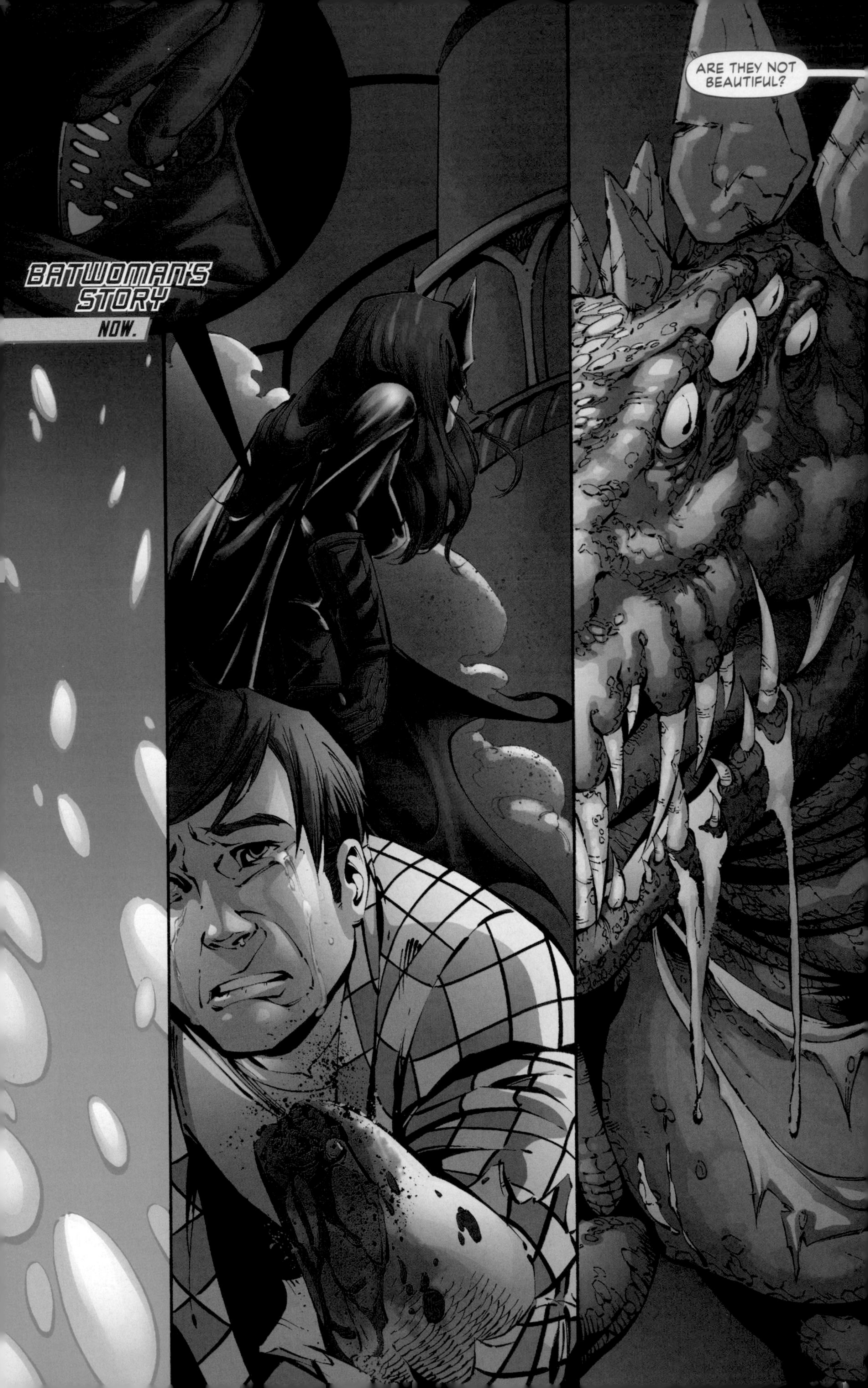
BATWOMAN'S STORY
NOW.
ARE THEY NOT BEAUTIFUL?

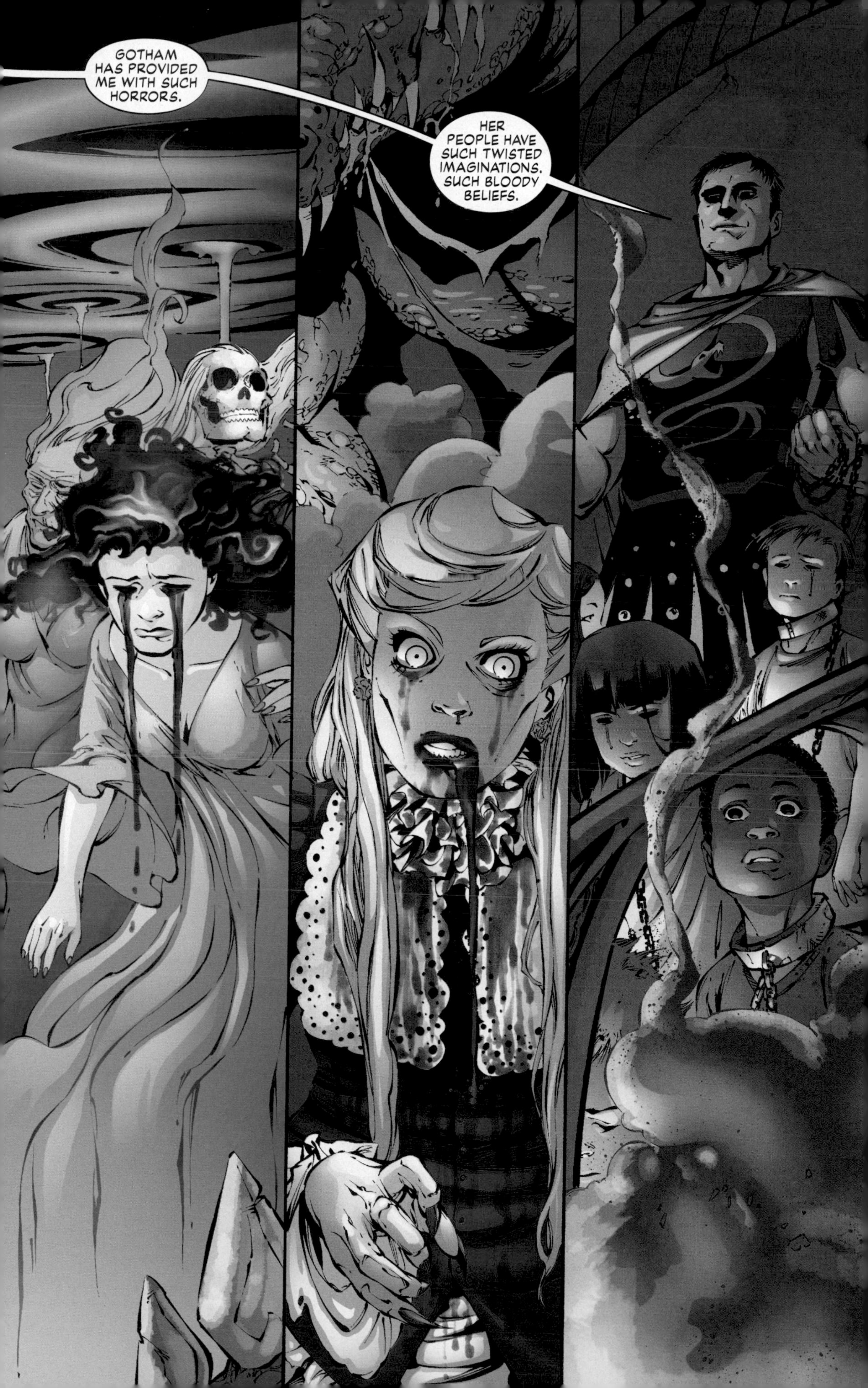
GOTHAM HAS PROVIDED ME WITH SUCH HORRORS.
HER PEOPLE HAVE SUCH TWISTED IMAGINATIONS. SUCH BLOODY BELIEFS.

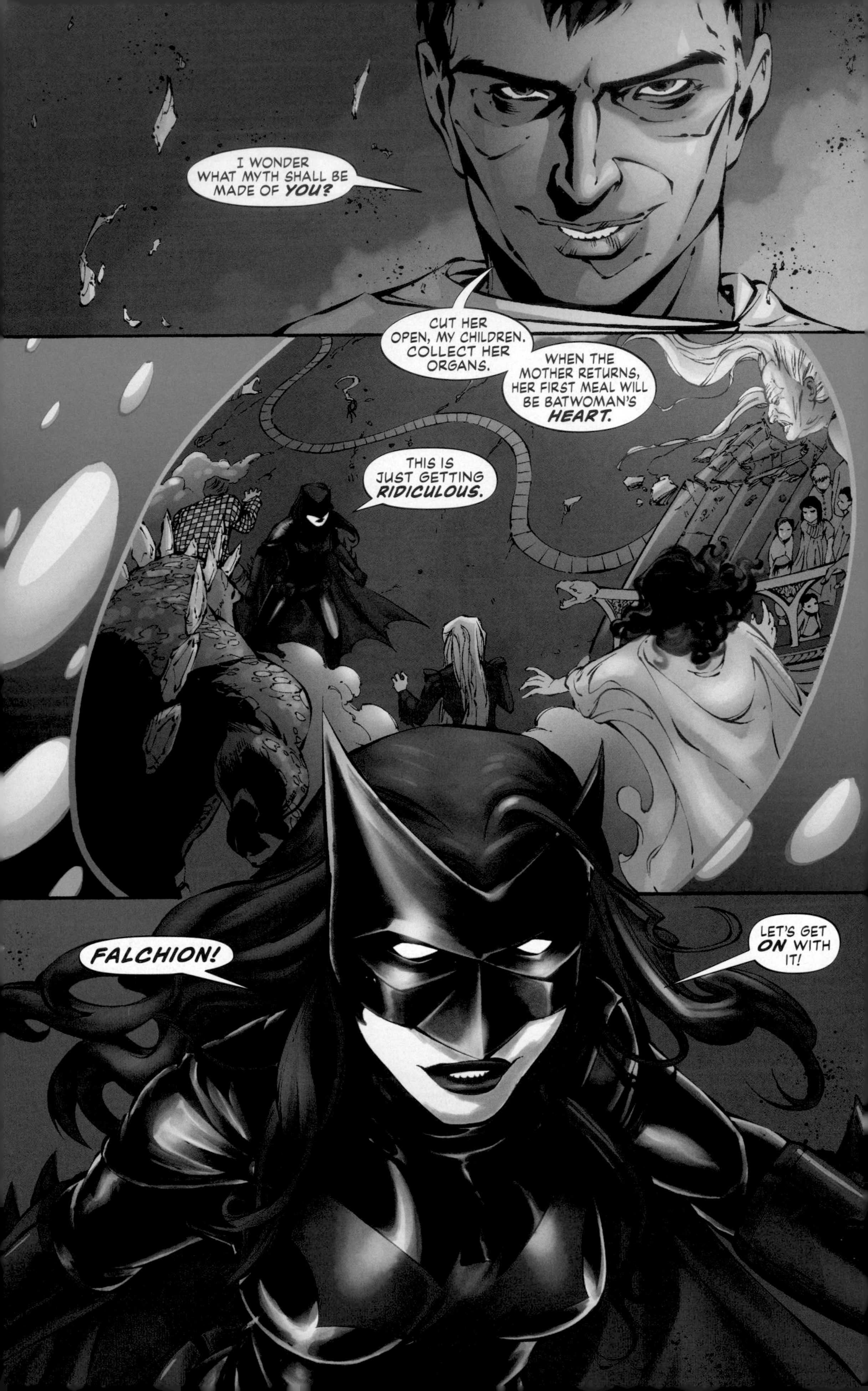
I WONDER WHAT MYTH SHALL BE MADE OF YOU?
CUT HER OPEN, MY CHILDREN. COLLECT HER ORGANS.
WHEN THE MOTHER RETURNS, HER FIRST MEAL WILL BE BATWOMAN'S HEART.
THIS IS JUST GETTING RIDICULOUS.
FALCHION!
LET'S GET ON WITH IT!

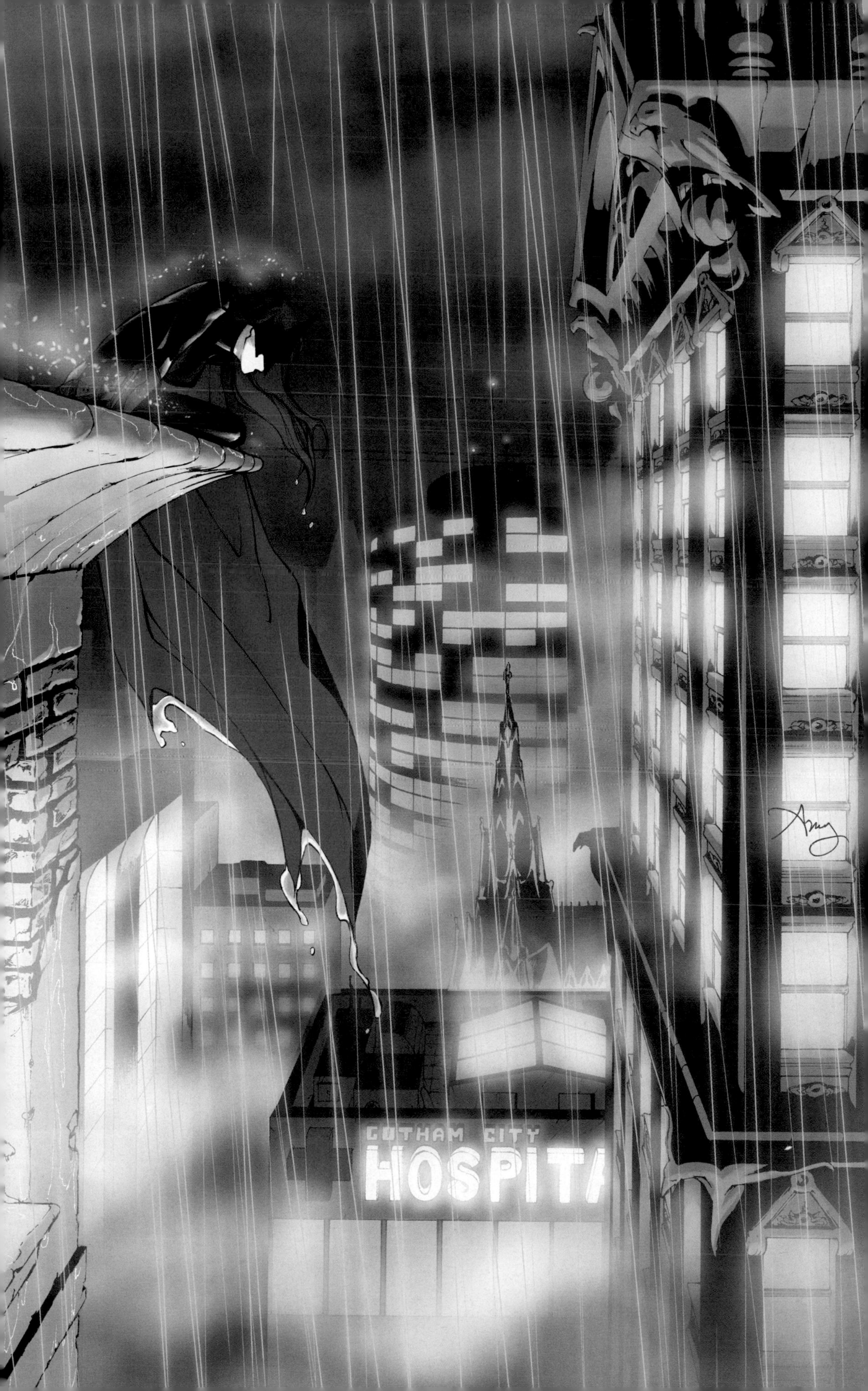
GOTHAM CITY
HOSPITA

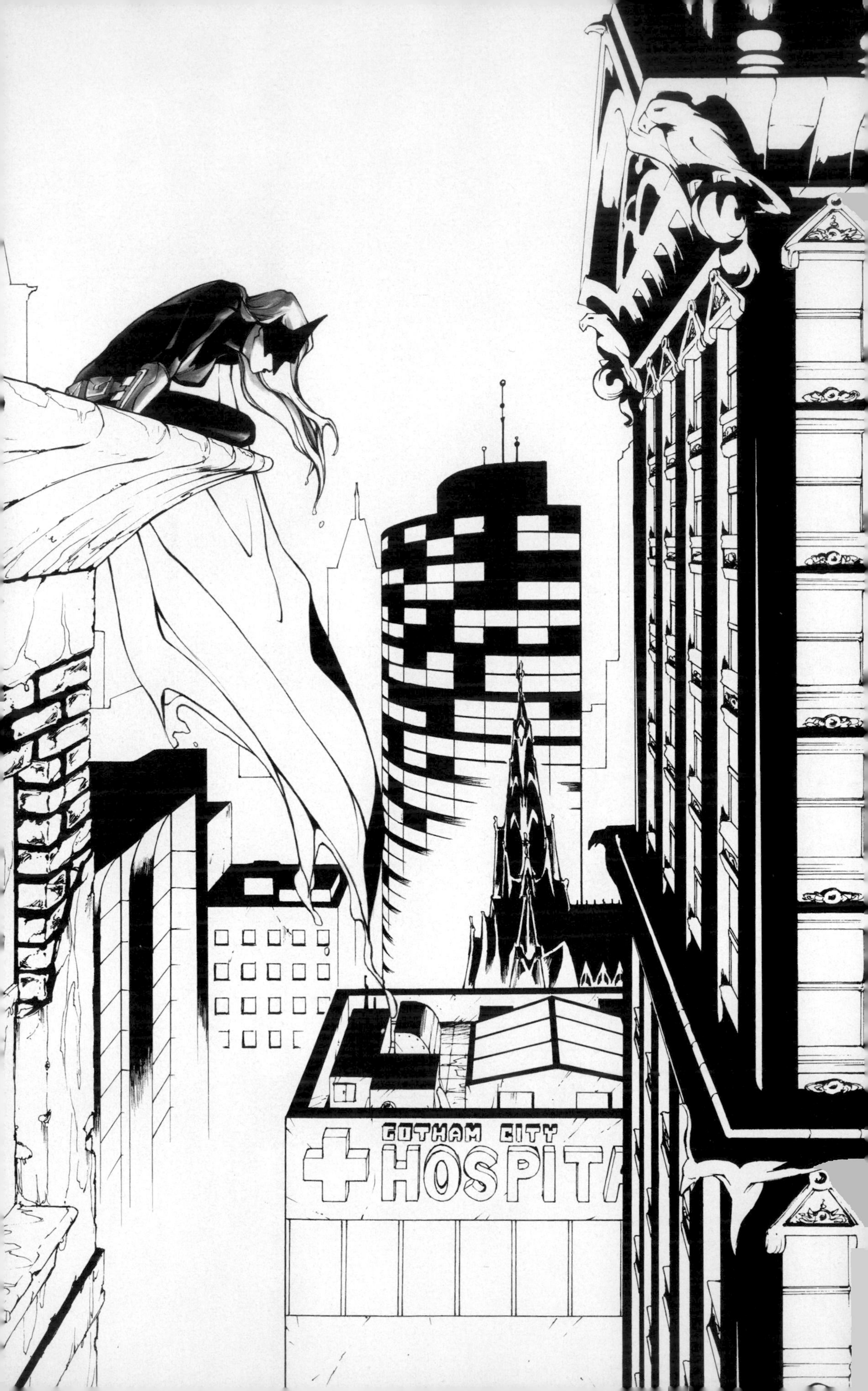
GOTHAM CITY
HOSPITA

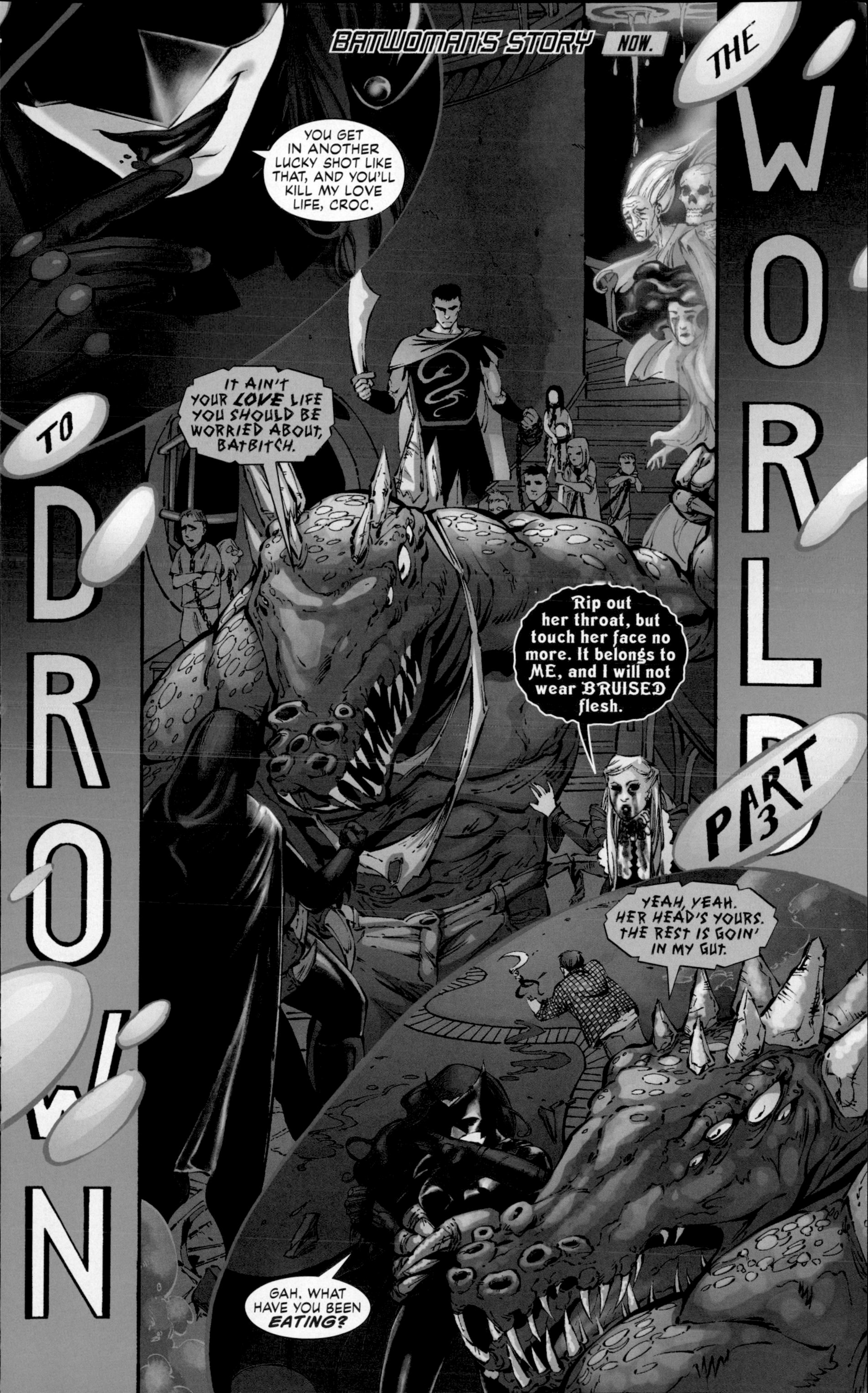
BATWOMAN'S STORY NOW.
THE WORLD TO DROWN PART 3
YOU GET IN ANOTHER LUCKY SHOT LIKE THAT, AND YOU'LL KILL MY LOVE LIFE, CROC.
IT AIN'T YOUR LOVE LIFE YOU SHOULD BE WORRIED ABOUT, BATBITCH.
Rip out her throat, but touch her face no more. It belongs to ME, and I will not wear BRUISED flesh.
YEAH, YEAH. HER HEAD'S YOURS. THE REST IS GOIN' IN MY GUT.
GAH, WHAT HAVE YOU BEEN EATING?

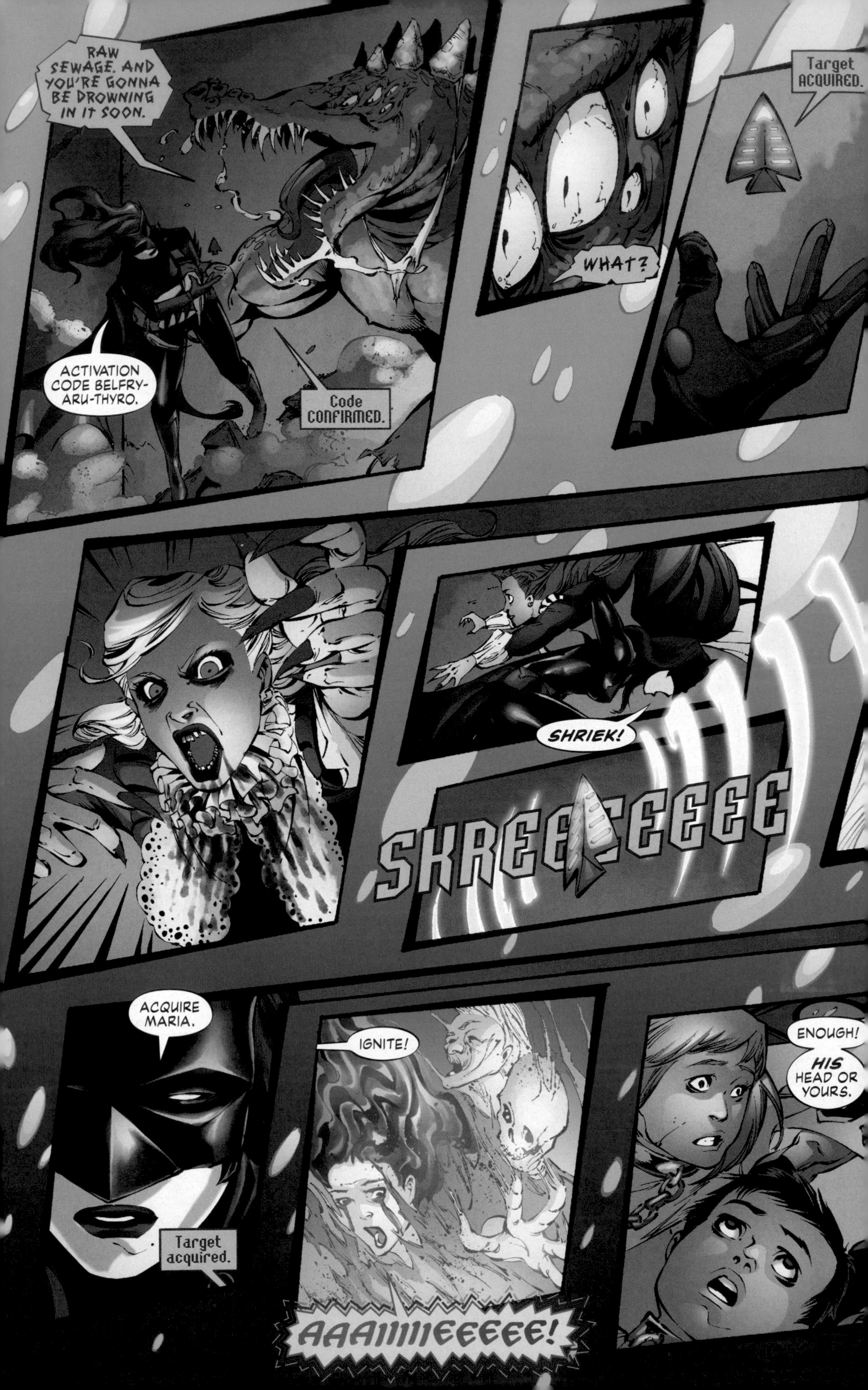
RAW SEWAGE. AND YOU'RE GONNA BE DROWNING IN IT SOON.
ACTIVATION CODE BELFRY-ARU-THYRO.
Code CONFIRMED.
WHAT?
Target ACQUIRED.
SHRIEK!
SKREEEEEEEE
ACQUIRE MARIA.
Target acquired.
IGNITE!
AAAIIIIIEEEEE!
ENOUGH! HIS HEAD OR YOURS.

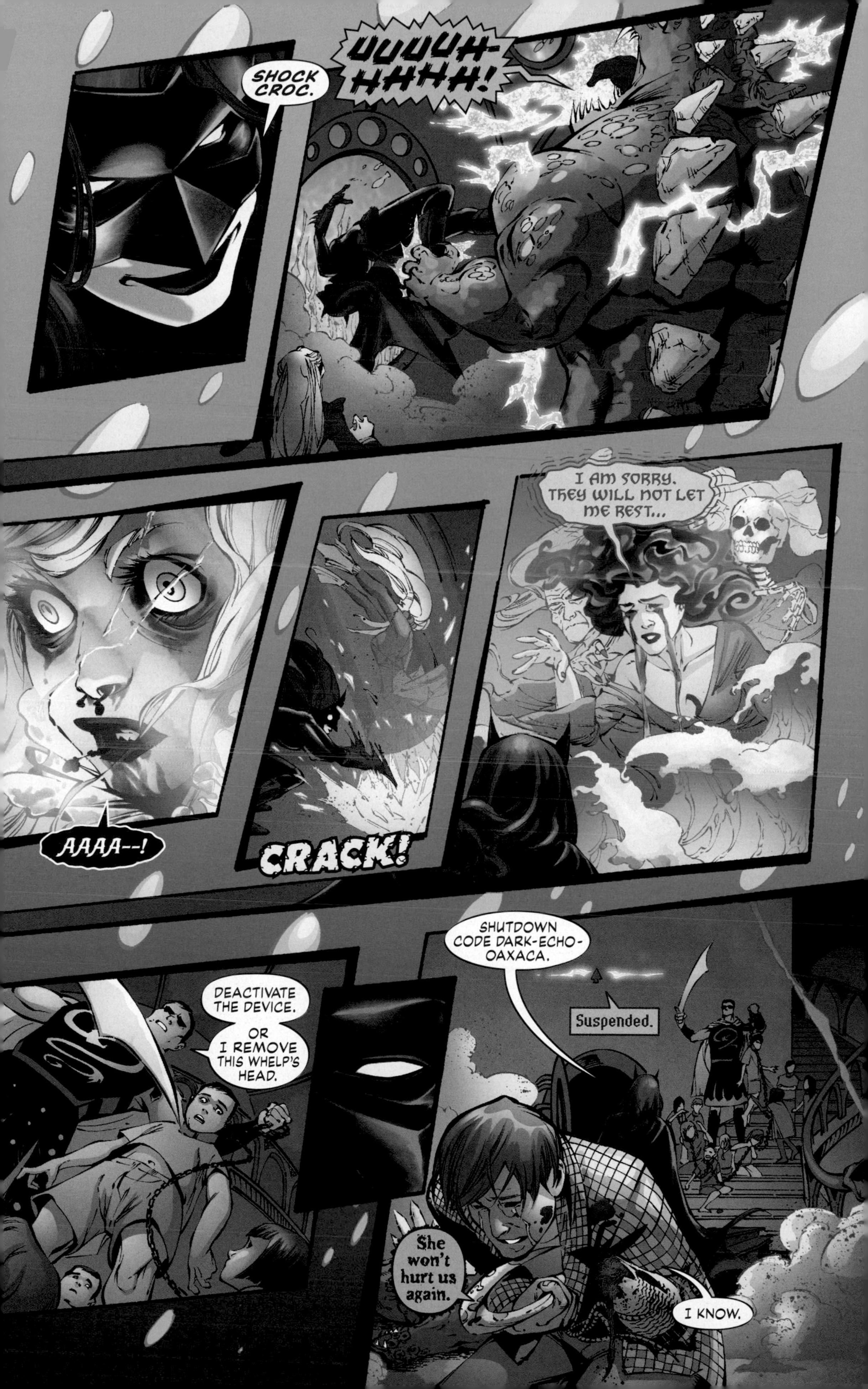
SHOCK CROC.
UUUUH-HHHH!
I AM SORRY. THEY WILL NOT LET ME REST...
AAAA--!
CRACK!
DEACTIVATE THE DEVICE. OR I REMOVE THIS WHELP'S HEAD.
SHUTDOWN CODE DARK-ECHO-OAXACA.
Suspended.
She won't hurt us again.
I KNOW.

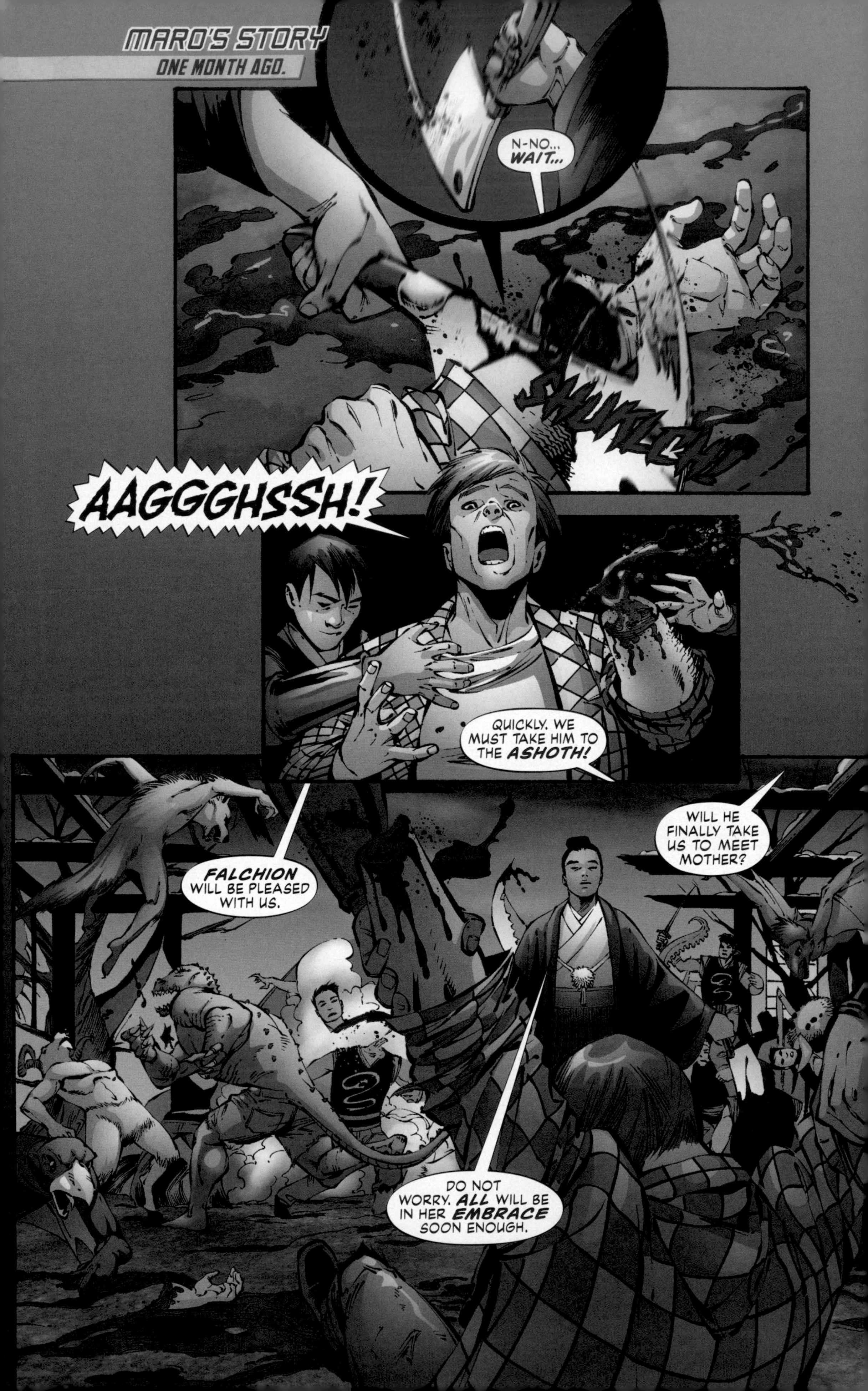
MARO'S STORY
ONE MONTH AGO.
N-NO... WAIT...
SHUKLCH!
AAGGGHSSH!
QUICKLY. WE MUST TAKE HIM TO THE ASHOTH!
FALCHION WILL BE PLEASED WITH US.
WILL HE FINALLY TAKE US TO MEET MOTHER?
DO NOT WORRY. ALL WILL BE IN HER EMBRACE SOON ENOUGH.

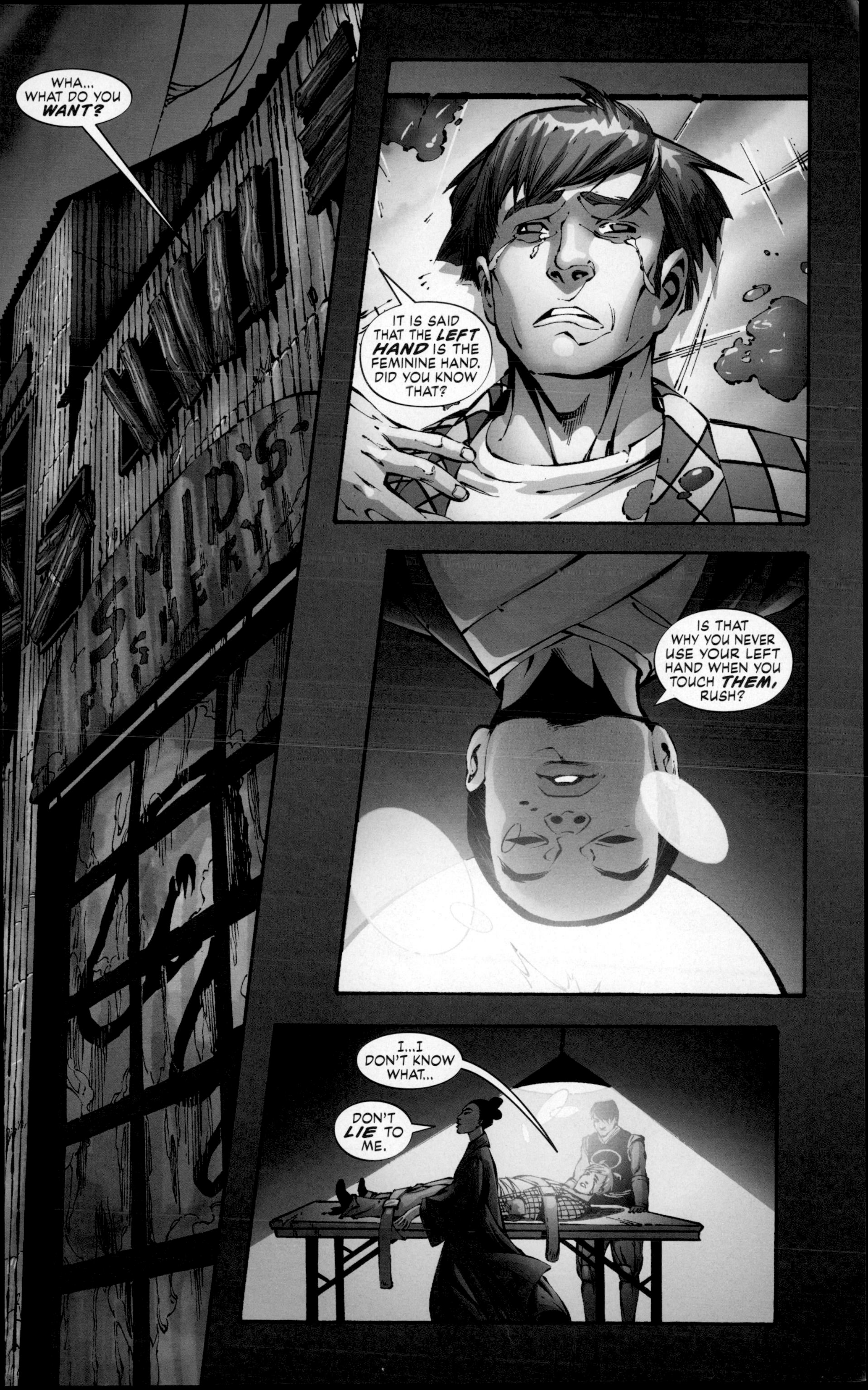
WHA... WHAT DO YOU **WANT?**
IT IS SAID THAT THE **LEFT HAND** IS THE FEMININE HAND. DID YOU KNOW THAT?
IS THAT WHY YOU NEVER USE YOUR LEFT HAND WHEN YOU TOUCH **THEM,** RUSH?
I...I DON'T KNOW WHAT...
DON'T **LIE** TO ME.

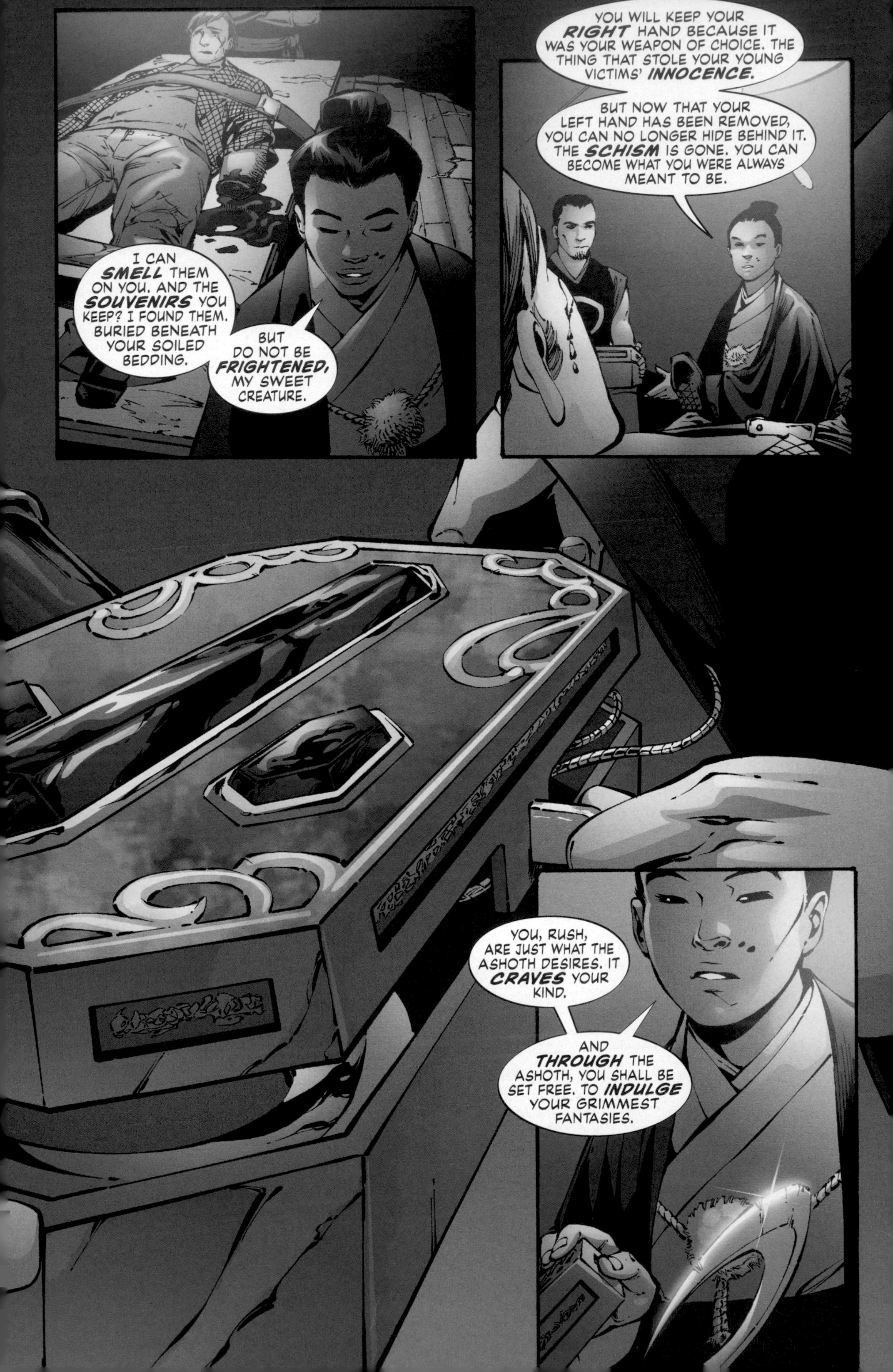
I CAN SMELL THEM ON YOU. AND THE SOUVENIRS YOU KEEP? I FOUND THEM. BURIED BENEATH YOUR SOILED BEDDING.
BUT DO NOT BE FRIGHTENED, MY SWEET CREATURE.
YOU WILL KEEP YOUR RIGHT HAND BECAUSE IT WAS YOUR WEAPON OF CHOICE. THE THING THAT STOLE YOUR YOUNG VICTIMS' INNOCENCE.
BUT NOW THAT YOUR LEFT HAND HAS BEEN REMOVED, YOU CAN NO LONGER HIDE BEHIND IT. THE SCHISM IS GONE. YOU CAN BECOME WHAT YOU WERE ALWAYS MEANT TO BE.
YOU, RUSH, ARE JUST WHAT THE ASHOTH DESIRES. IT CRAVES YOUR KIND.
AND THROUGH THE ASHOTH, YOU SHALL BE SET FREE. TO INDULGE YOUR GRIMMEST FANTASIES.

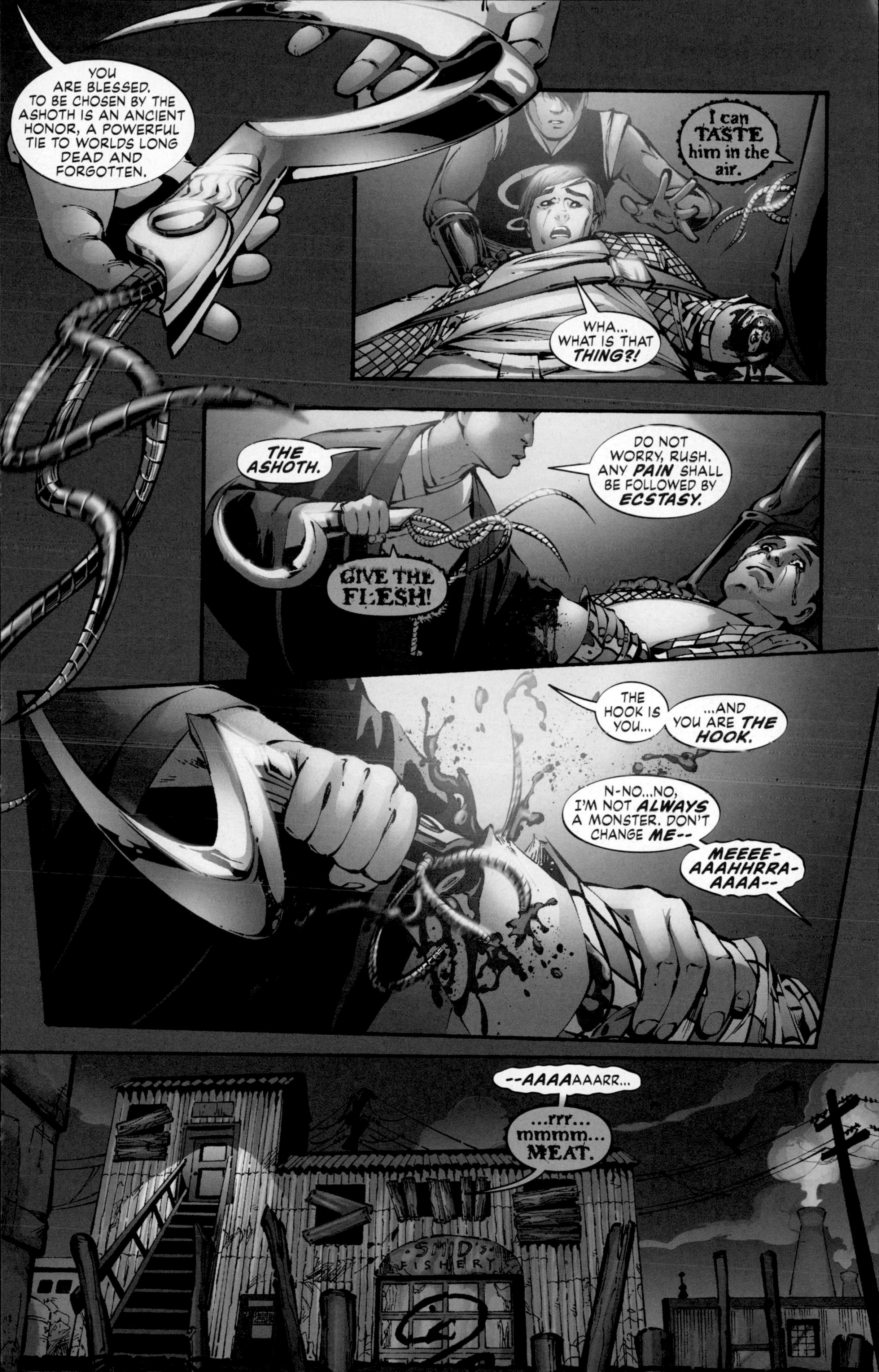
YOU ARE BLESSED. TO BE CHOSEN BY THE ASHOTH IS AN ANCIENT HONOR, A POWERFUL TIE TO WORLDS LONG DEAD AND FORGOTTEN.
I can TASTE him in the air.
WHA... WHAT IS THAT THING?!
THE ASHOTH.
DO NOT WORRY, RUSH. ANY PAIN SHALL BE FOLLOWED BY ECSTASY.
GIVE THE FLESH!
THE HOOK IS YOU...
...AND YOU ARE THE HOOK.
N-NO...NO, I'M NOT ALWAYS A MONSTER. DON'T CHANGE ME--
MEEEE-AAAHHRRA-AAAA--
--AAAAAAARR...
...rrr... mmmm... MEAT.
SMID'S FISHERY

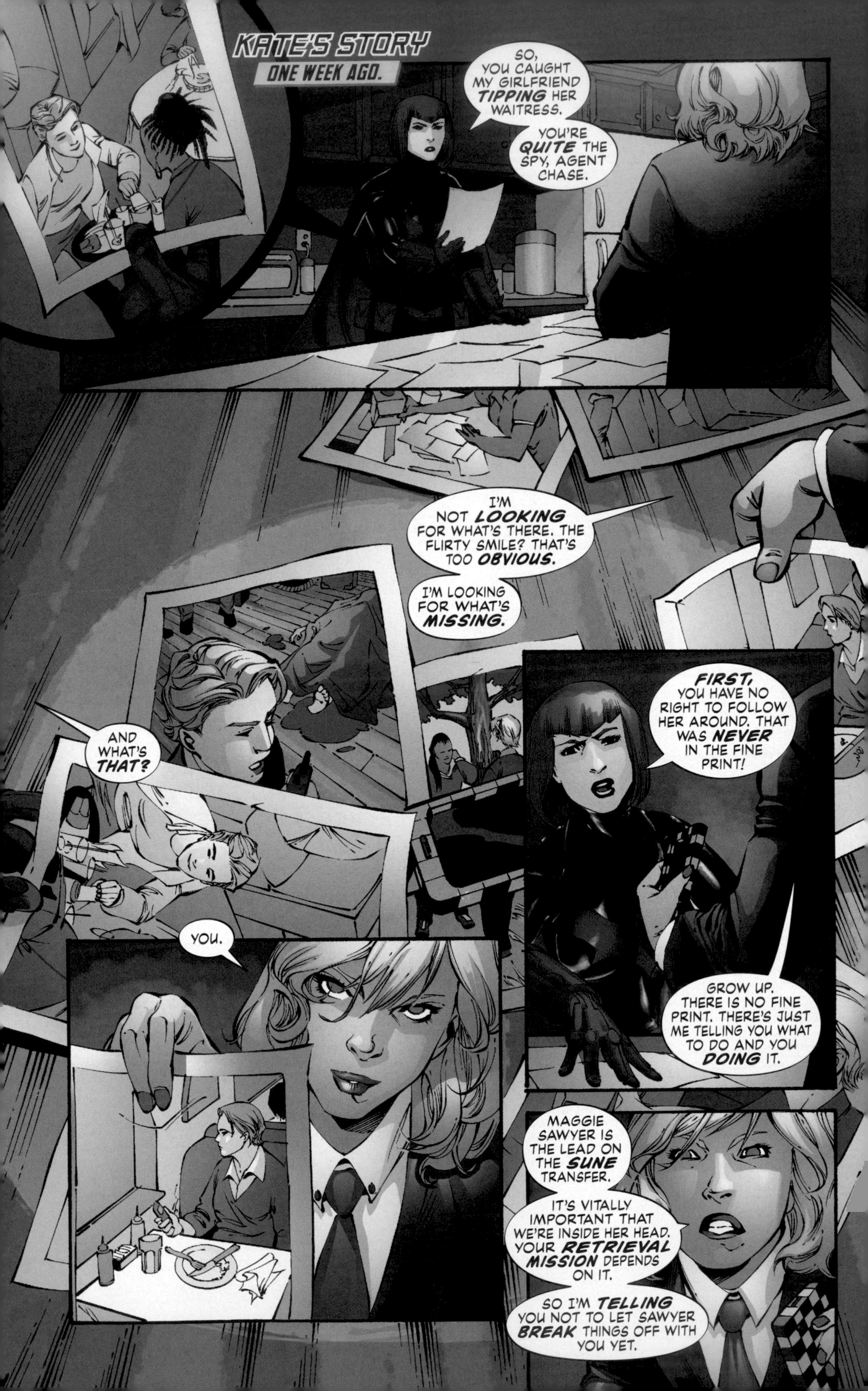
KATE'S STORY
ONE WEEK AGO.
SO, YOU CAUGHT MY GIRLFRIEND TIPPING HER WAITRESS.
YOU'RE QUITE THE SPY, AGENT CHASE.
I'M NOT LOOKING FOR WHAT'S THERE. THE FLIRTY SMILE? THAT'S TOO OBVIOUS.
I'M LOOKING FOR WHAT'S MISSING.
AND WHAT'S THAT?
YOU.
FIRST, YOU HAVE NO RIGHT TO FOLLOW HER AROUND. THAT WAS NEVER IN THE FINE PRINT!
GROW UP. THERE IS NO FINE PRINT. THERE'S JUST ME TELLING YOU WHAT TO DO AND YOU DOING IT.
MAGGIE SAWYER IS THE LEAD ON THE SUNE TRANSFER.
IT'S VITALLY IMPORTANT THAT WE'RE INSIDE HER HEAD. YOUR RETRIEVAL MISSION DEPENDS ON IT.
SO I'M TELLING YOU NOT TO LET SAWYER BREAK THINGS OFF WITH YOU YET.

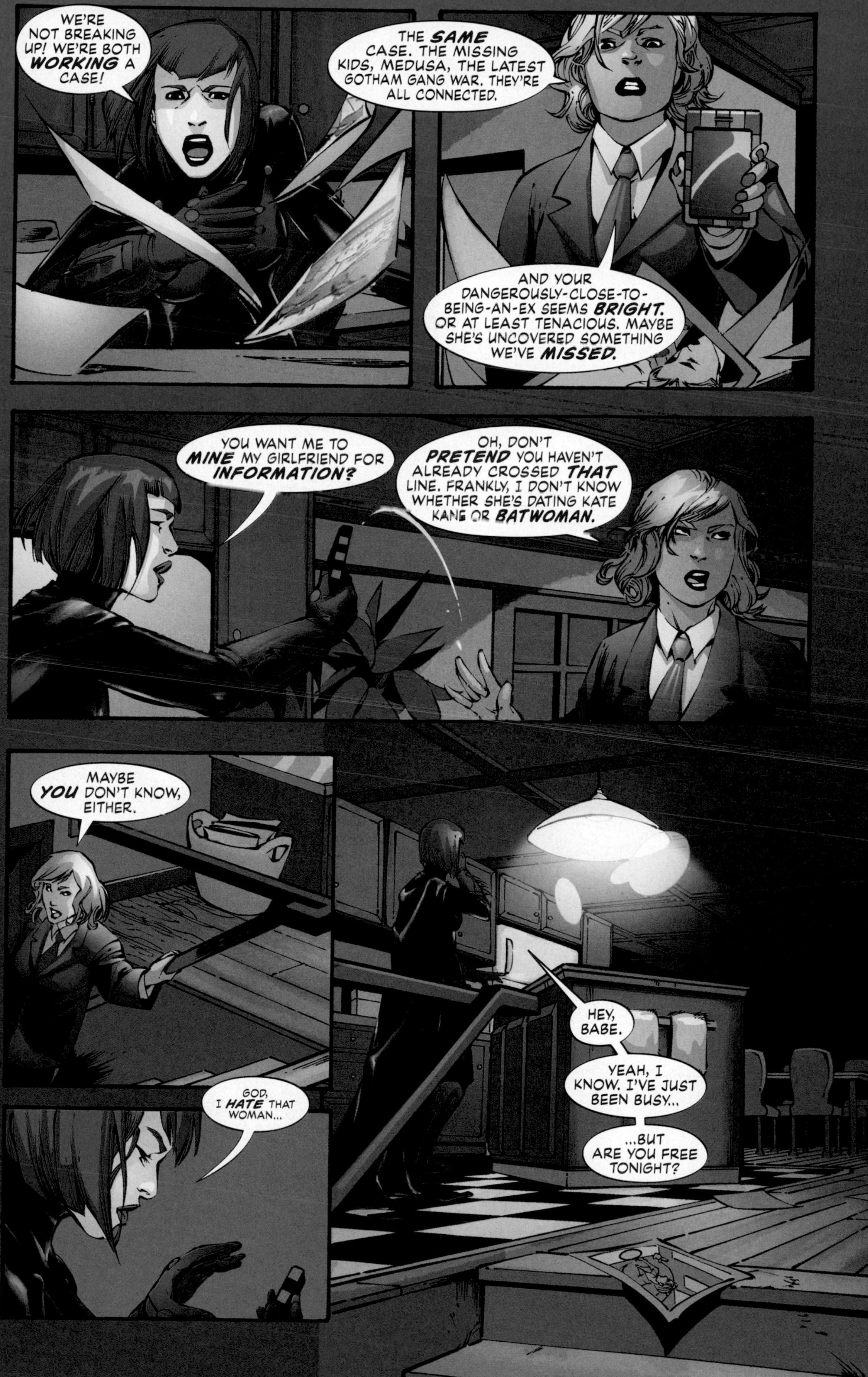
WE'RE NOT BREAKING UP! WE'RE BOTH WORKING A CASE!
THE SAME CASE. THE MISSING KIDS, MEDUSA, THE LATEST GOTHAM GANG WAR. THEY'RE ALL CONNECTED.
AND YOUR DANGEROUSLY-CLOSE-TO-BEING-AN-EX SEEMS BRIGHT. OR AT LEAST TENACIOUS. MAYBE SHE'S UNCOVERED SOMETHING WE'VE MISSED.
YOU WANT ME TO MINE MY GIRLFRIEND FOR INFORMATION?
OH, DON'T PRETEND YOU HAVEN'T ALREADY CROSSED THAT LINE. FRANKLY, I DON'T KNOW WHETHER SHE'S DATING KATE KANE OR BATWOMAN.
MAYBE YOU DON'T KNOW, EITHER.
GOD, I HATE THAT WOMAN...
HEY, BABE.
YEAH, I KNOW. I'VE JUST BEEN BUSY...
...BUT ARE YOU FREE TONIGHT?

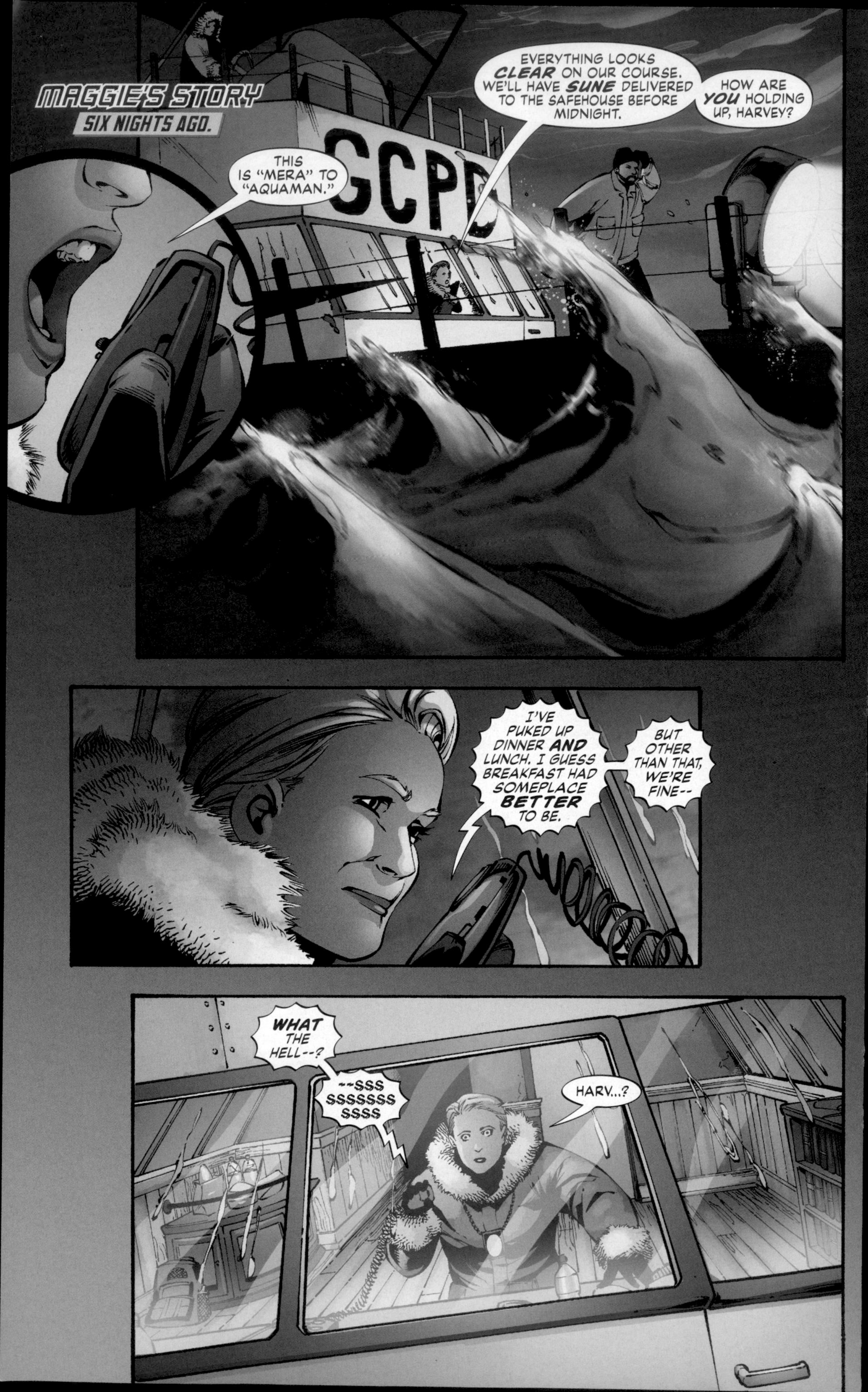
MAGGIE'S STORY
SIX NIGHTS AGO.
THIS IS "MERA" TO "AQUAMAN."
EVERYTHING LOOKS CLEAR ON OUR COURSE. WE'LL HAVE SUNE DELIVERED TO THE SAFEHOUSE BEFORE MIDNIGHT.
HOW ARE YOU HOLDING UP, HARVEY?
GCPD
I'VE PUKED UP DINNER AND LUNCH. I GUESS BREAKFAST HAD SOMEPLACE BETTER TO BE.
BUT OTHER THAN THAT, WE'RE FINE--
WHAT THE HELL--?
--SSS SSSSSSS SSSS
HARV...?

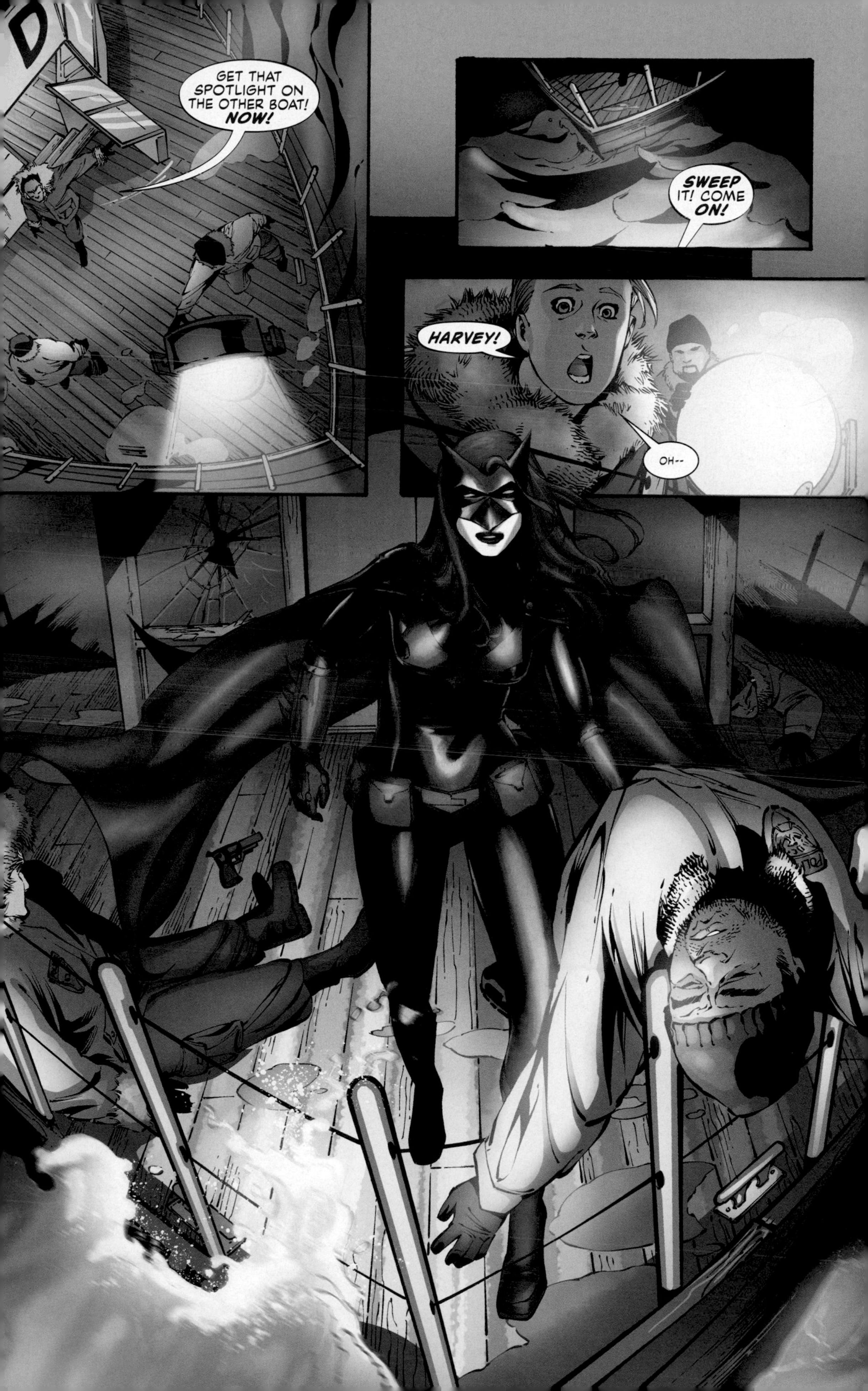
GET THAT SPOTLIGHT ON THE OTHER BOAT! NOW!
SWEEP IT! COME ON!
HARVEY!
OH--

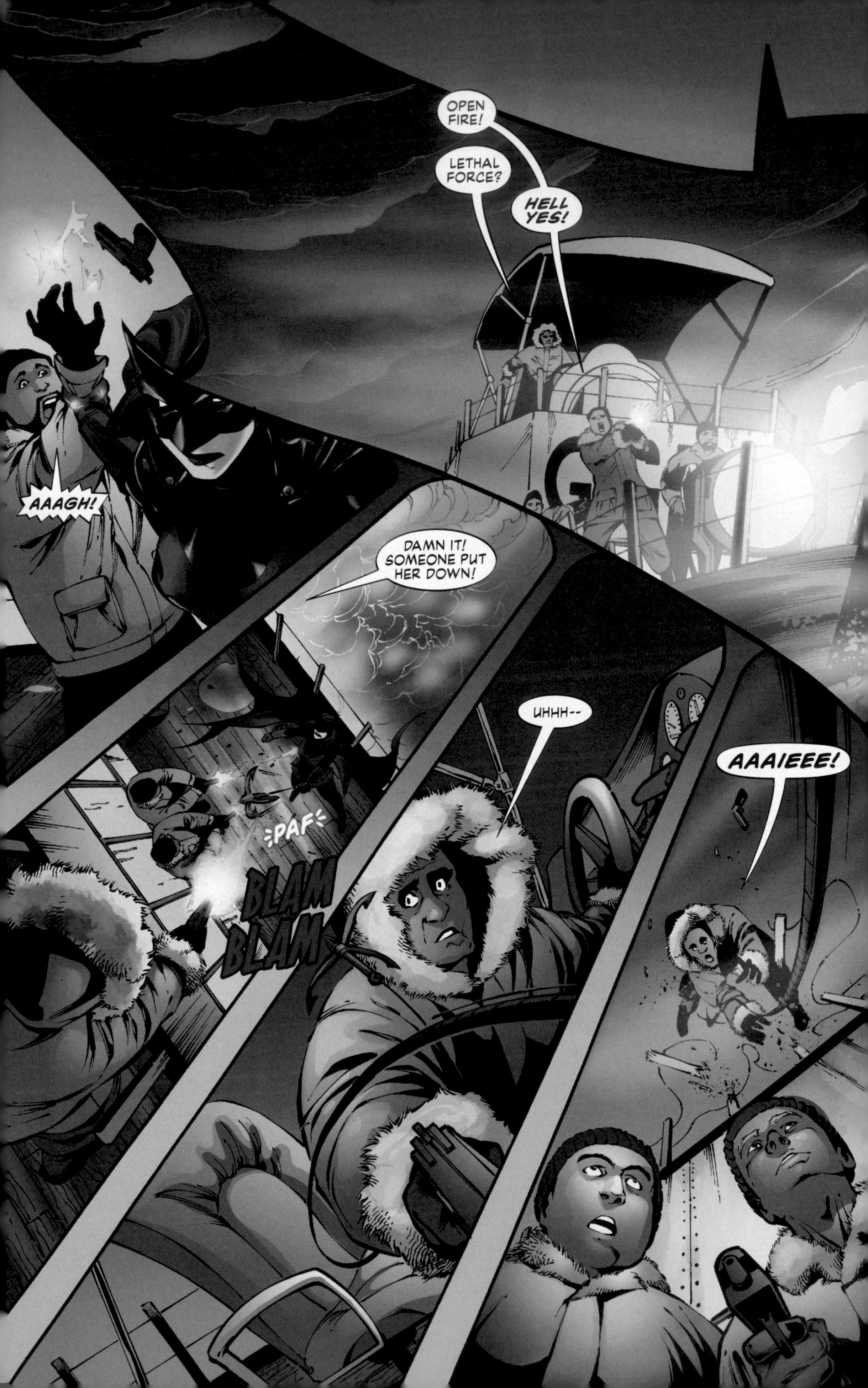
OPEN FIRE!
LETHAL FORCE?
HELL YES!
AAAGH!
DAMN IT! SOMEONE PUT HER DOWN!
PAF
BLAM BLAM
UHHH--
AAAIEEE!

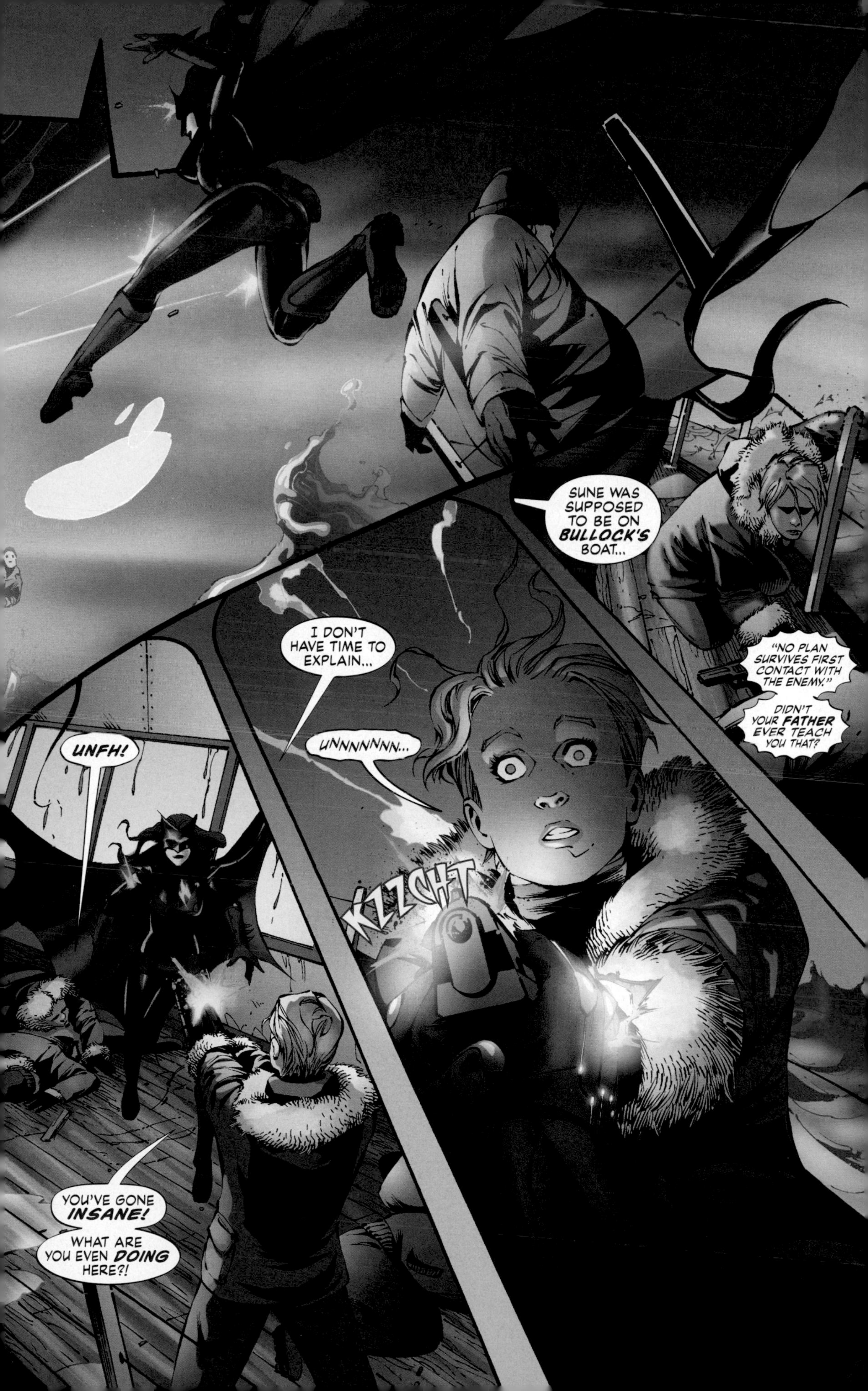
SUNE WAS SUPPOSED TO BE ON BULLOCK'S BOAT...
"NO PLAN SURVIVES FIRST CONTACT WITH THE ENEMY."
DIDN'T YOUR FATHER EVER TEACH YOU THAT?
I DON'T HAVE TIME TO EXPLAIN...
UNNNNNNN...
KZZCHT
UNFH!
YOU'VE GONE INSANE!
WHAT ARE YOU EVEN DOING HERE?!

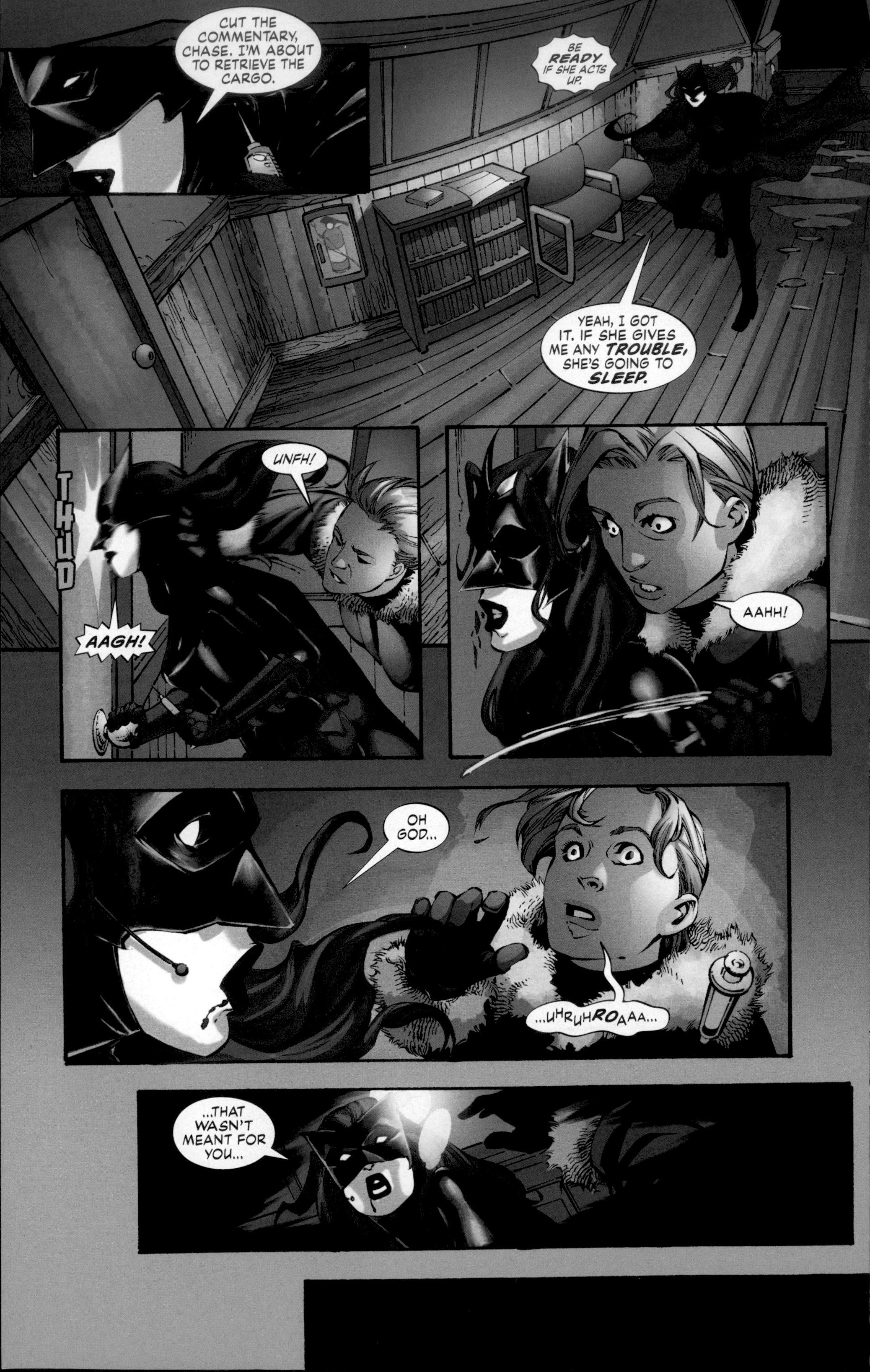
CUT THE COMMENTARY, CHASE. I'M ABOUT TO RETRIEVE THE CARGO.
BE READY IF SHE ACTS UP.
YEAH, I GOT IT. IF SHE GIVES ME ANY TROUBLE, SHE'S GOING TO SLEEP.
THUD
AAGH!
UNFH!
AAHH!
OH GOD...
...UHRUHROAAA...
...THAT WASN'T MEANT FOR YOU...

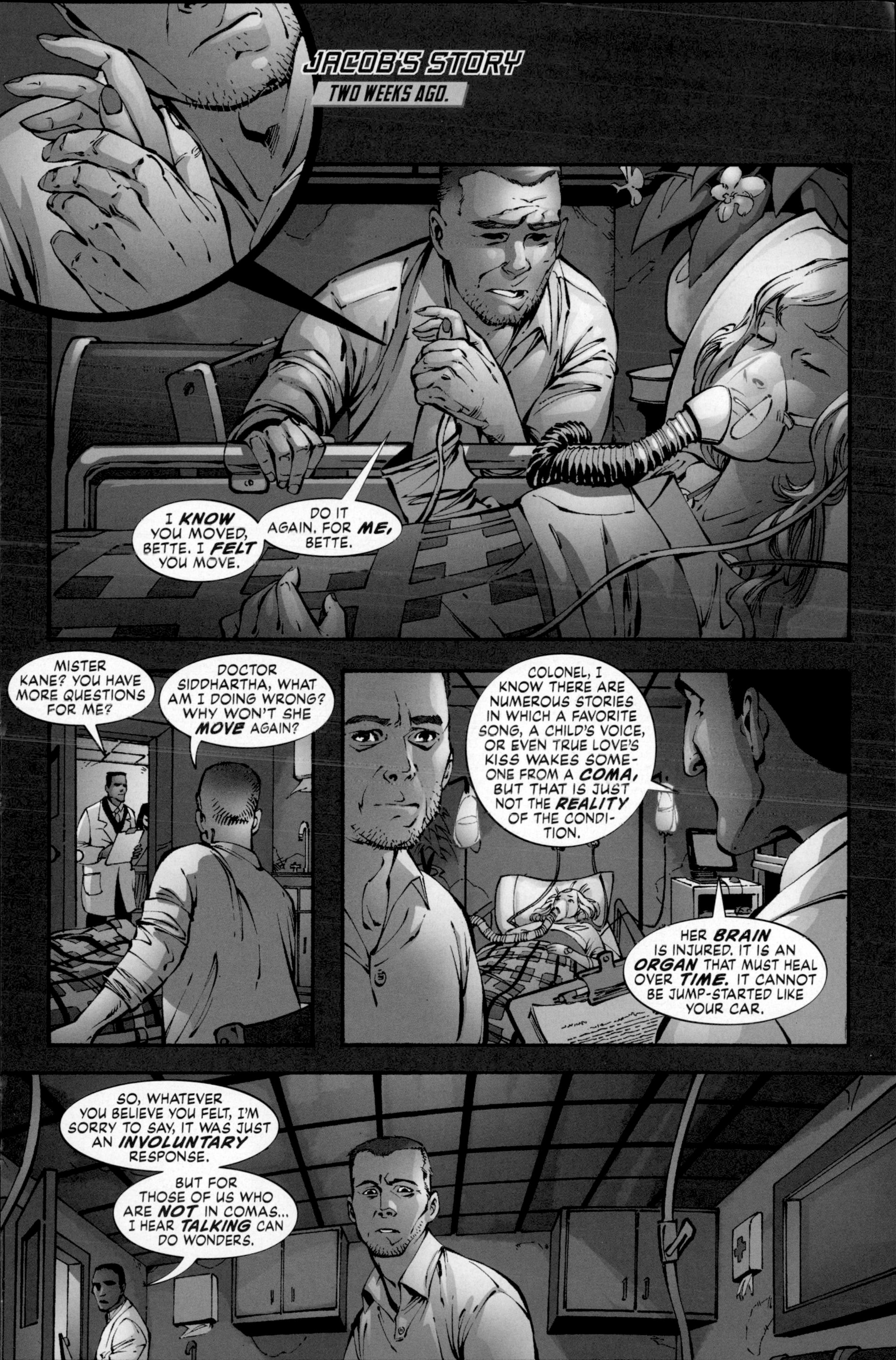
JACOB'S STORY
TWO WEEKS AGO.
I KNOW YOU MOVED, BETTE. I FELT YOU MOVE.
DO IT AGAIN. FOR ME, BETTE.
MISTER KANE? YOU HAVE MORE QUESTIONS FOR ME?
DOCTOR SIDDHARTHA, WHAT AM I DOING WRONG? WHY WON'T SHE MOVE AGAIN?
COLONEL, I KNOW THERE ARE NUMEROUS STORIES IN WHICH A FAVORITE SONG, A CHILD'S VOICE, OR EVEN TRUE LOVE'S KISS WAKES SOME-ONE FROM A COMA, BUT THAT IS JUST NOT THE REALITY OF THE CONDI-TION.
HER BRAIN IS INJURED. IT IS AN ORGAN THAT MUST HEAL OVER TIME. IT CANNOT BE JUMP-STARTED LIKE YOUR CAR.
SO, WHATEVER YOU BELIEVE YOU FELT, I'M SORRY TO SAY, IT WAS JUST AN INVOLUNTARY RESPONSE.
BUT FOR THOSE OF US WHO ARE NOT IN COMAS... I HEAR TALKING CAN DO WONDERS.

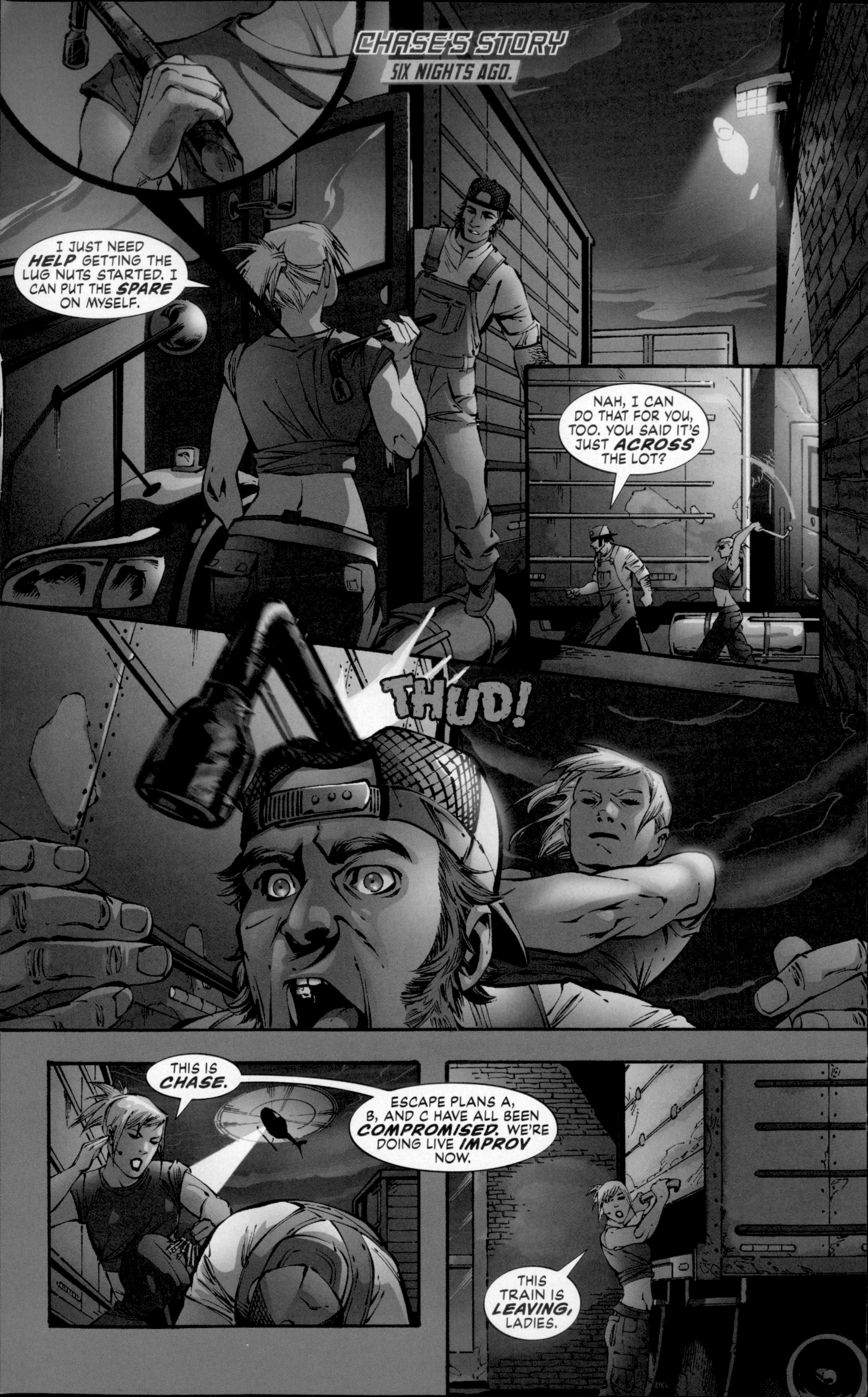
CHASE'S STORY
SIX NIGHTS AGO.
I JUST NEED HELP GETTING THE LUG NUTS STARTED. I CAN PUT THE SPARE ON MYSELF.
NAH, I CAN DO THAT FOR YOU, TOO. YOU SAID IT'S JUST ACROSS THE LOT?
THUD!
THIS IS CHASE.
ESCAPE PLANS A, B, AND C HAVE ALL BEEN COMPROMISED. WE'RE DOING LIVE IMPROV NOW.
THIS TRAIN IS LEAVING, LADIES.

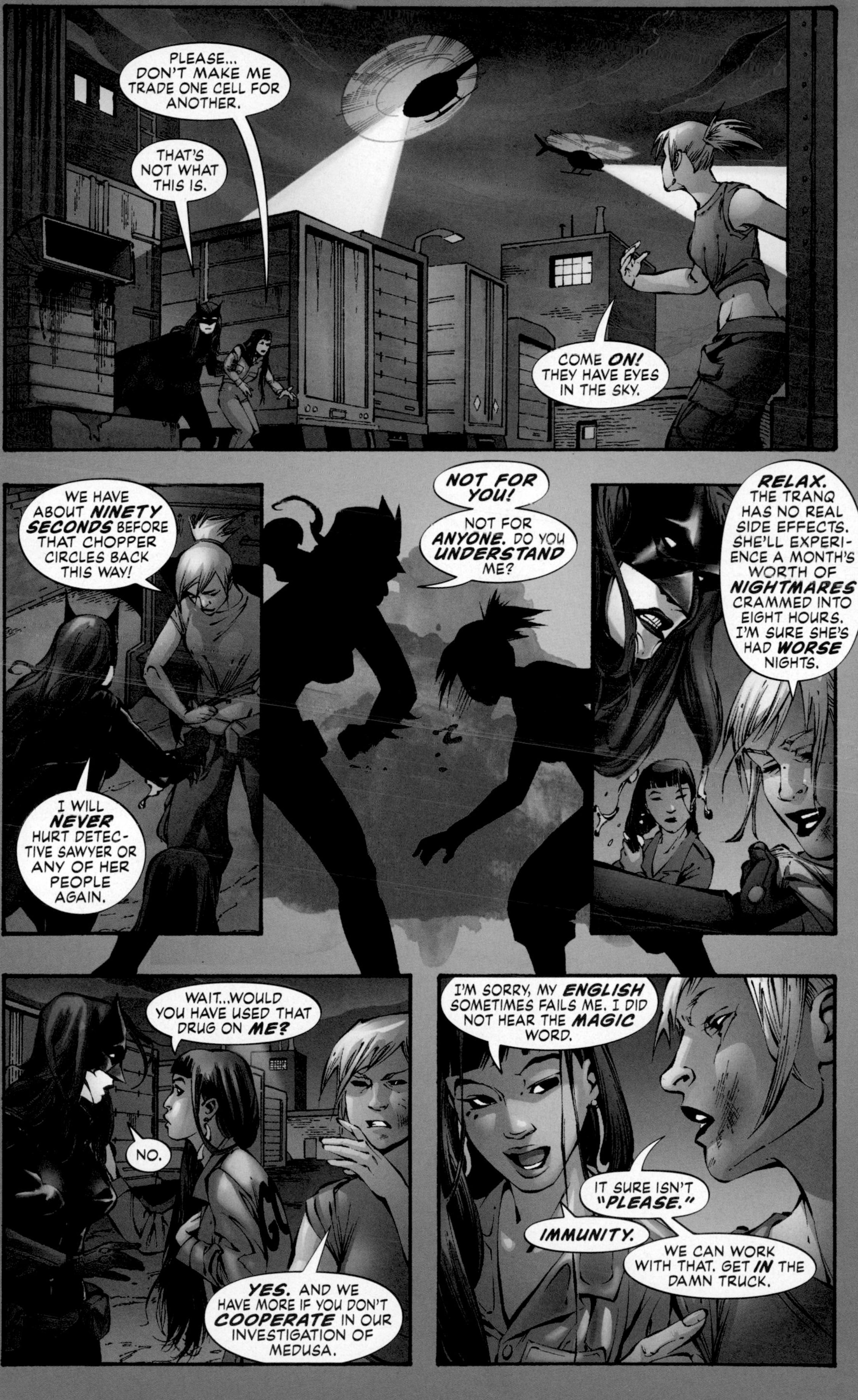
PLEASE... DON'T MAKE ME TRADE ONE CELL FOR ANOTHER.
THAT'S NOT WHAT THIS IS.
COME ON! THEY HAVE EYES IN THE SKY.
WE HAVE ABOUT NINETY SECONDS BEFORE THAT CHOPPER CIRCLES BACK THIS WAY!
I WILL NEVER HURT DETECTIVE SAWYER OR ANY OF HER PEOPLE AGAIN.
NOT FOR YOU!
NOT FOR ANYONE. DO YOU UNDERSTAND ME?
RELAX. THE TRANQ HAS NO REAL SIDE EFFECTS. SHE'LL EXPERIENCE A MONTH'S WORTH OF NIGHTMARES CRAMMED INTO EIGHT HOURS. I'M SURE SHE'S HAD WORSE NIGHTS.
WAIT..WOULD YOU HAVE USED THAT DRUG ON ME?
NO.
YES. AND WE HAVE MORE IF YOU DON'T COOPERATE IN OUR INVESTIGATION OF MEDUSA.
I'M SORRY, MY ENGLISH SOMETIMES FAILS ME. I DID NOT HEAR THE MAGIC WORD.
IT SURE ISN'T "PLEASE."
IMMUNITY.
WE CAN WORK WITH THAT. GET IN THE DAMN TRUCK.

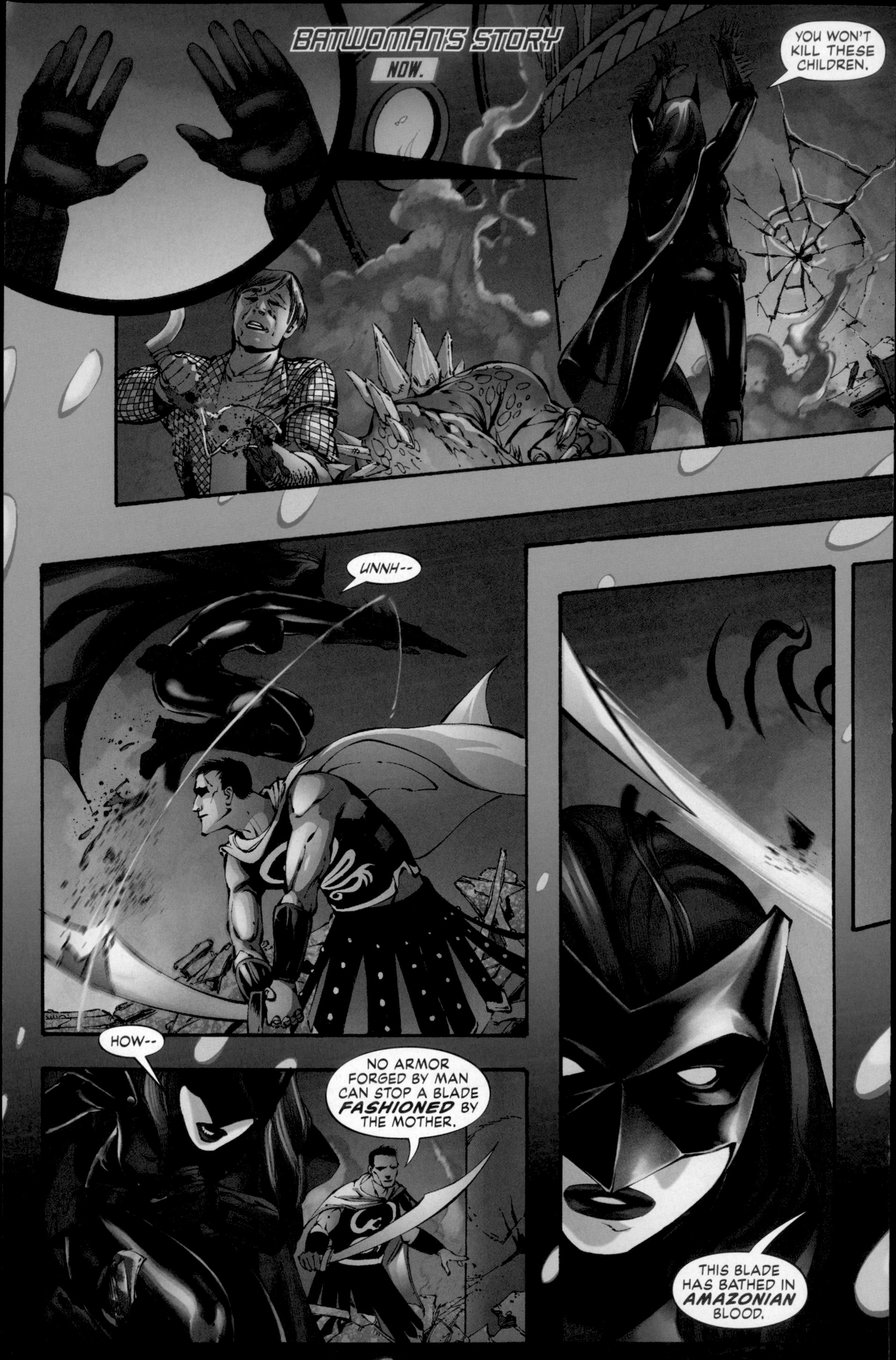
BATWOMAN'S STORY
NOW.
YOU WON'T KILL THESE CHILDREN.
UNNH--
HOW--
NO ARMOR FORGED BY MAN CAN STOP A BLADE FASHIONED BY THE MOTHER.
THIS BLADE HAS BATHED IN AMAZONIAN BLOOD.

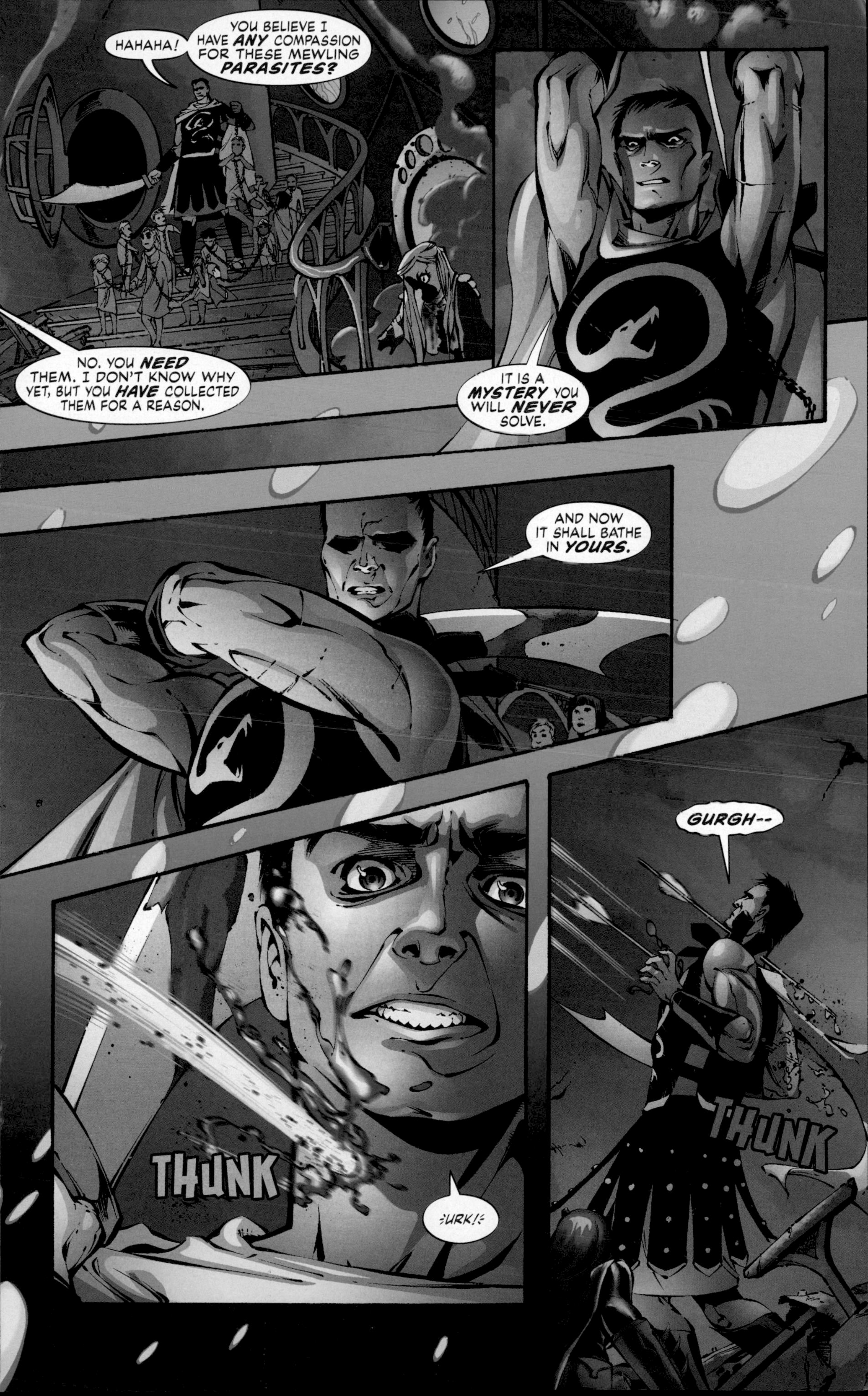
HAHAHA!
YOU BELIEVE I HAVE ANY COMPASSION FOR THESE MEWLING PARASITES?
NO. YOU NEED THEM. I DON'T KNOW WHY YET, BUT YOU HAVE COLLECTED THEM FOR A REASON.
IT IS A MYSTERY YOU WILL NEVER SOLVE.
AND NOW IT SHALL BATHE IN YOURS.
GURGH--
THUNK
THUNK
URK!

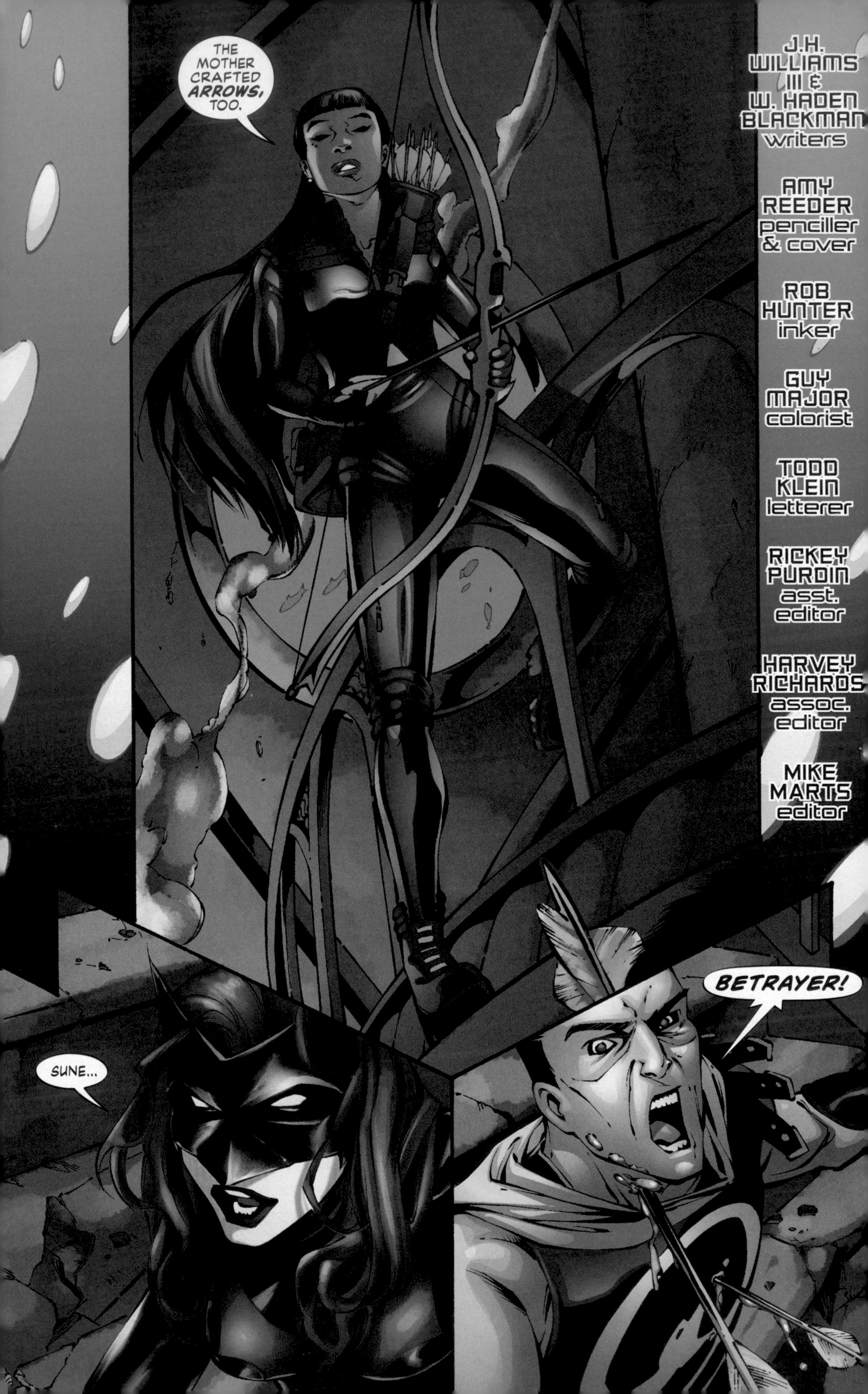

THE MOTHER CRAFTED ARROWS, TOO.
J.H. WILLIAMS III & W. HADEN BLACKMAN writers
AMY REEDER penciller & cover
ROB HUNTER inker
GUY MAJOR colorist
TODD KLEIN letterer
RICKEY PURDIN asst. editor
HARVEY RICHARDS assoc. editor
MIKE MARTS editor
SUNE...
BETRAYER!

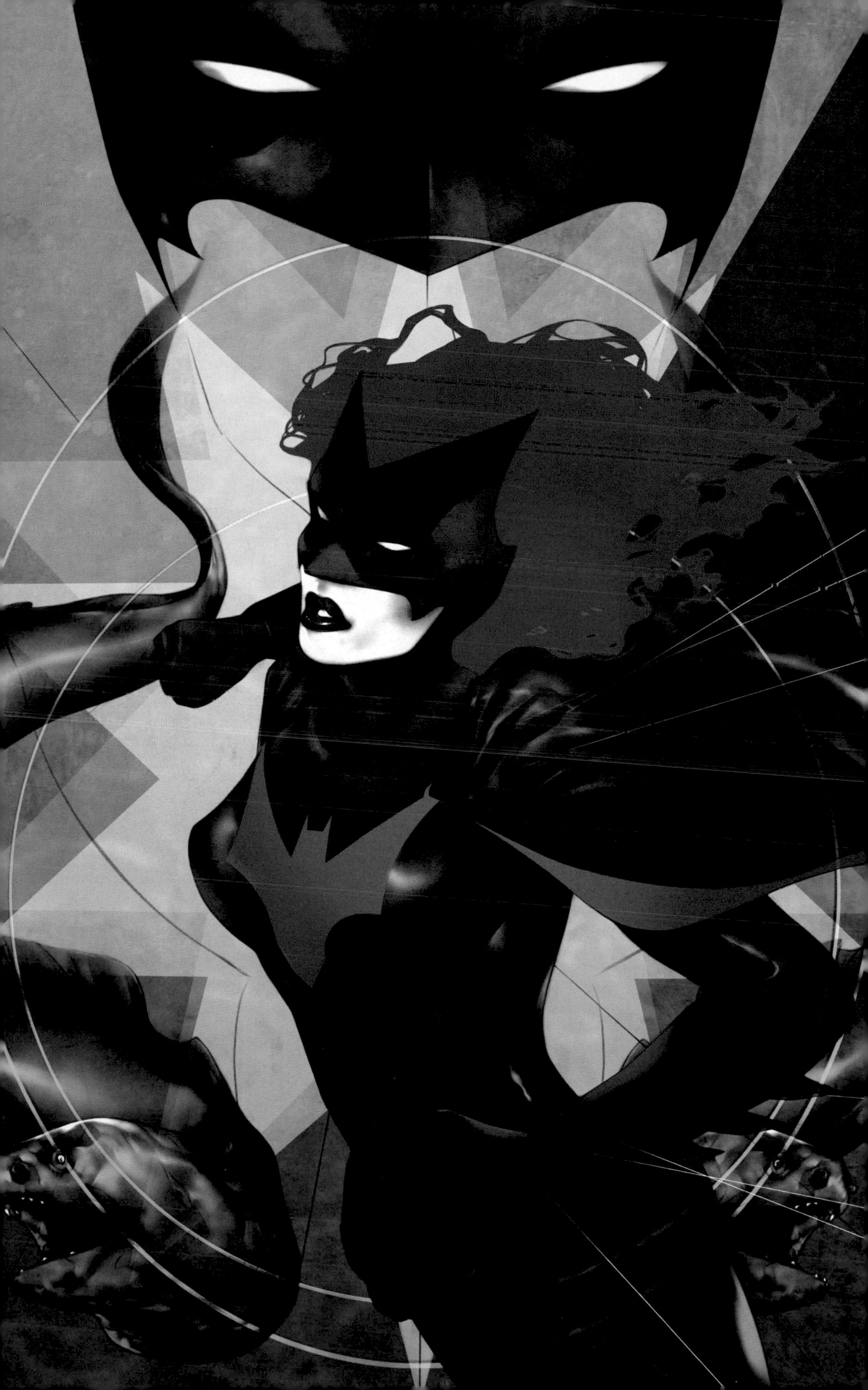

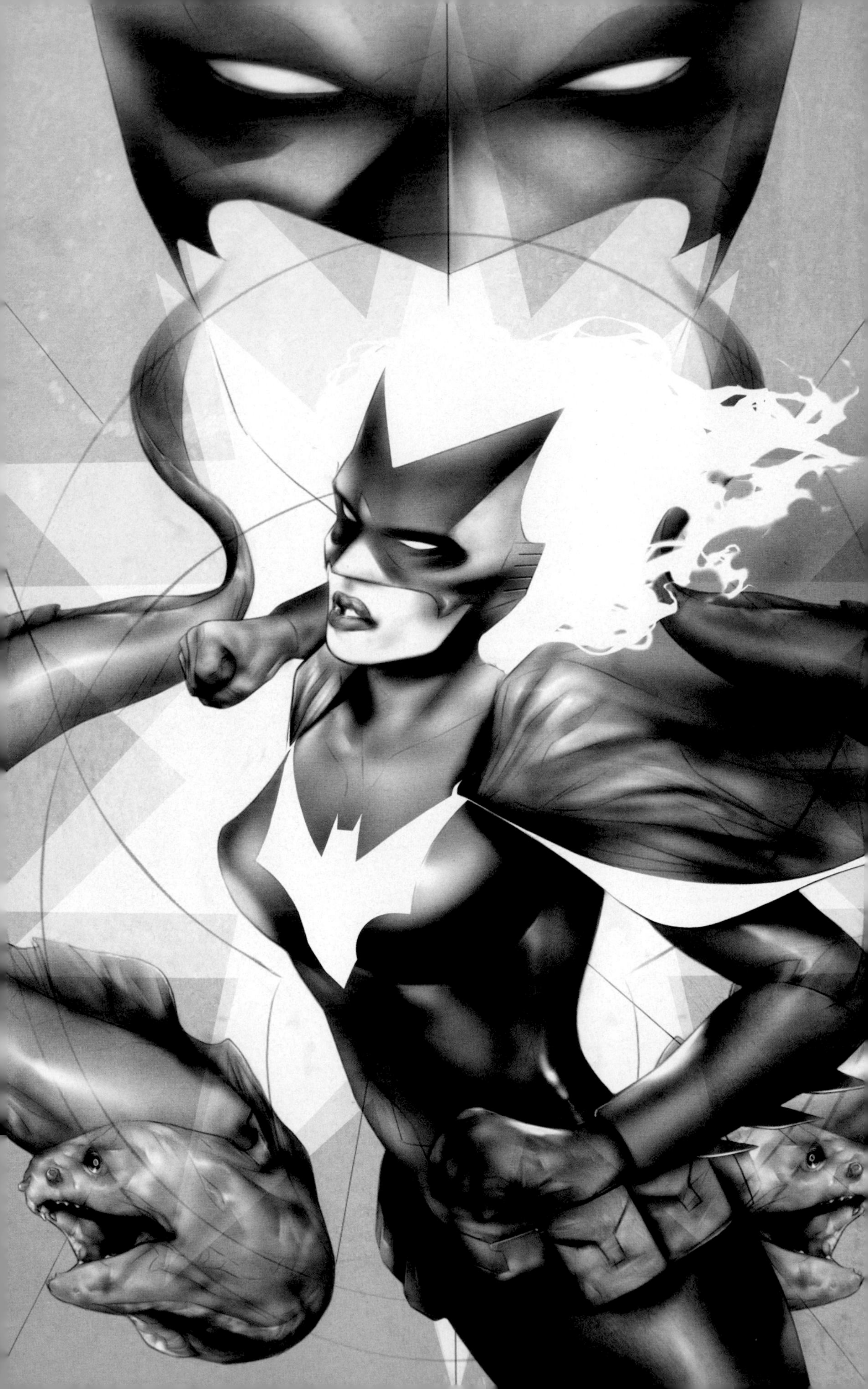

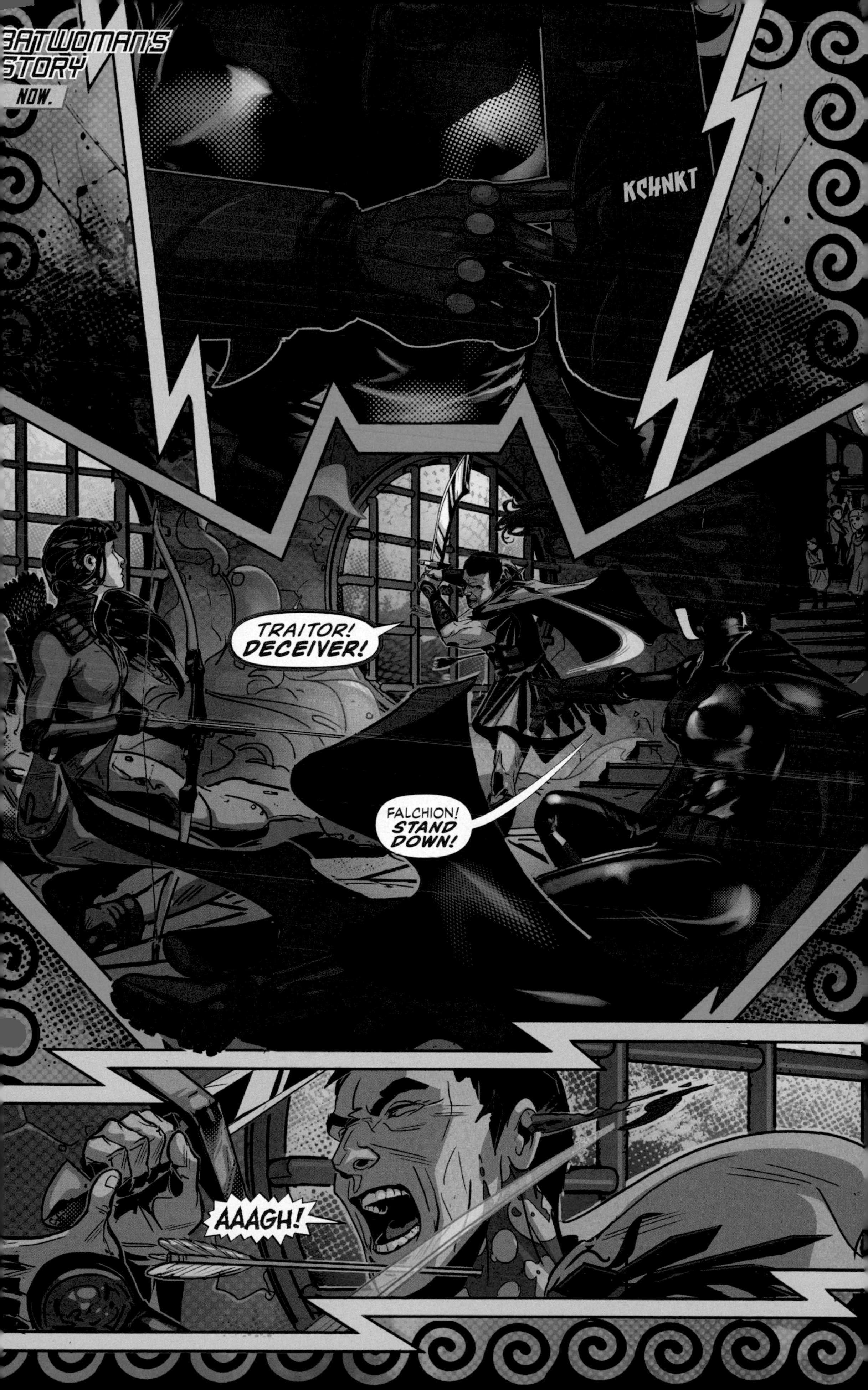
BATWOMAN'S STORY
NOW.
KCHNKT
TRAITOR! DECEIVER!
FALCHION! STAND DOWN!
AAAGH!

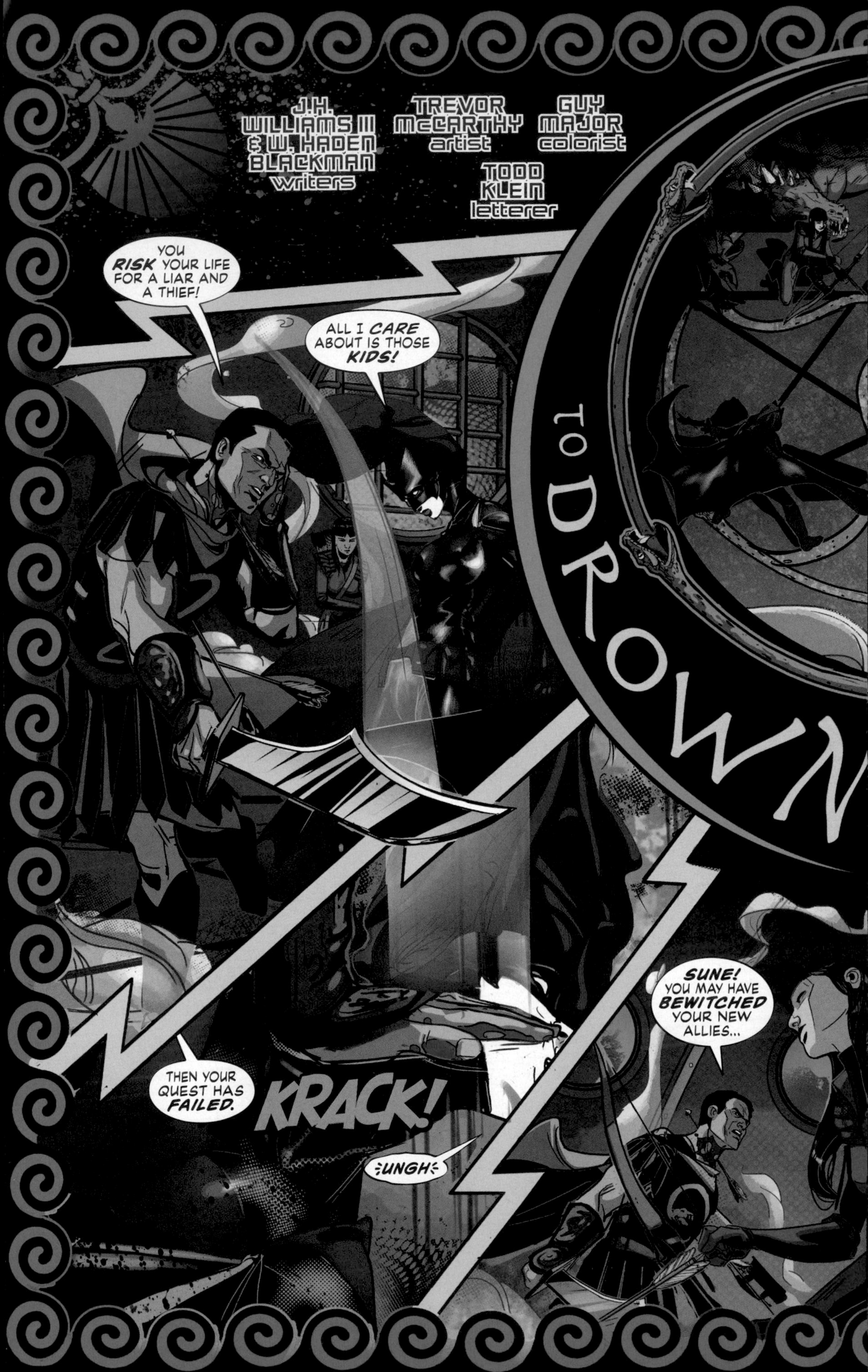
J.H. WILLIAMS III & W. HADEN BLACKMAN writers
TREVOR McCARTHY artist
GUY MAJOR colorist
TODD KLEIN letterer
TO DROWN
YOU RISK YOUR LIFE FOR A LIAR AND A THIEF!
ALL I CARE ABOUT IS THOSE KIDS!
THEN YOUR QUEST HAS FAILED.
KRACK!
UNGH
SUNE! YOU MAY HAVE BEWITCHED YOUR NEW ALLIES...

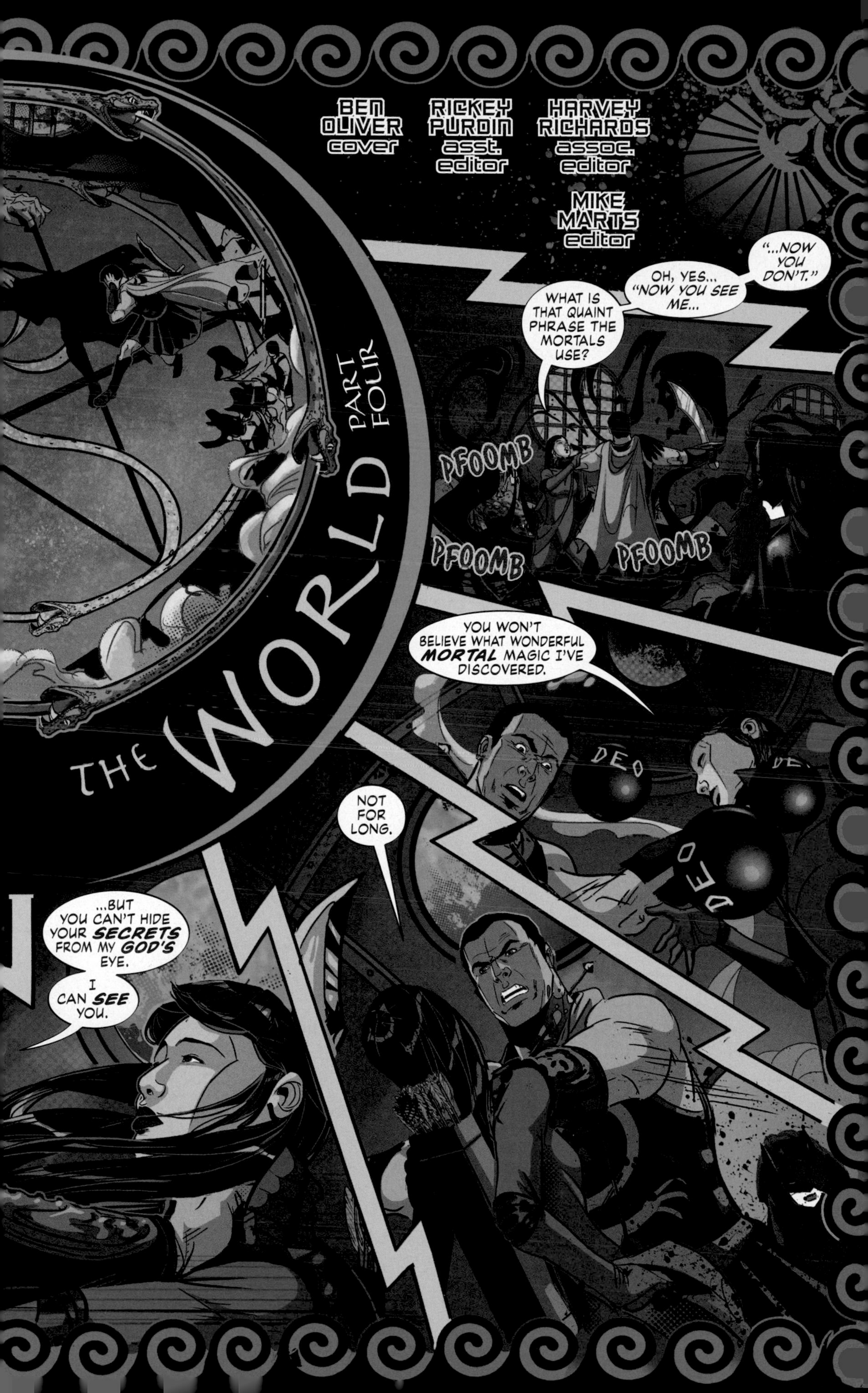
BEN OLIVER cover
RICKEY PURDIN asst. editor
HARVEY RICHARDS assoc. editor
MIKE MARTS editor
THE WORLD PART FOUR
WHAT IS THAT QUAINT PHRASE THE MORTALS USE?
OH, YES... "NOW YOU SEE ME...
"...NOW YOU DON'T."
PFOOMB
PFOOMB
PFOOMB
YOU WON'T BELIEVE WHAT WONDERFUL MORTAL MAGIC I'VE DISCOVERED.
DEO
NOT FOR LONG.
...BUT YOU CAN'T HIDE YOUR SECRETS FROM MY GOD'S EYE.
I CAN SEE YOU.

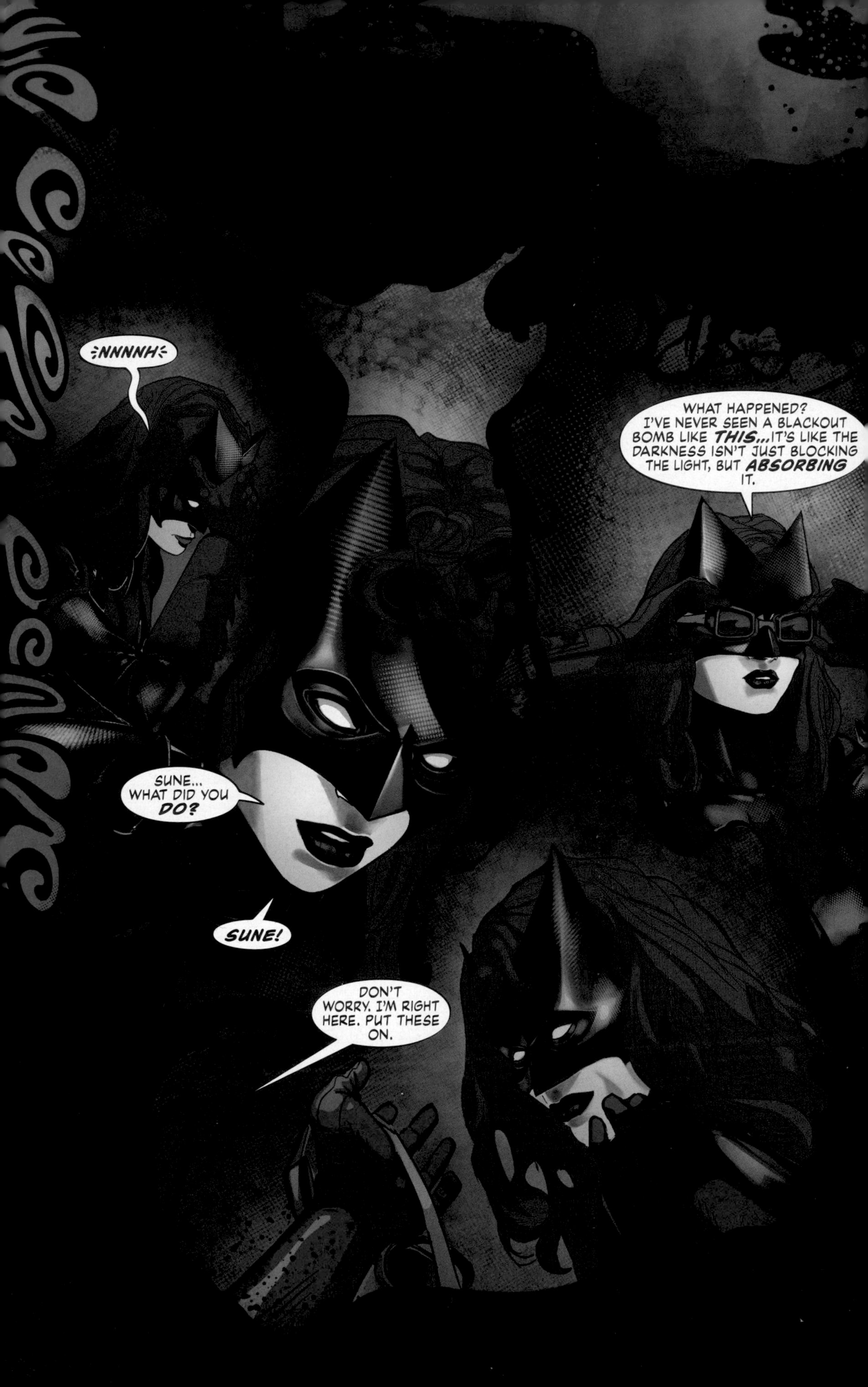

NNNNH
WHAT HAPPENED? I'VE NEVER SEEN A BLACKOUT BOMB LIKE THIS... IT'S LIKE THE DARKNESS ISN'T JUST BLOCKING THE LIGHT, BUT ABSORBING IT.
SUNE... WHAT DID YOU DO?
SUNE!
DON'T WORRY. I'M RIGHT HERE. PUT THESE ON.

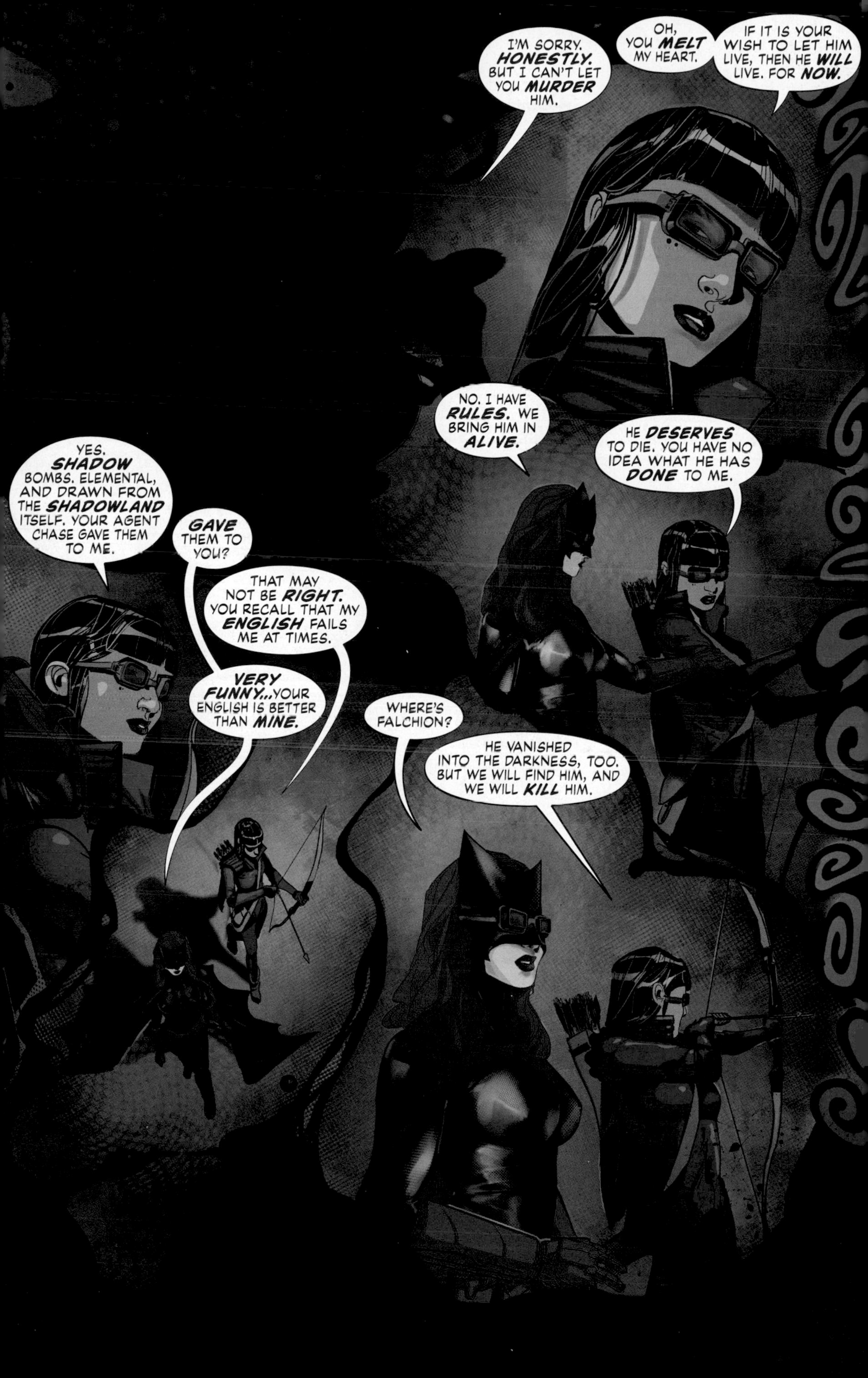
I'M SORRY. HONESTLY. BUT I CAN'T LET YOU MURDER HIM.
OH, YOU MELT MY HEART.
IF IT IS YOUR WISH TO LET HIM LIVE, THEN HE WILL LIVE. FOR NOW.
NO. I HAVE RULES. WE BRING HIM IN ALIVE.
HE DESERVES TO DIE. YOU HAVE NO IDEA WHAT HE HAS DONE TO ME.
YES. SHADOW BOMBS. ELEMENTAL, AND DRAWN FROM THE SHADOWLAND ITSELF. YOUR AGENT CHASE GAVE THEM TO ME.
GAVE THEM TO YOU?
THAT MAY NOT BE RIGHT. YOU RECALL THAT MY ENGLISH FAILS ME AT TIMES.
VERY FUNNY... YOUR ENGLISH IS BETTER THAN MINE.
WHERE'S FALCHION?
HE VANISHED INTO THE DARKNESS, TOO. BUT WE WILL FIND HIM, AND WE WILL KILL HIM.

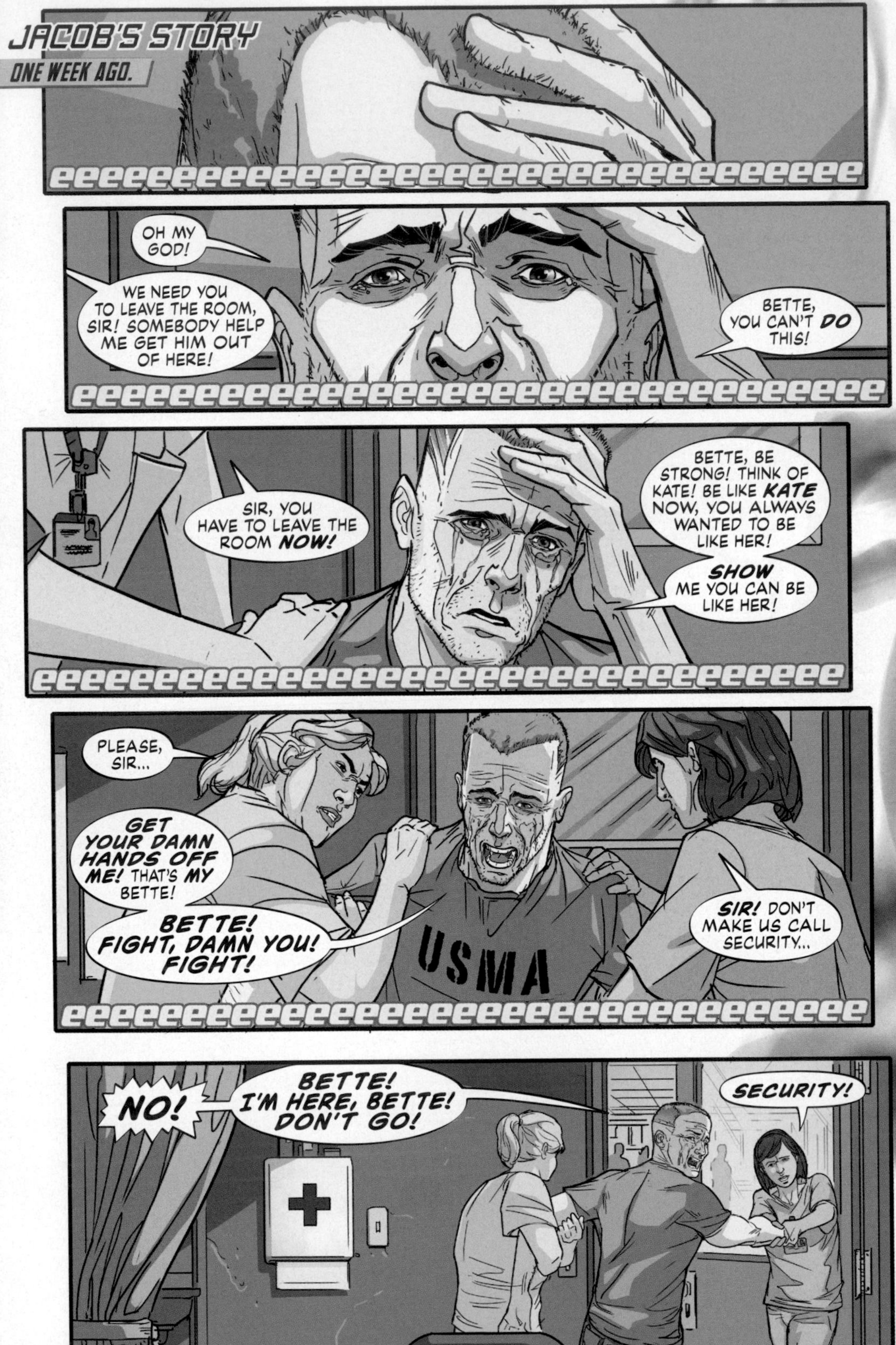
JACOB'S STORY
ONE WEEK AGO.
eeeeeeeeeeeeeeeeeeeeeeeeeeeeeeeeeeeeeee
OH MY GOD!
WE NEED YOU TO LEAVE THE ROOM, SIR! SOMEBODY HELP ME GET HIM OUT OF HERE!
BETTE, YOU CAN'T DO THIS!
eeeeeeeeeeeeeeeeeeeeeeeeeeeeeeeeeeeeeee
SIR, YOU HAVE TO LEAVE THE ROOM NOW!
BETTE, BE STRONG! THINK OF KATE! BE LIKE KATE NOW, YOU ALWAYS WANTED TO BE LIKE HER!
SHOW ME YOU CAN BE LIKE HER!
eeeeeeeeeeeeeeeeeeeeeeeeeeeeeeeeeeeeeee
PLEASE, SIR...
GET YOUR DAMN HANDS OFF ME! THAT'S MY BETTE!
BETTE! FIGHT, DAMN YOU! FIGHT!
USMA
SIR! DON'T MAKE US CALL SECURITY...
eeeeeeeeeeeeeeeeeeeeeeeeeeeeeeeeeeeeeee
NO!
BETTE! I'M HERE, BETTE! DON'T GO!
SECURITY!
eeeeeeeeeeeeeeeeeeeeeeeeeeeeeeeeeeeeeee

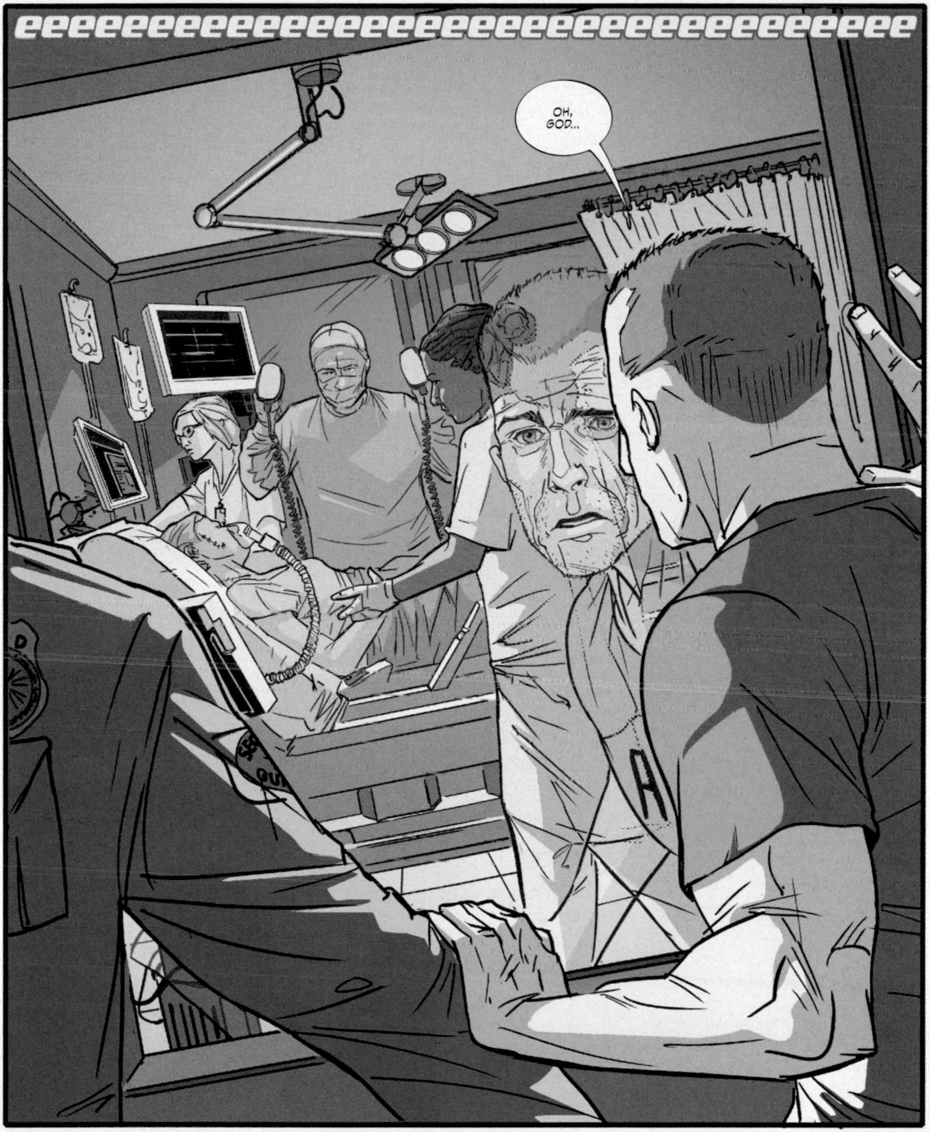
eeeeeeeeeeeeeeeeeeeeeeeeeeeeeeeeeeeeeee
OH, GOD...

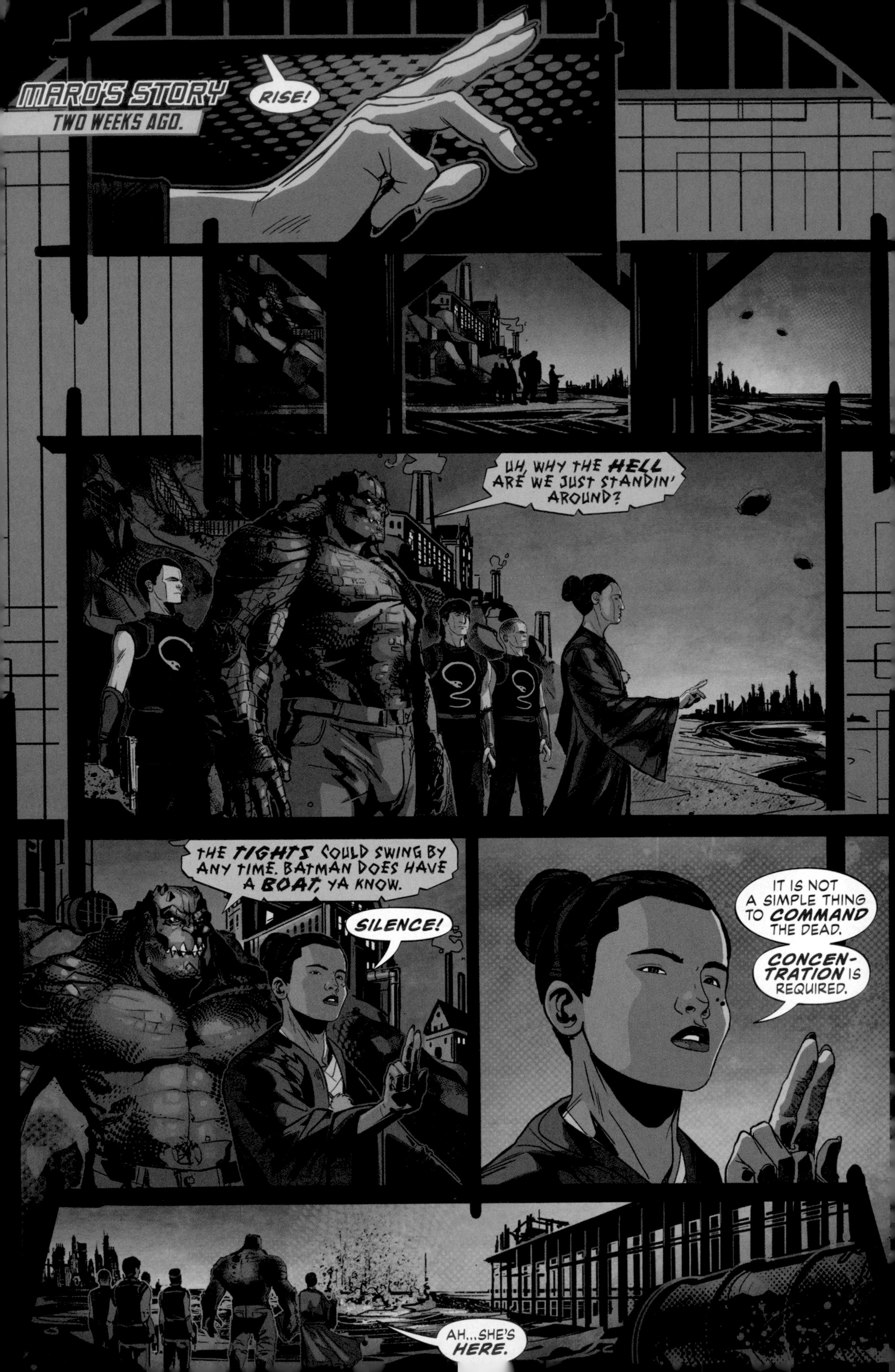
MARO'S STORY
TWO WEEKS AGO.
RISE!
UH, WHY THE HELL ARE WE JUST STANDIN' AROUND?
THE TIGHTS COULD SWING BY ANY TIME. BATMAN DOES HAVE A BOAT, YA KNOW.
SILENCE!
IT IS NOT A SIMPLE THING TO COMMAND THE DEAD.
CONCENTRATION IS REQUIRED.
AH...SHE'S HERE.

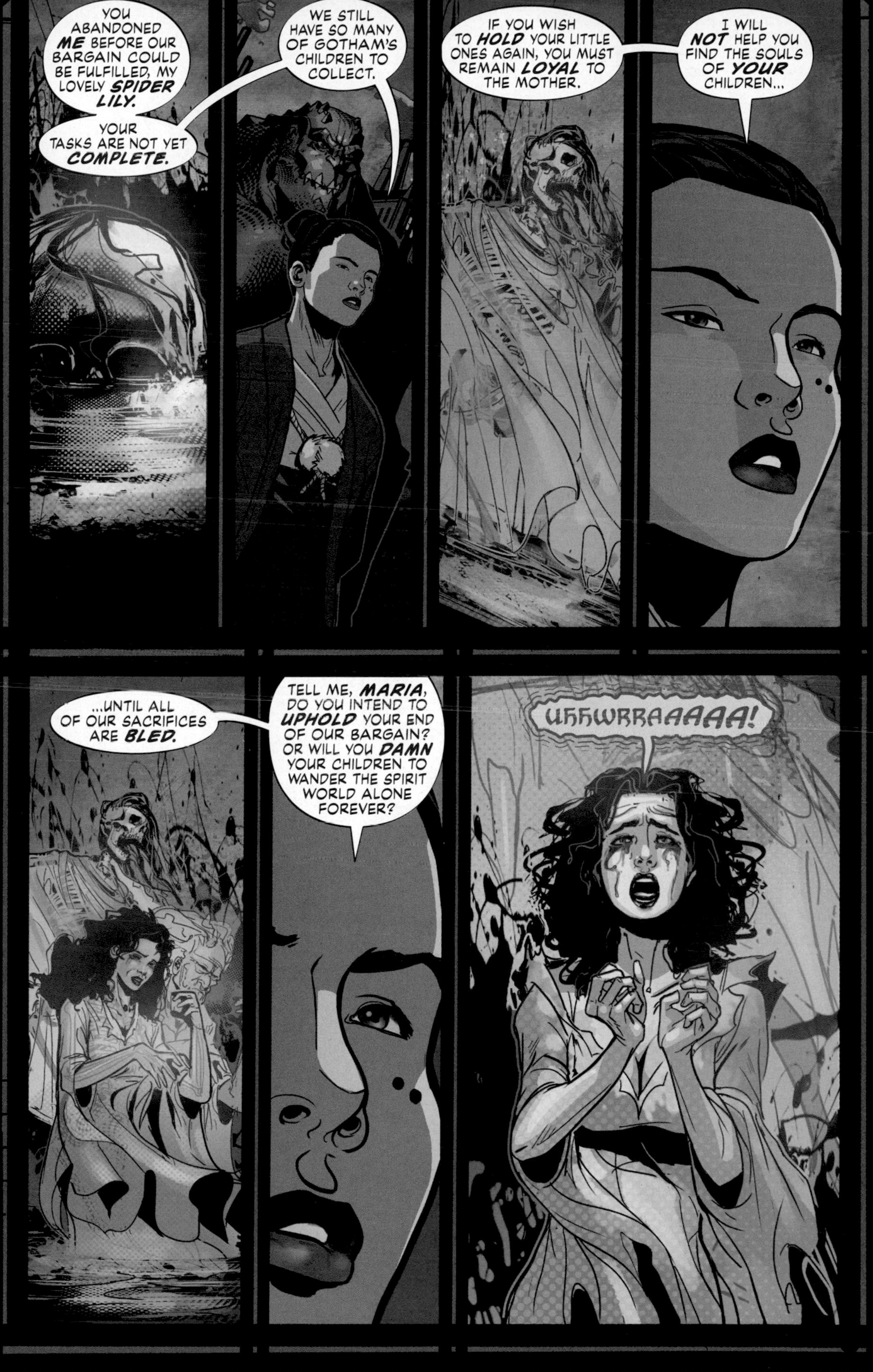
YOU ABANDONED ME BEFORE OUR BARGAIN COULD BE FULFILLED, MY LOVELY SPIDER LILY.
YOUR TASKS ARE NOT YET COMPLETE.
WE STILL HAVE SO MANY OF GOTHAM'S CHILDREN TO COLLECT.
IF YOU WISH TO HOLD YOUR LITTLE ONES AGAIN, YOU MUST REMAIN LOYAL TO THE MOTHER.
I WILL NOT HELP YOU FIND THE SOULS OF YOUR CHILDREN...
...UNTIL ALL OF OUR SACRIFICES ARE BLED.
TELL ME, MARIA, DO YOU INTEND TO UPHOLD YOUR END OF OUR BARGAIN? OR WILL YOU DAMN YOUR CHILDREN TO WANDER THE SPIRIT WORLD ALONE FOREVER?
UHHWRRAAAAAA!

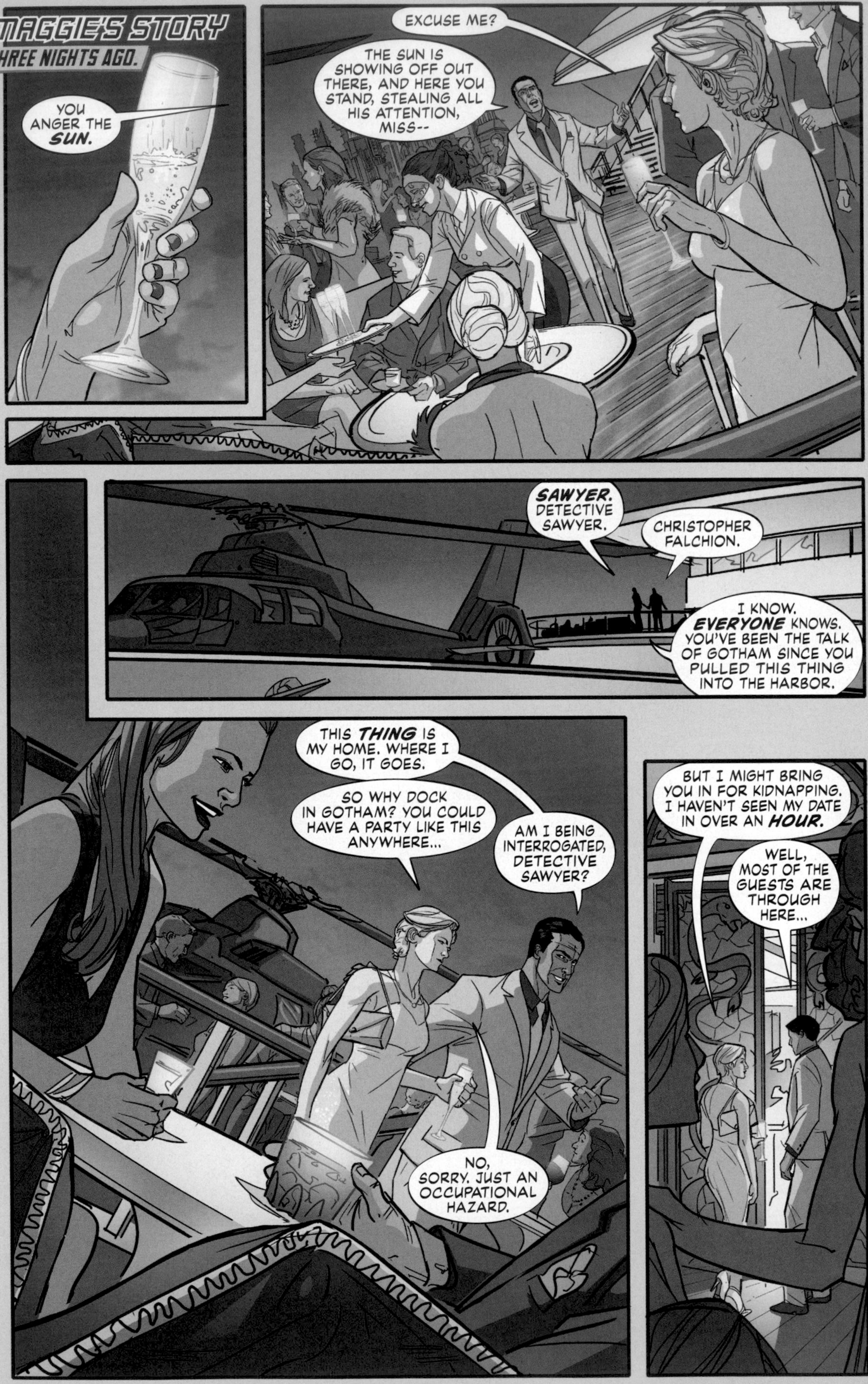
MAGGIE'S STORY
THREE NIGHTS AGO.
YOU ANGER THE SUN.
EXCUSE ME?
THE SUN IS SHOWING OFF OUT THERE, AND HERE YOU STAND, STEALING ALL HIS ATTENTION, MISS--
SAWYER. DETECTIVE SAWYER.
CHRISTOPHER FALCHION.
I KNOW. EVERYONE KNOWS. YOU'VE BEEN THE TALK OF GOTHAM SINCE YOU PULLED THIS THING INTO THE HARBOR.
THIS THING IS MY HOME. WHERE I GO, IT GOES.
SO WHY DOCK IN GOTHAM? YOU COULD HAVE A PARTY LIKE THIS ANYWHERE...
AM I BEING INTERROGATED, DETECTIVE SAWYER?
NO, SORRY. JUST AN OCCUPATIONAL HAZARD.
BUT I MIGHT BRING YOU IN FOR KIDNAPPING. I HAVEN'T SEEN MY DATE IN OVER AN HOUR.
WELL, MOST OF THE GUESTS ARE THROUGH HERE...

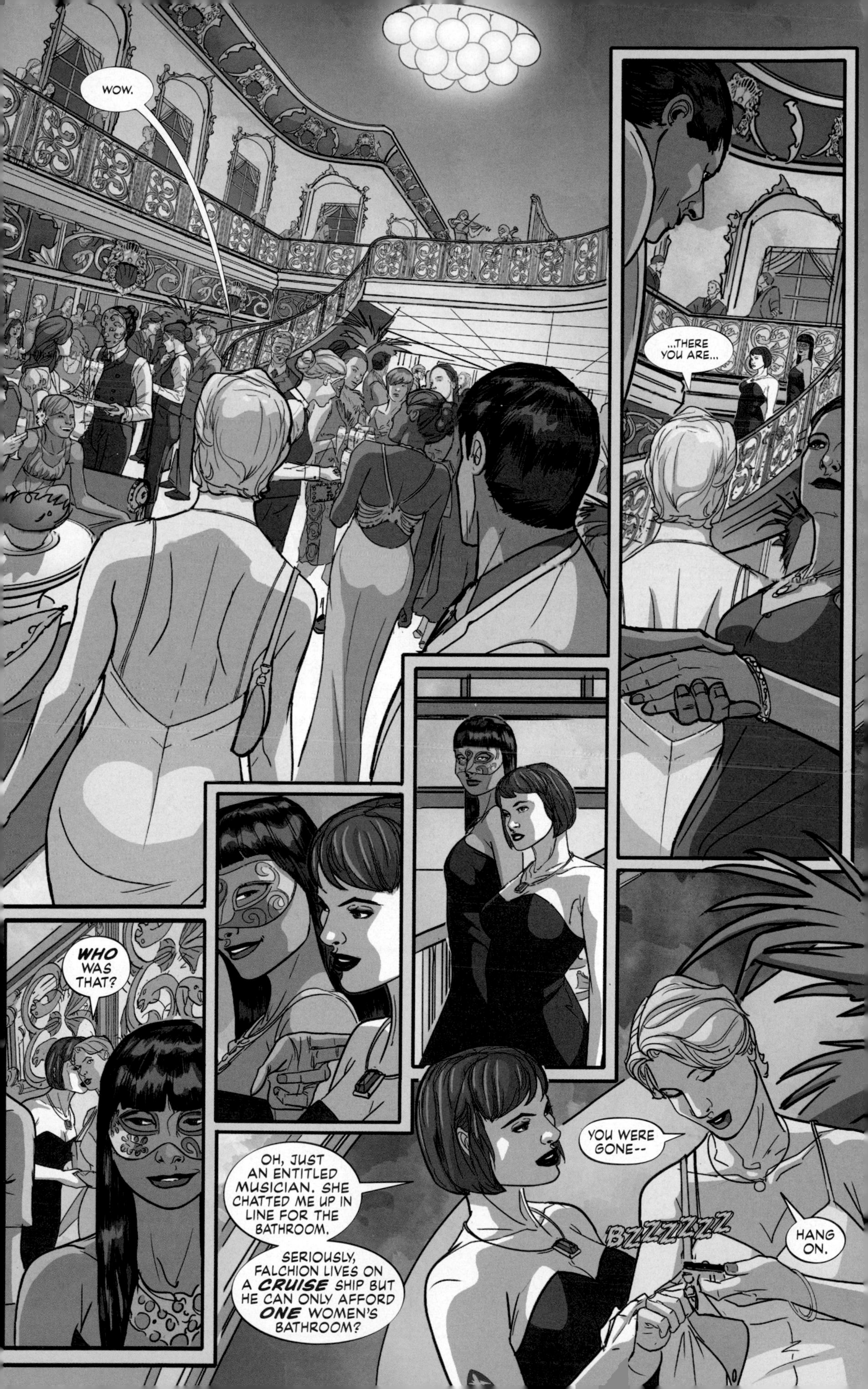
WOW.
...THERE YOU ARE...
WHO WAS THAT?
OH, JUST AN ENTITLED MUSICIAN. SHE CHATTED ME UP IN LINE FOR THE BATHROOM.
SERIOUSLY, FALCHION LIVES ON A CRUISE SHIP BUT HE CAN ONLY AFFORD ONE WOMEN'S BATHROOM?
YOU WERE GONE--
BZZZZZZ
HANG ON.

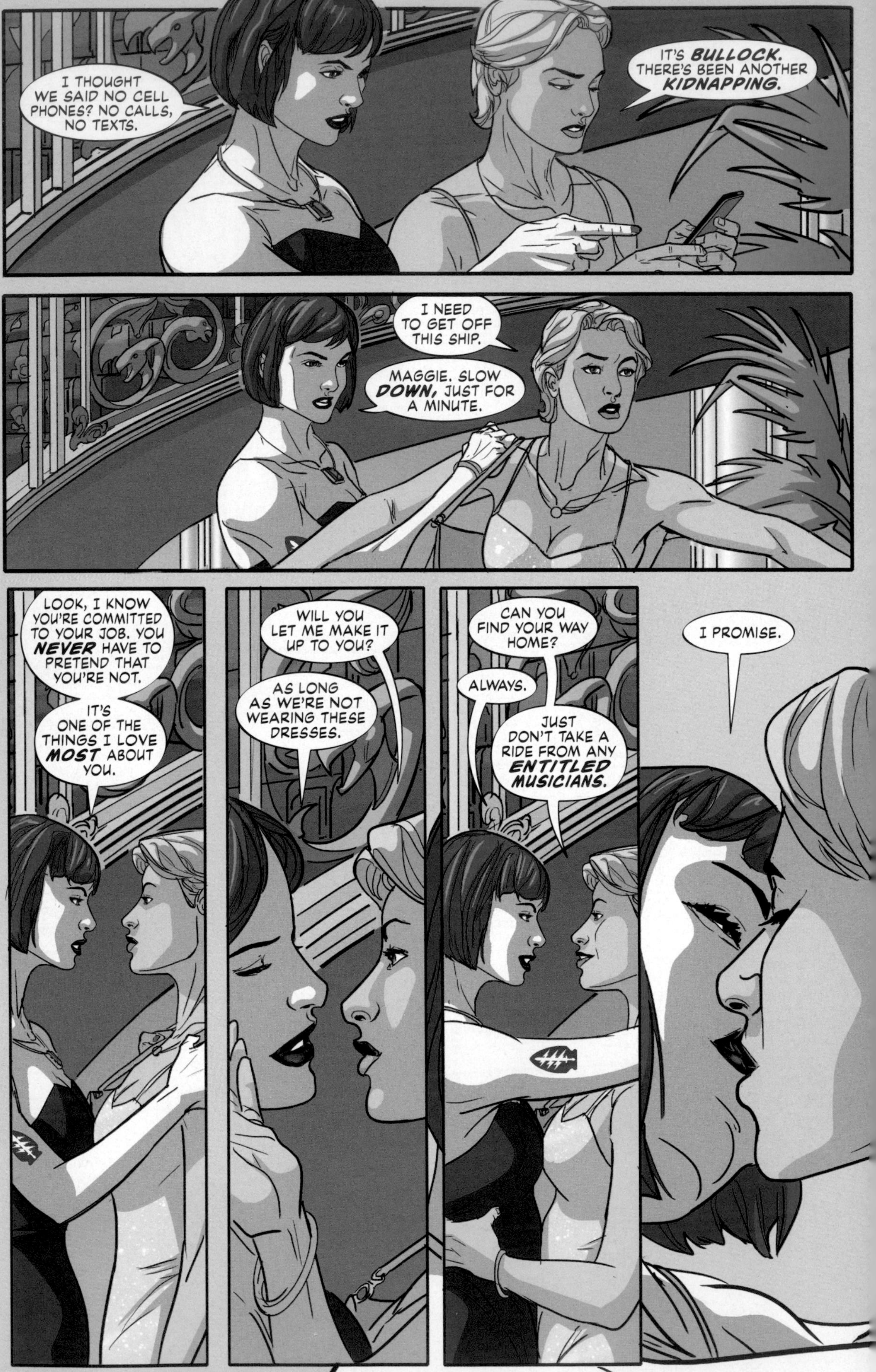
I THOUGHT WE SAID NO CELL PHONES? NO CALLS, NO TEXTS.
IT'S **BULLOCK.** THERE'S BEEN ANOTHER **KIDNAPPING.**
I NEED TO GET OFF THIS SHIP.
MAGGIE. SLOW **DOWN,** JUST FOR A MINUTE.
LOOK, I KNOW YOU'RE COMMITTED TO YOUR JOB. YOU **NEVER** HAVE TO PRETEND THAT YOU'RE NOT.
IT'S ONE OF THE THINGS I LOVE **MOST** ABOUT YOU.
WILL YOU LET ME MAKE IT UP TO YOU?
AS LONG AS WE'RE NOT WEARING THESE DRESSES.
CAN YOU FIND YOUR WAY HOME?
ALWAYS.
JUST DON'T TAKE A RIDE FROM ANY **ENTITLED MUSICIANS.**
I PROMISE.

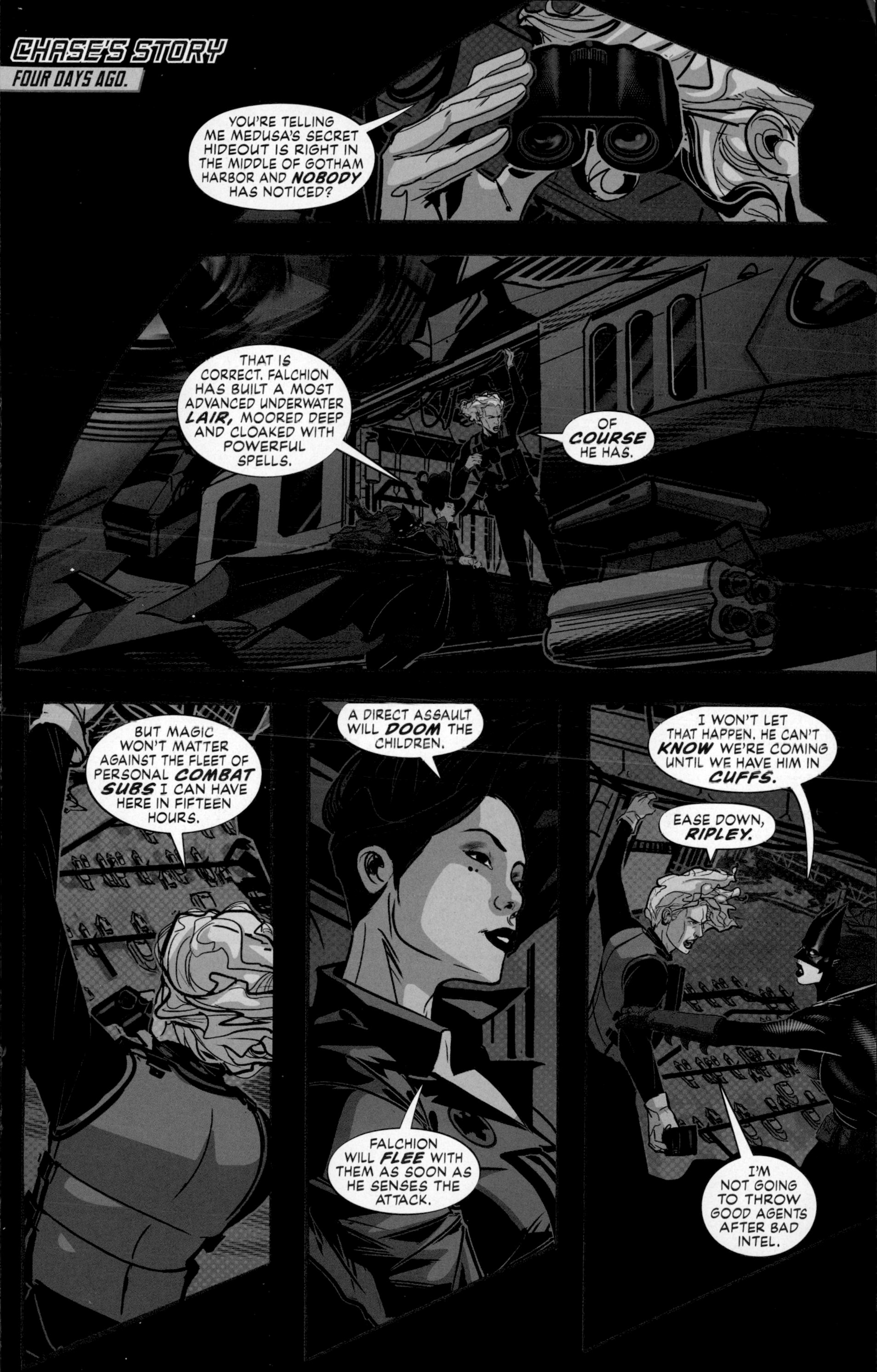
CHASE'S STORY
FOUR DAYS AGO.
YOU'RE TELLING ME MEDUSA'S SECRET HIDEOUT IS RIGHT IN THE MIDDLE OF GOTHAM HARBOR AND NOBODY HAS NOTICED?
THAT IS CORRECT. FALCHION HAS BUILT A MOST ADVANCED UNDERWATER LAIR, MOORED DEEP AND CLOAKED WITH POWERFUL SPELLS.
OF COURSE HE HAS.
BUT MAGIC WON'T MATTER AGAINST THE FLEET OF PERSONAL COMBAT SUBS I CAN HAVE HERE IN FIFTEEN HOURS.
A DIRECT ASSAULT WILL DOOM THE CHILDREN.
FALCHION WILL FLEE WITH THEM AS SOON AS HE SENSES THE ATTACK.
I WON'T LET THAT HAPPEN. HE CAN'T KNOW WE'RE COMING UNTIL WE HAVE HIM IN CUFFS.
EASE DOWN, RIPLEY.
I'M NOT GOING TO THROW GOOD AGENTS AFTER BAD INTEL.

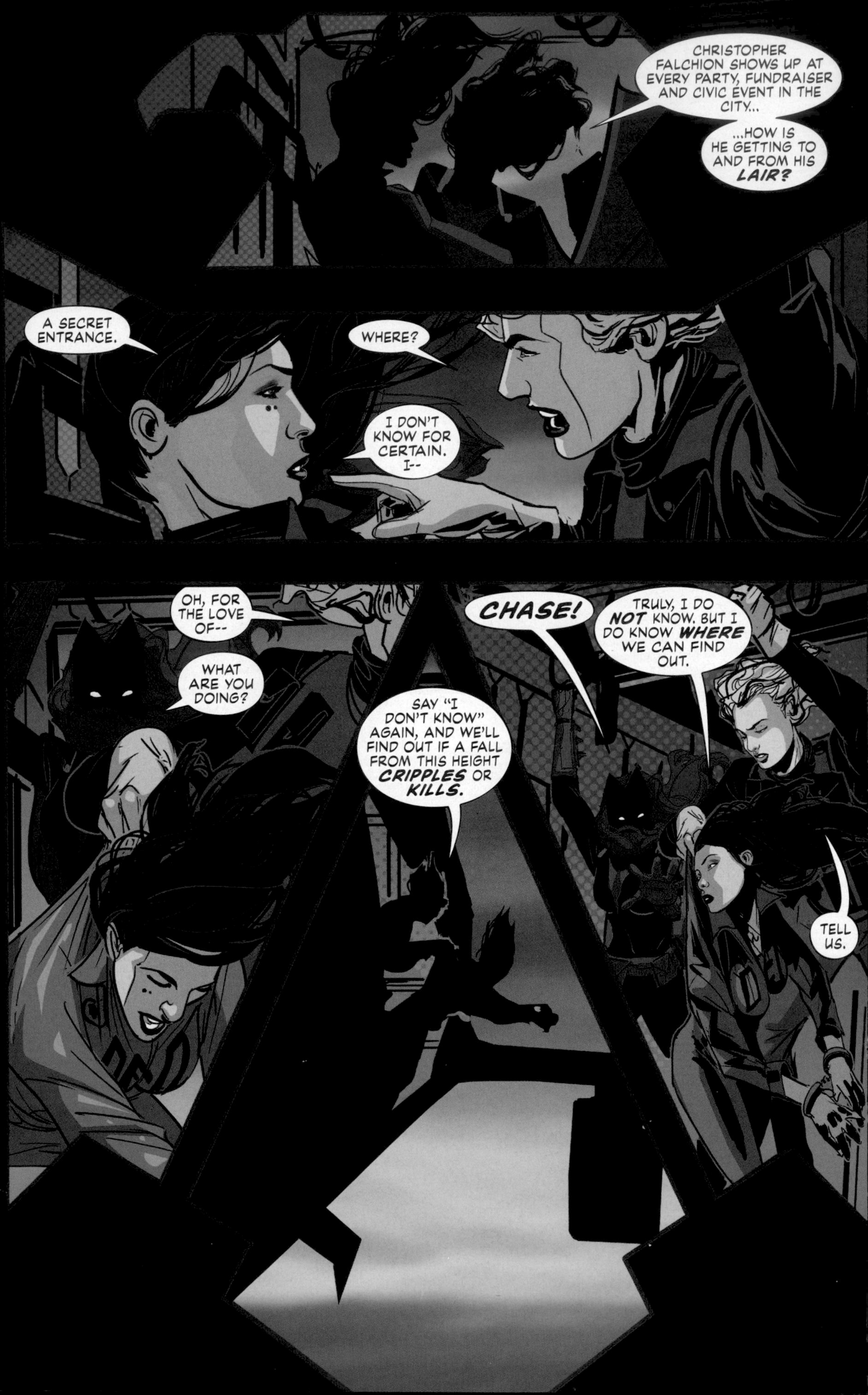
CHRISTOPHER FALCHION SHOWS UP AT EVERY PARTY, FUNDRAISER AND CIVIC EVENT IN THE CITY...
...HOW IS HE GETTING TO AND FROM HIS LAIR?
A SECRET ENTRANCE.
WHERE?
I DON'T KNOW FOR CERTAIN. I--
OH, FOR THE LOVE OF--
WHAT ARE YOU DOING?
SAY "I DON'T KNOW" AGAIN, AND WE'LL FIND OUT IF A FALL FROM THIS HEIGHT CRIPPLES OR KILLS.
CHASE!
TRULY, I DO NOT KNOW. BUT I DO KNOW WHERE WE CAN FIND OUT.
TELL US.

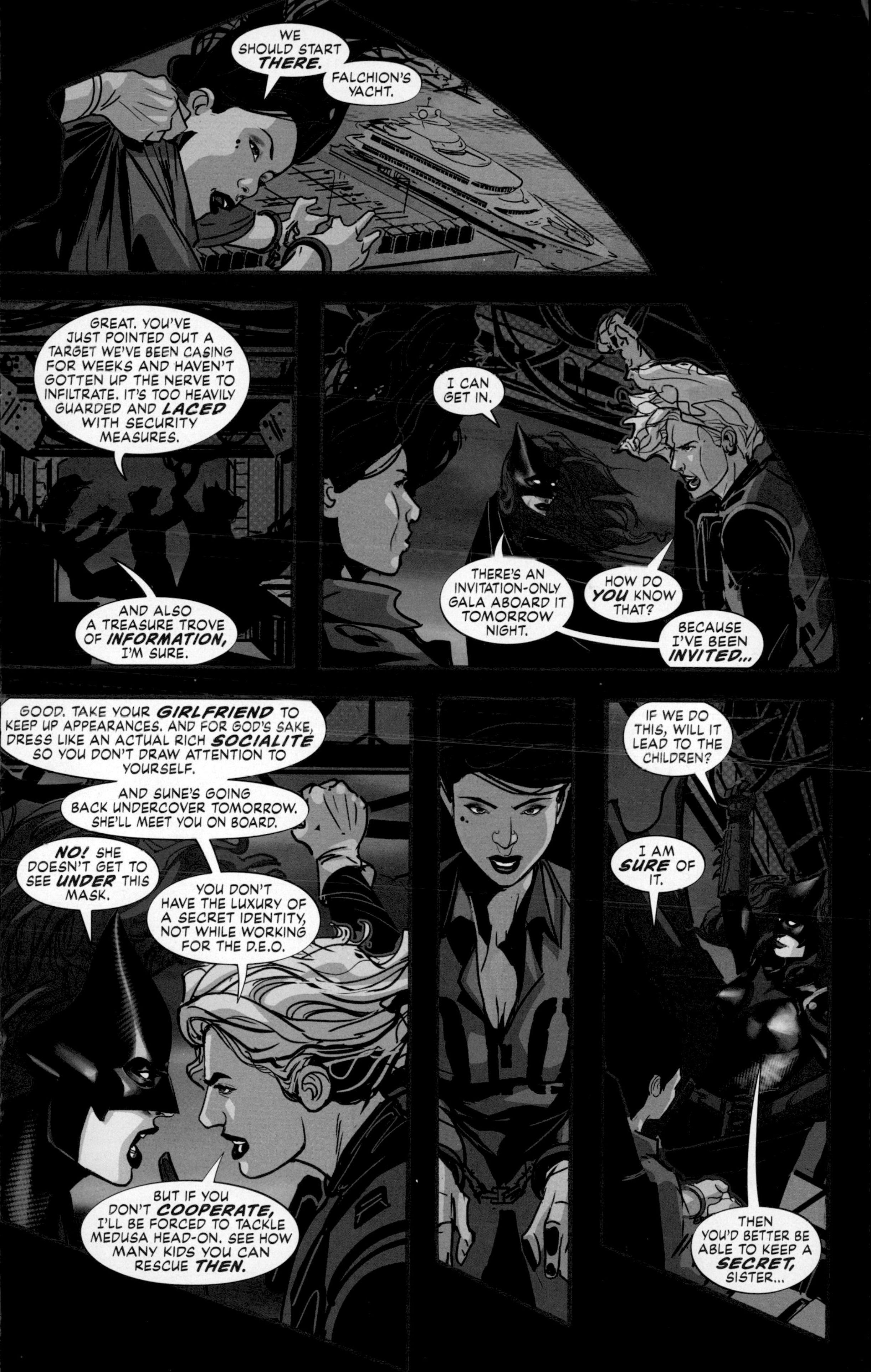
WE SHOULD START THERE.
FALCHION'S YACHT.
GREAT. YOU'VE JUST POINTED OUT A TARGET WE'VE BEEN CASING FOR WEEKS AND HAVEN'T GOTTEN UP THE NERVE TO INFILTRATE. IT'S TOO HEAVILY GUARDED AND LACED WITH SECURITY MEASURES.
AND ALSO A TREASURE TROVE OF INFORMATION, I'M SURE.
I CAN GET IN.
THERE'S AN INVITATION-ONLY GALA ABOARD IT TOMORROW NIGHT.
HOW DO YOU KNOW THAT?
BECAUSE I'VE BEEN INVITED...
GOOD. TAKE YOUR GIRLFRIEND TO KEEP UP APPEARANCES. AND FOR GOD'S SAKE, DRESS LIKE AN ACTUAL RICH SOCIALITE SO YOU DON'T DRAW ATTENTION TO YOURSELF.
AND SUNE'S GOING BACK UNDERCOVER TOMORROW. SHE'LL MEET YOU ON BOARD.
NO! SHE DOESN'T GET TO SEE UNDER THIS MASK.
YOU DON'T HAVE THE LUXURY OF A SECRET IDENTITY, NOT WHILE WORKING FOR THE D.E.O.
BUT IF YOU DON'T COOPERATE, I'LL BE FORCED TO TACKLE MEDUSA HEAD-ON. SEE HOW MANY KIDS YOU CAN RESCUE THEN.
IF WE DO THIS, WILL IT LEAD TO THE CHILDREN?
I AM SURE OF IT.
THEN YOU'D BETTER BE ABLE TO KEEP A SECRET, SISTER...

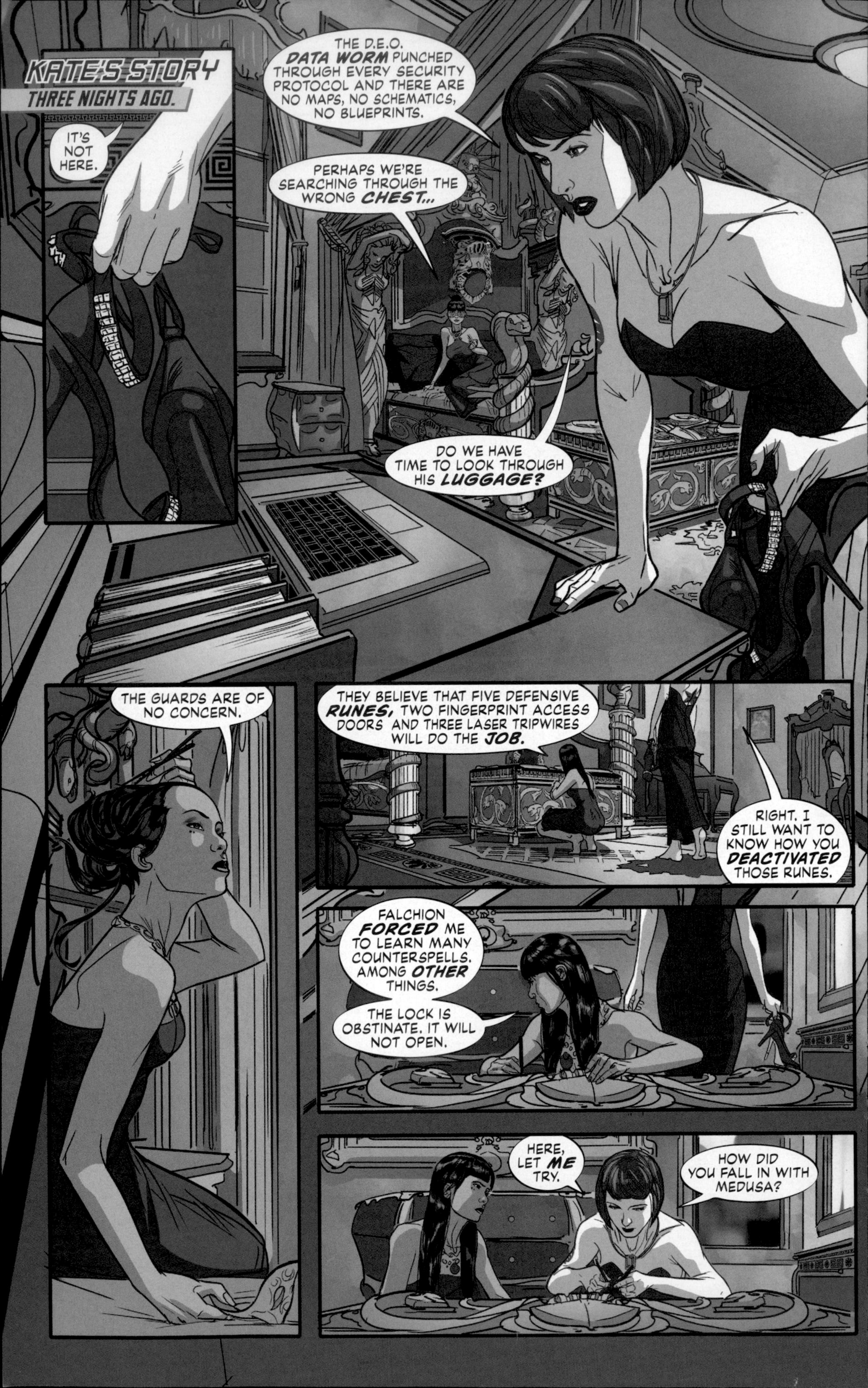
KATE'S STORY
THREE NIGHTS AGO.
IT'S NOT HERE.
THE D.E.O. DATA WORM PUNCHED THROUGH EVERY SECURITY PROTOCOL AND THERE ARE NO MAPS, NO SCHEMATICS, NO BLUEPRINTS.
PERHAPS WE'RE SEARCHING THROUGH THE WRONG CHEST...
DO WE HAVE TIME TO LOOK THROUGH HIS LUGGAGE?
THE GUARDS ARE OF NO CONCERN.
THEY BELIEVE THAT FIVE DEFENSIVE RUNES, TWO FINGERPRINT ACCESS DOORS AND THREE LASER TRIPWIRES WILL DO THE JOB.
RIGHT. I STILL WANT TO KNOW HOW YOU DEACTIVATED THOSE RUNES.
FALCHION FORCED ME TO LEARN MANY COUNTERSPELLS. AMONG OTHER THINGS.
THE LOCK IS OBSTINATE. IT WILL NOT OPEN.
HERE, LET ME TRY.
HOW DID YOU FALL IN WITH MEDUSA?

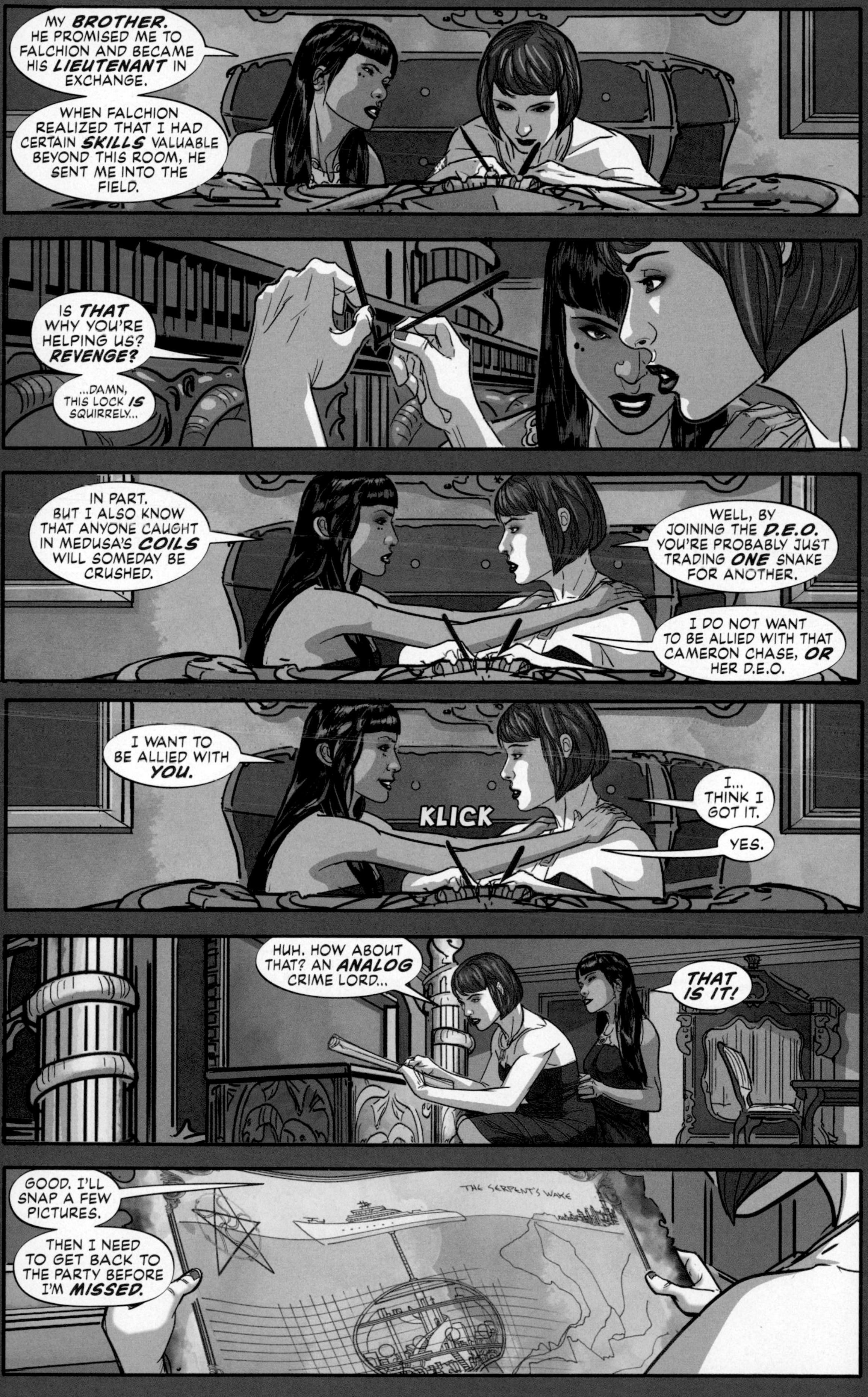
MY BROTHER. HE PROMISED ME TO FALCHION AND BECAME HIS LIEUTENANT IN EXCHANGE.
WHEN FALCHION REALIZED THAT I HAD CERTAIN SKILLS VALUABLE BEYOND THIS ROOM, HE SENT ME INTO THE FIELD.
IS THAT WHY YOU'RE HELPING US? REVENGE?
...DAMN, THIS LOCK IS SQUIRRELY...
IN PART. BUT I ALSO KNOW THAT ANYONE CAUGHT IN MEDUSA'S COILS WILL SOMEDAY BE CRUSHED.
WELL, BY JOINING THE D.E.O. YOU'RE PROBABLY JUST TRADING ONE SNAKE FOR ANOTHER.
I DO NOT WANT TO BE ALLIED WITH THAT CAMERON CHASE, OR HER D.E.O.
I WANT TO BE ALLIED WITH YOU.
KLICK
I... THINK I GOT IT.
YES.
HUH. HOW ABOUT THAT? AN ANALOG CRIME LORD...
THAT IS IT!
GOOD. I'LL SNAP A FEW PICTURES.
THEN I NEED TO GET BACK TO THE PARTY BEFORE I'M MISSED.
THE SERPENT'S WAKE

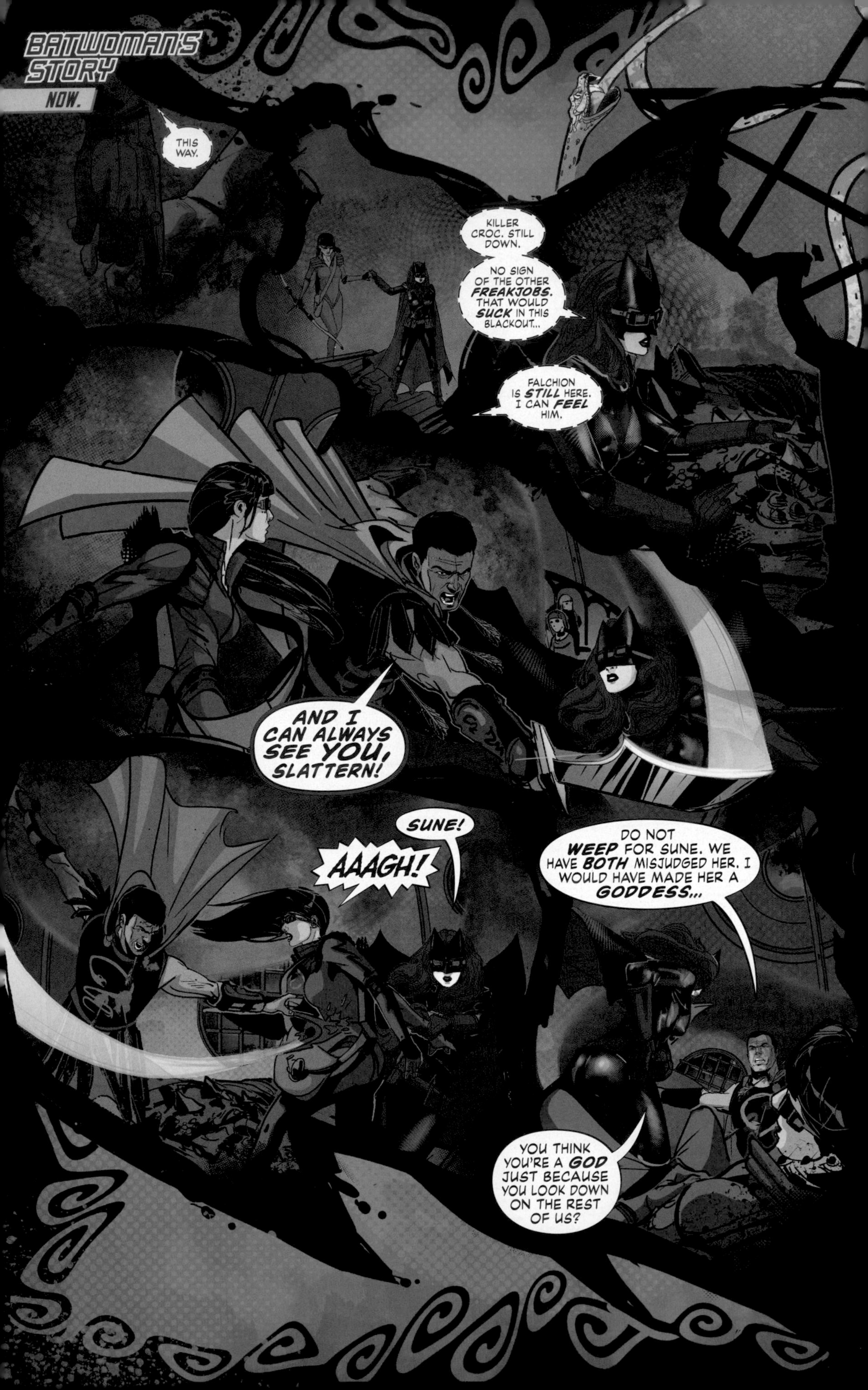
BATWOMAN'S STORY
NOW.
THIS WAY.
KILLER CROC. STILL DOWN.
NO SIGN OF THE OTHER FREAKJOBS. THAT WOULD SUCK IN THIS BLACKOUT...
FALCHION IS STILL HERE. I CAN FEEL HIM.
AND I CAN ALWAYS SEE YOU, SLATTERN!
AAAGH!
SUNE!
DO NOT WEEP FOR SUNE. WE HAVE BOTH MISJUDGED HER. I WOULD HAVE MADE HER A GODDESS...
YOU THINK YOU'RE A GOD JUST BECAUSE YOU LOOK DOWN ON THE REST OF US?

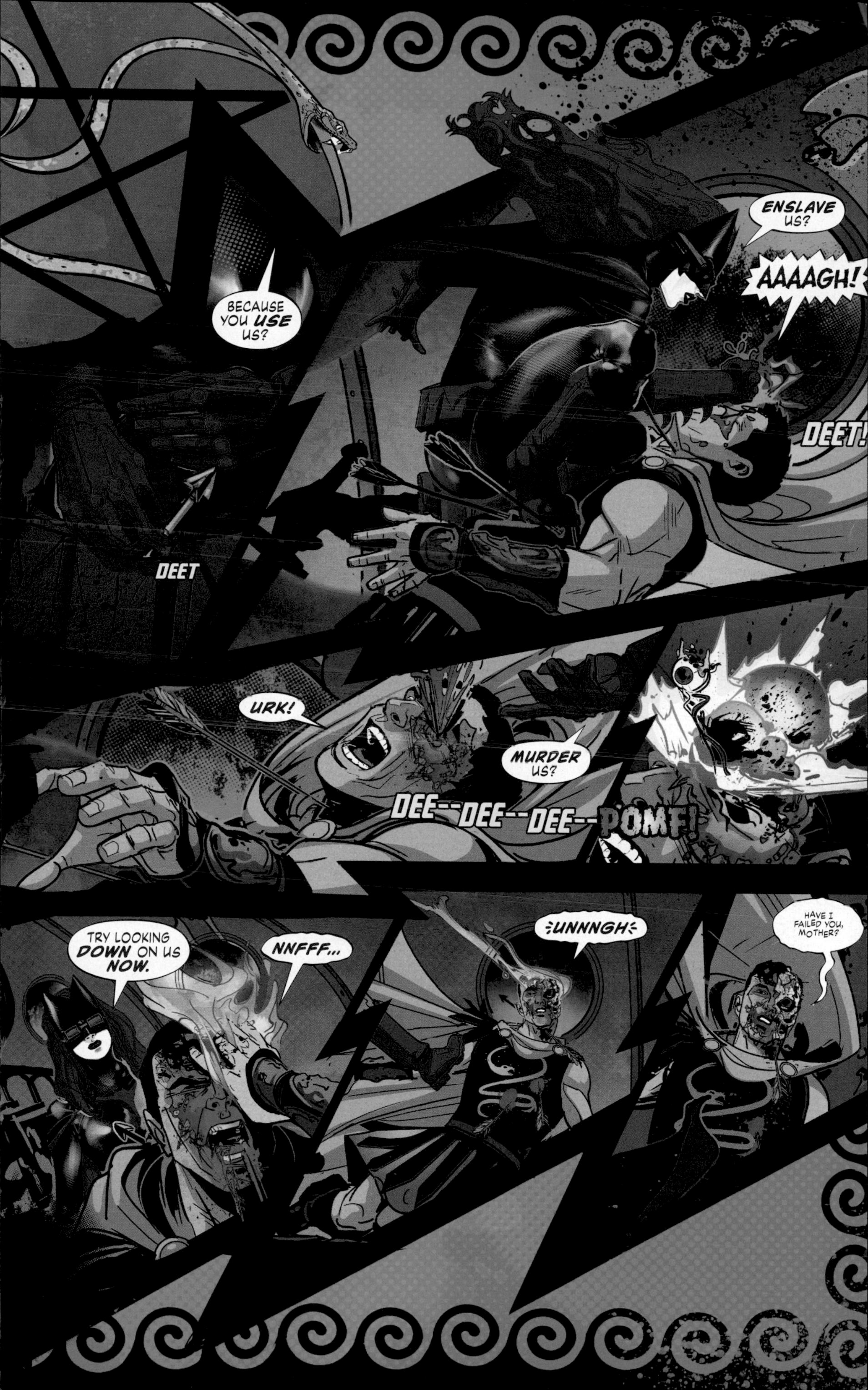
BECAUSE YOU USE US?
ENSLAVE US?
AAAAGH!
DEET!
DEET
URK!
MURDER US?
DEE--DEE--DEE--POMF!
TRY LOOKING DOWN ON US NOW.
NNFFF...
UNNNGH
HAVE I FAILED YOU, MOTHER?

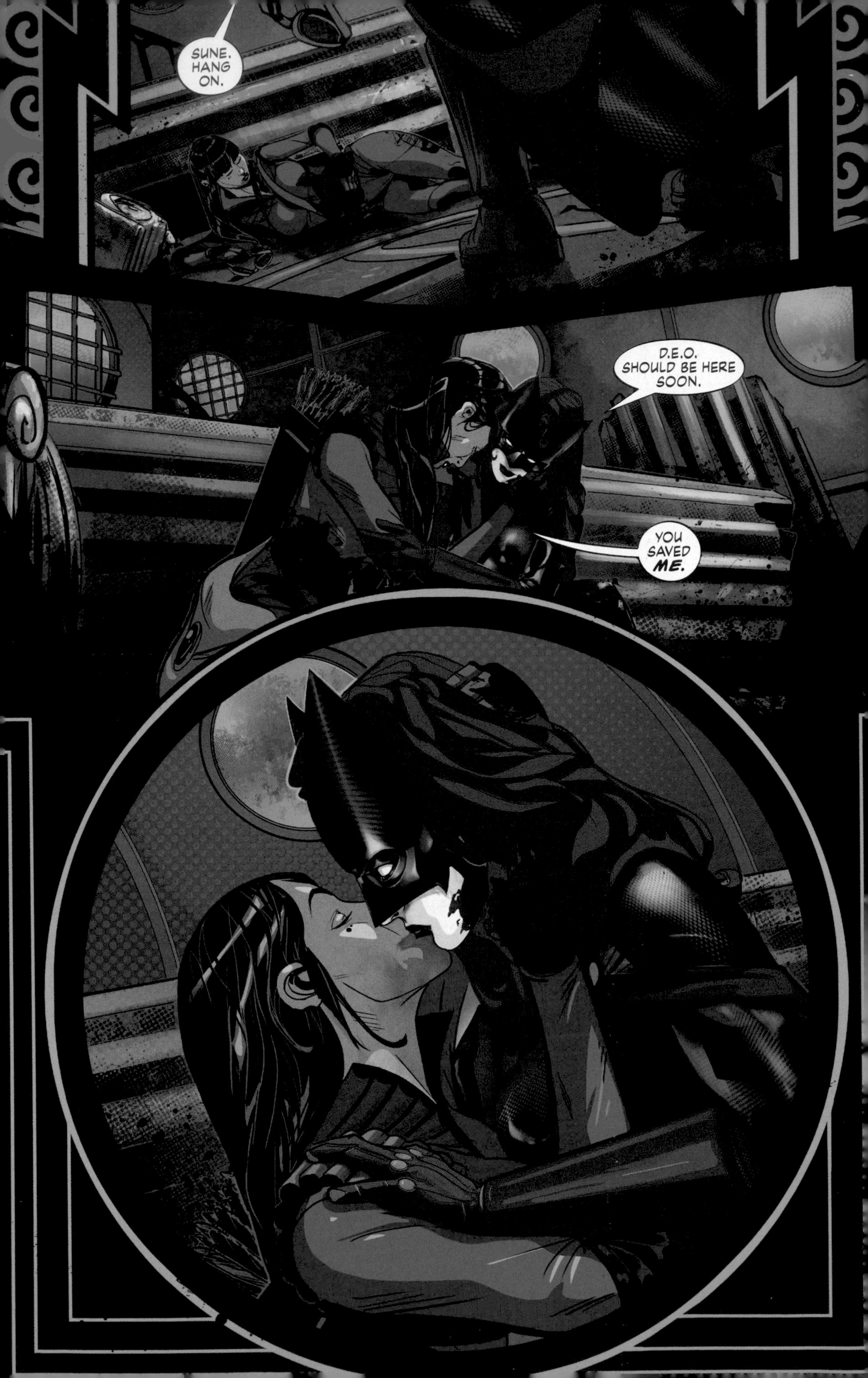
SUNE. HANG ON.
D.E.O. SHOULD BE HERE SOON.
YOU SAVED ME.

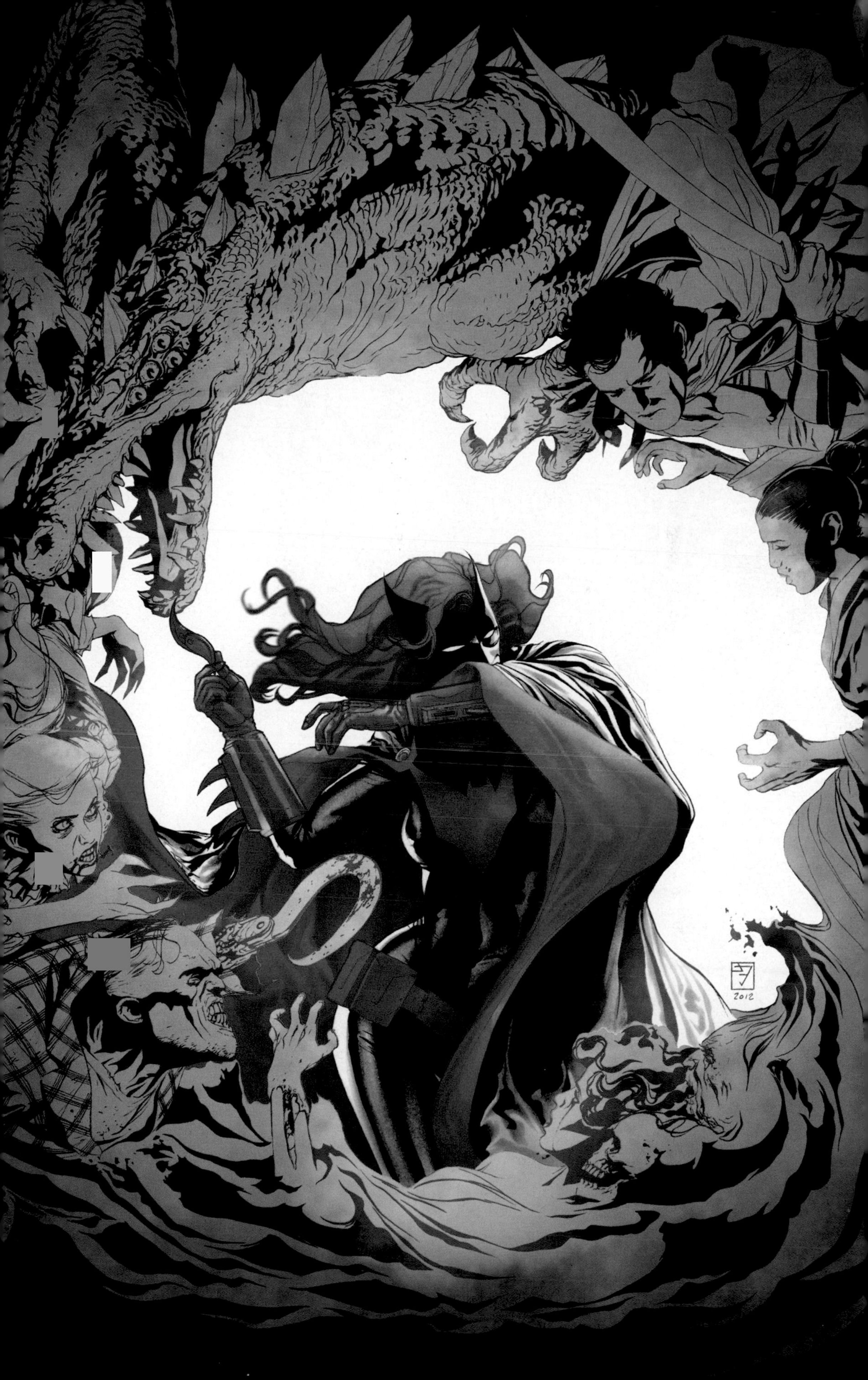
2012

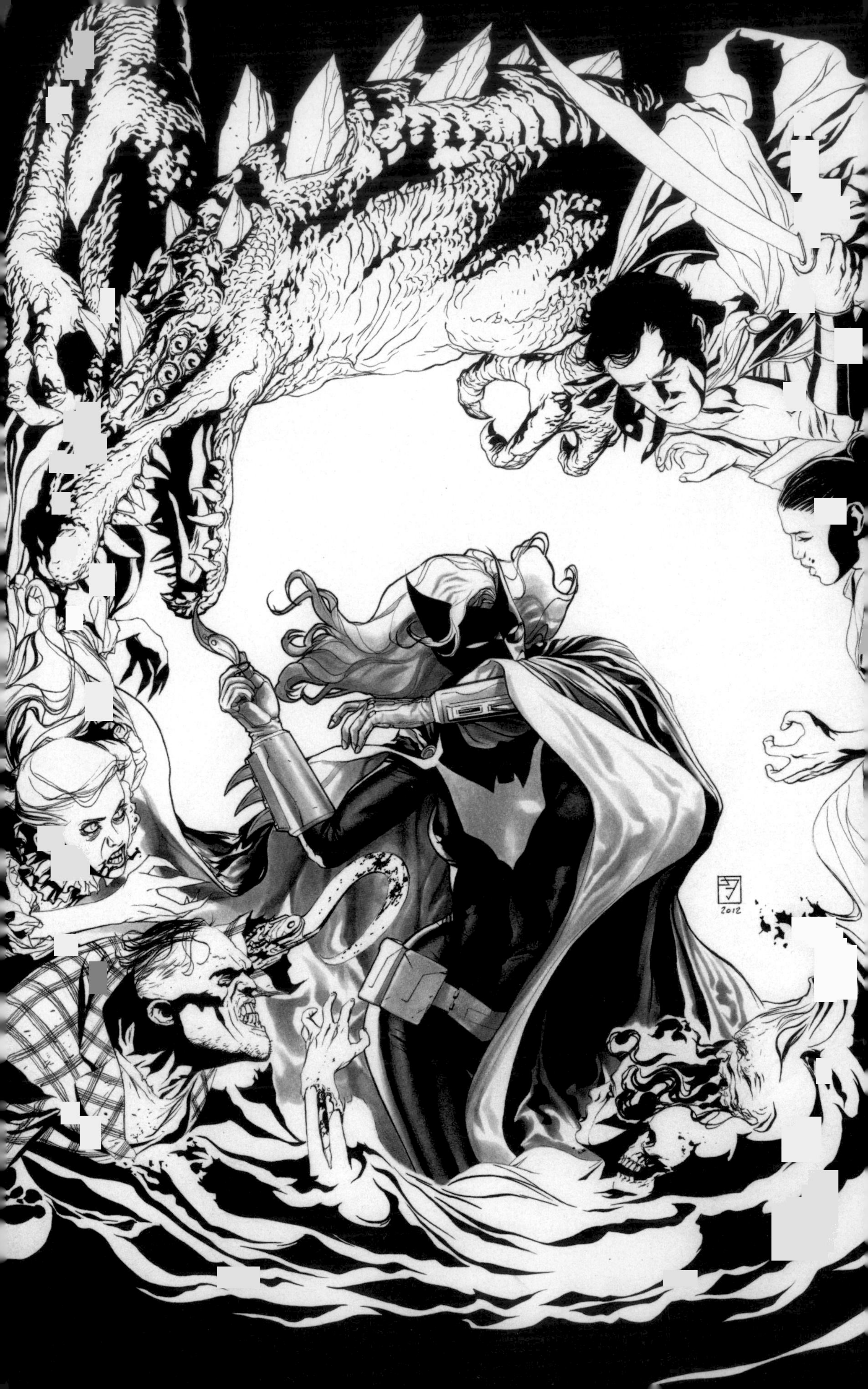
2012

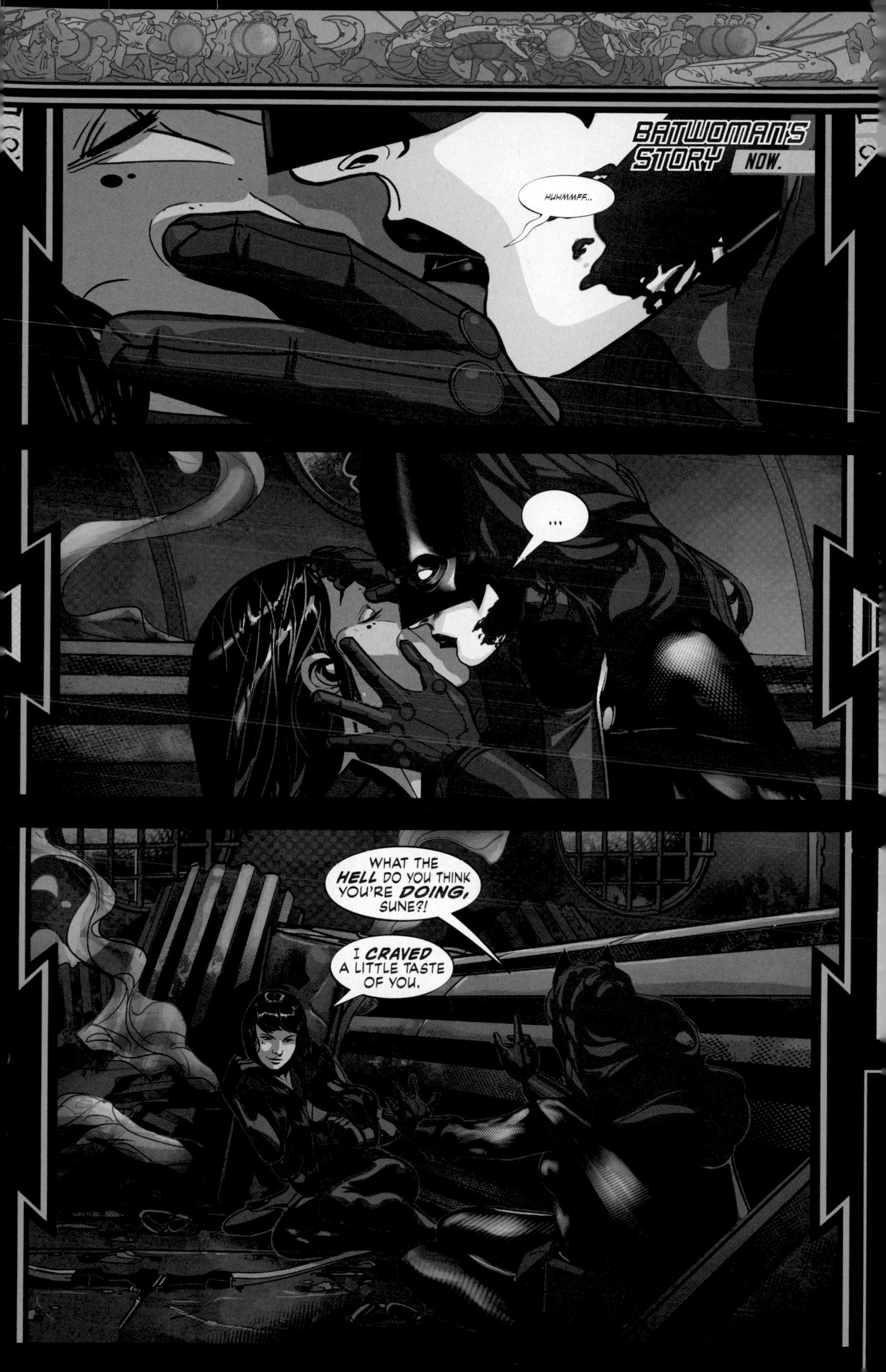
BATWOMAN'S STORY NOW.
HUHMMFF...
...
WHAT THE HELL DO YOU THINK YOU'RE DOING, SUNE?!
I CRAVED A LITTLE TASTE OF YOU.

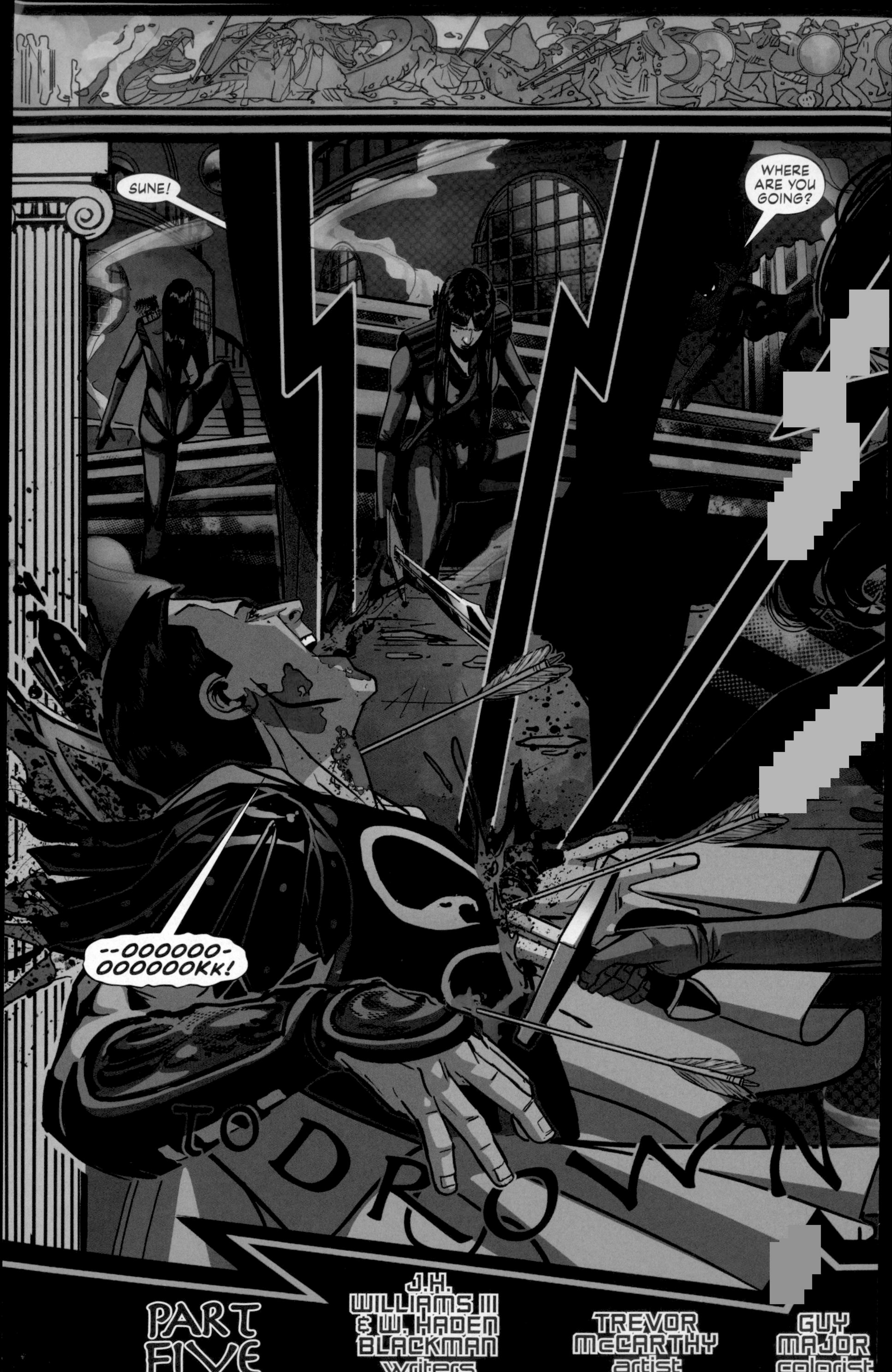
SUNE!
WHERE ARE YOU GOING?
--OOOOOO-OOOOOOKk!
TO DROWN
PART FIVE
J.H. WILLIAMS III & W. HADEN BLACKMAN writers
TREVOR McCARTHY artist
GUY MAJOR colorist

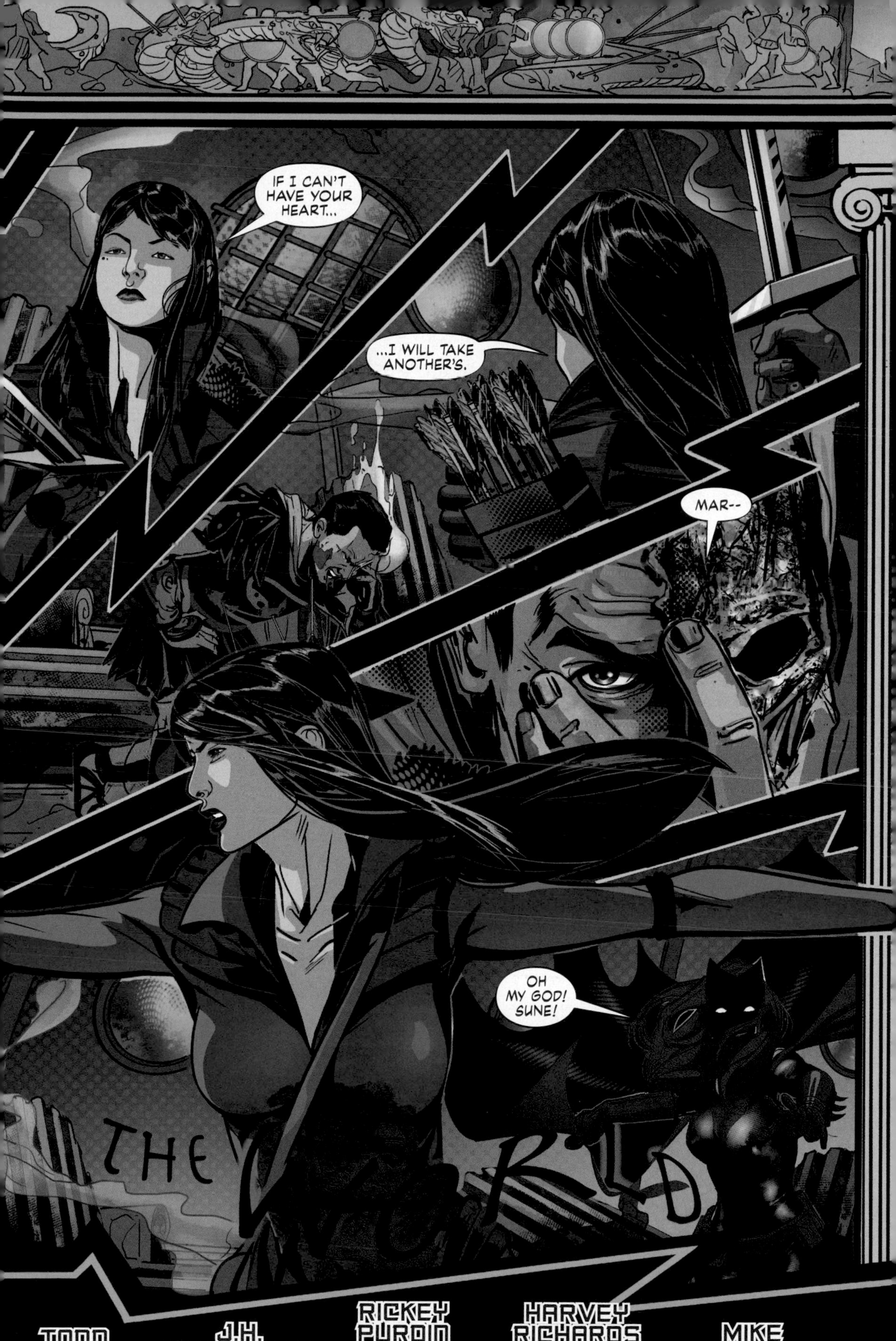
IF I CAN'T HAVE YOUR HEART...
...I WILL TAKE ANOTHER'S.
MAR--
OH MY GOD! SUNE!
THE

TODD KLEIN letterer

J.H. WILLIAMS III cover

RICKEY PURDIN asst. editor

HARVEY RICHARDS assoc. editor

MIKE MARTS editor

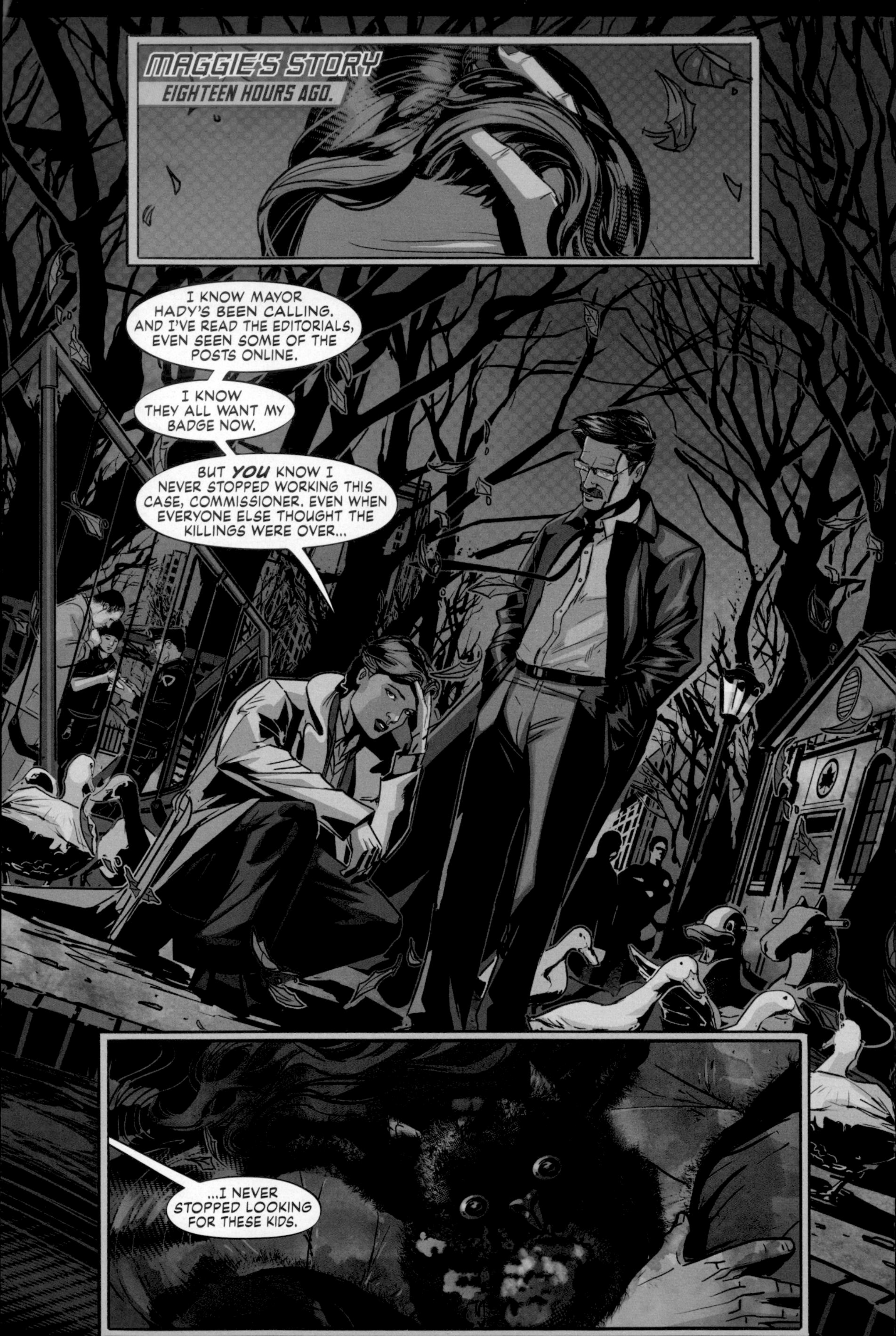
MAGGIE'S STORY
EIGHTEEN HOURS AGO.
I KNOW MAYOR HADY'S BEEN CALLING. AND I'VE READ THE EDITORIALS, EVEN SEEN SOME OF THE POSTS ONLINE.
I KNOW THEY ALL WANT MY BADGE NOW.
BUT YOU KNOW I NEVER STOPPED WORKING THIS CASE, COMMISSIONER. EVEN WHEN EVERYONE ELSE THOUGHT THE KILLINGS WERE OVER...
...I NEVER STOPPED LOOKING FOR THESE KIDS.

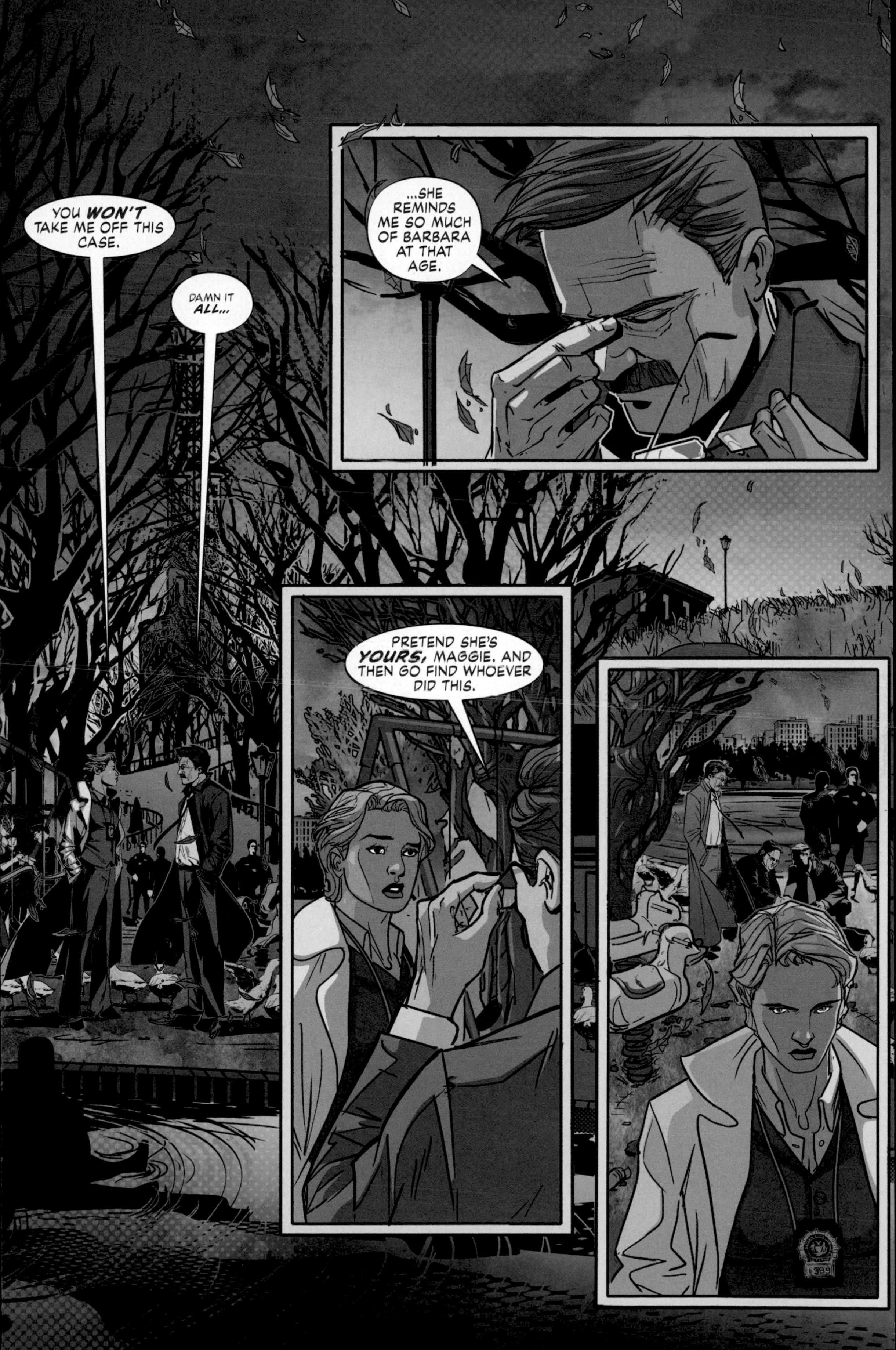
YOU **WON'T** TAKE ME OFF THIS CASE.
DAMN IT **ALL**...
...SHE REMINDS ME SO MUCH OF BARBARA AT THAT AGE.
PRETEND SHE'S **YOURS,** MAGGIE. AND THEN GO FIND WHOEVER DID THIS.

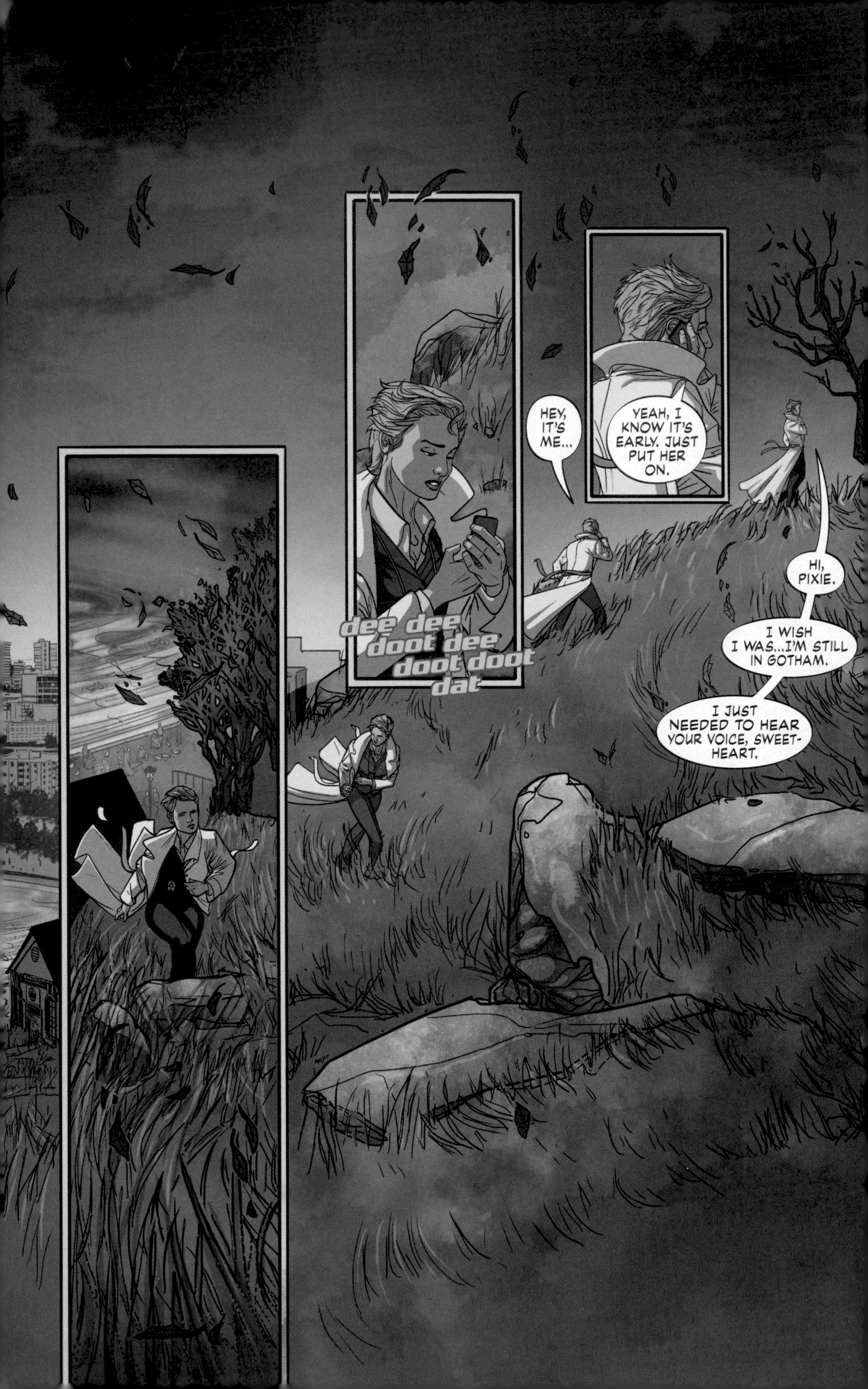
dee dee doot dee doot doot dat
HEY, IT'S ME...
YEAH, I KNOW IT'S EARLY. JUST PUT HER ON.
HI, PIXIE.
I WISH I WAS...I'M STILL IN GOTHAM.
I JUST NEEDED TO HEAR YOUR VOICE, SWEET-HEART.

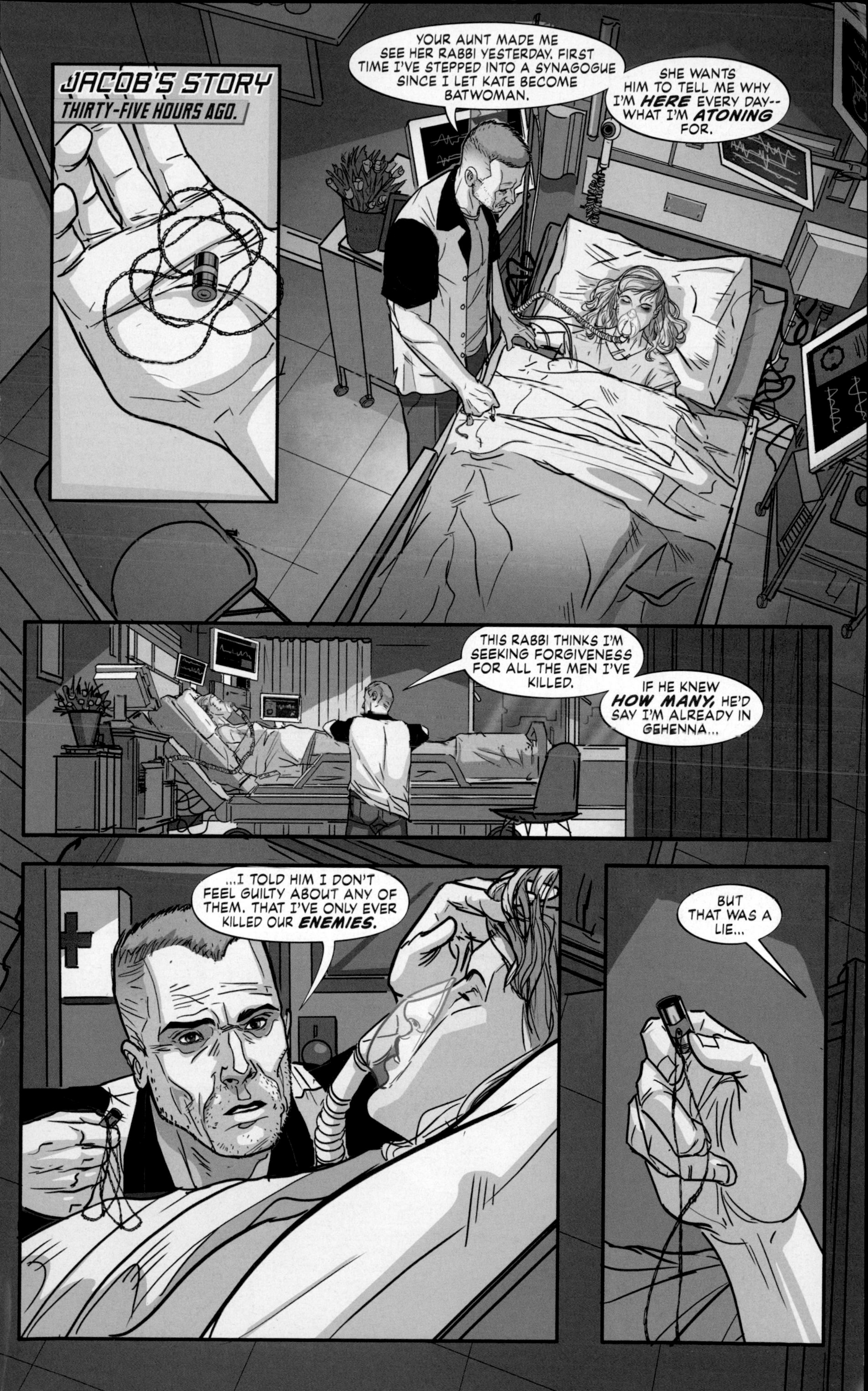
JACOB'S STORY
THIRTY-FIVE HOURS AGO.
YOUR AUNT MADE ME SEE HER RABBI YESTERDAY. FIRST TIME I'VE STEPPED INTO A SYNAGOGUE SINCE I LET KATE BECOME BATWOMAN.
SHE WANTS HIM TO TELL ME WHY I'M HERE EVERY DAY-- WHAT I'M ATONING FOR.
THIS RABBI THINKS I'M SEEKING FORGIVENESS FOR ALL THE MEN I'VE KILLED.
IF HE KNEW HOW MANY, HE'D SAY I'M ALREADY IN GEHENNA...
...I TOLD HIM I DON'T FEEL GUILTY ABOUT ANY OF THEM. THAT I'VE ONLY EVER KILLED OUR ENEMIES.
BUT THAT WAS A LIE...

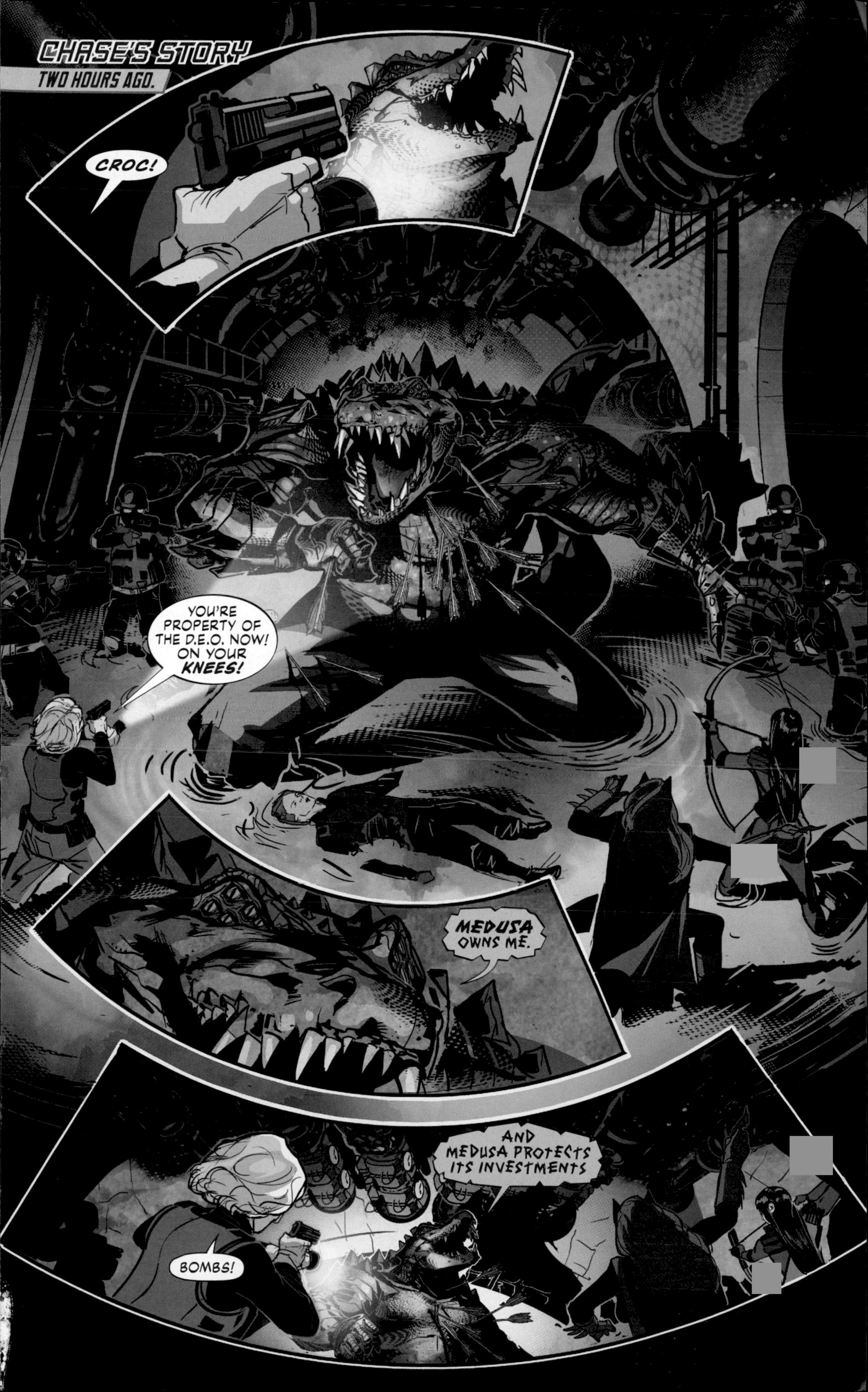
CHASE'S STORY
TWO HOURS AGO.
CROC!
YOU'RE PROPERTY OF THE D.E.O. NOW! ON YOUR KNEES!
MEDUSA OWNS ME.
AND MEDUSA PROTECTS ITS INVESTMENTS
BOMBS!

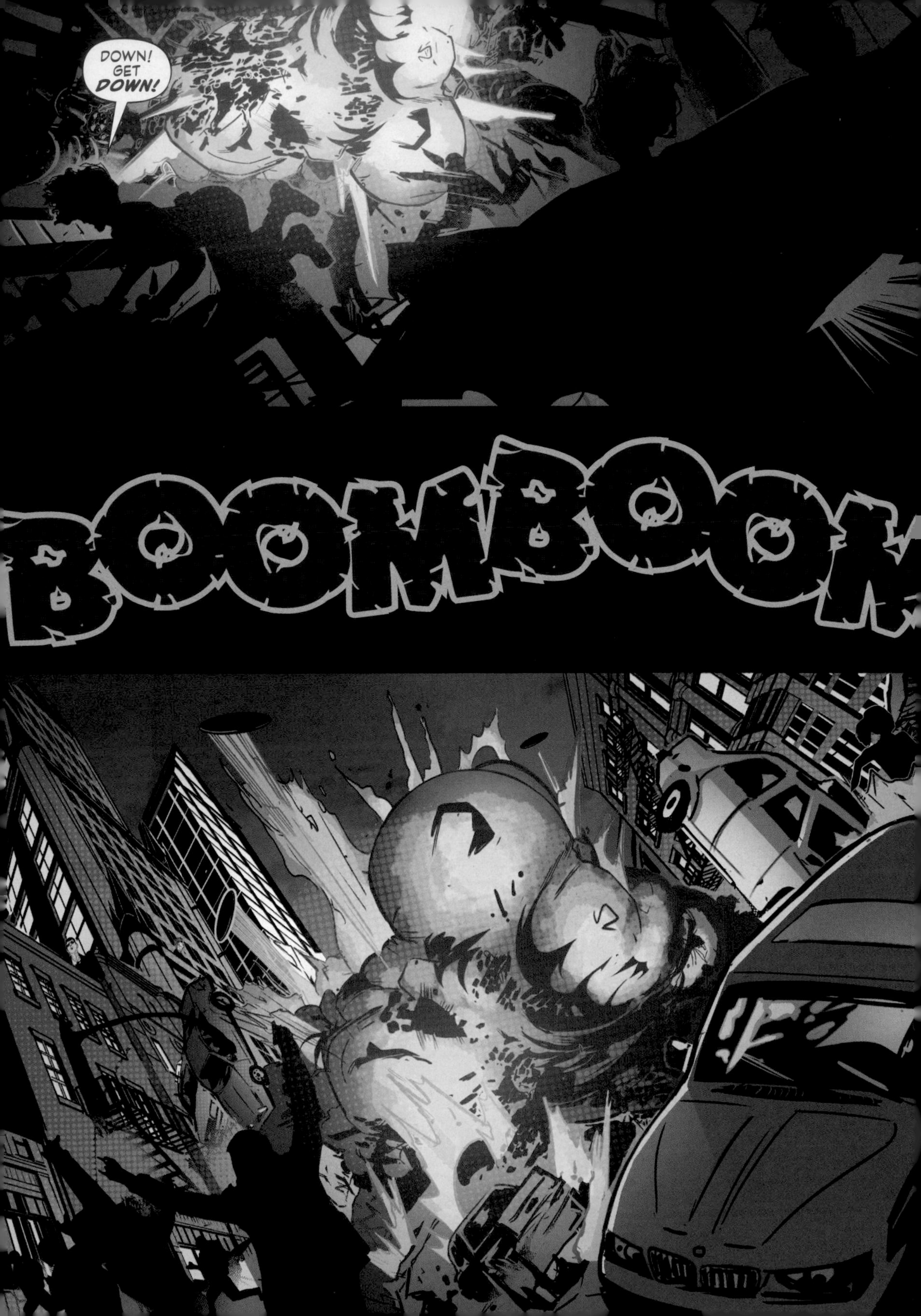
DOWN! GET DOWN!
BOOMBOOM

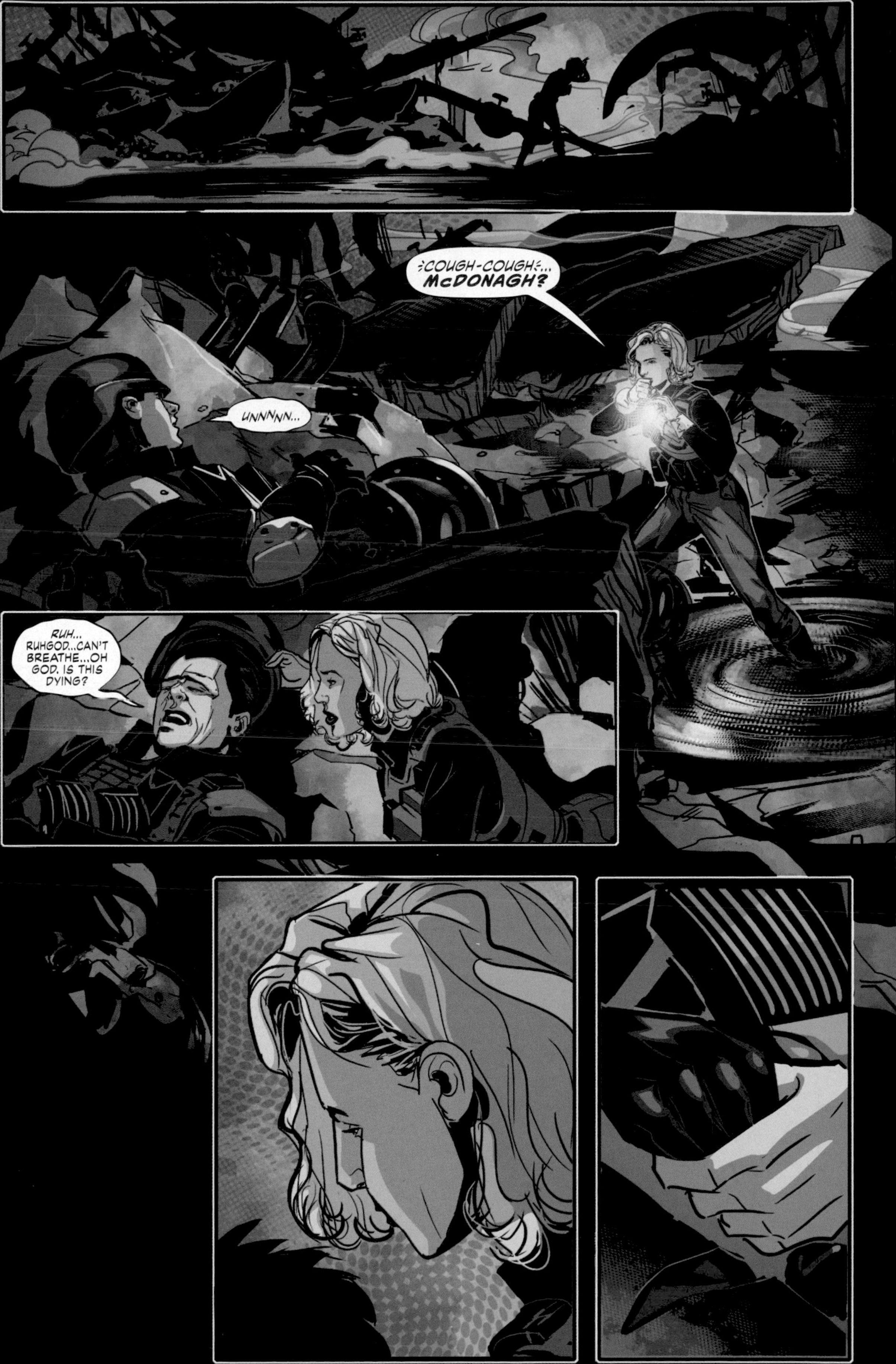

COUGH-COUGH... McDONAGH?
UNNNNN...
RUH... RUHGOD...CAN'T BREATHE...OH GOD. IS THIS DYING?

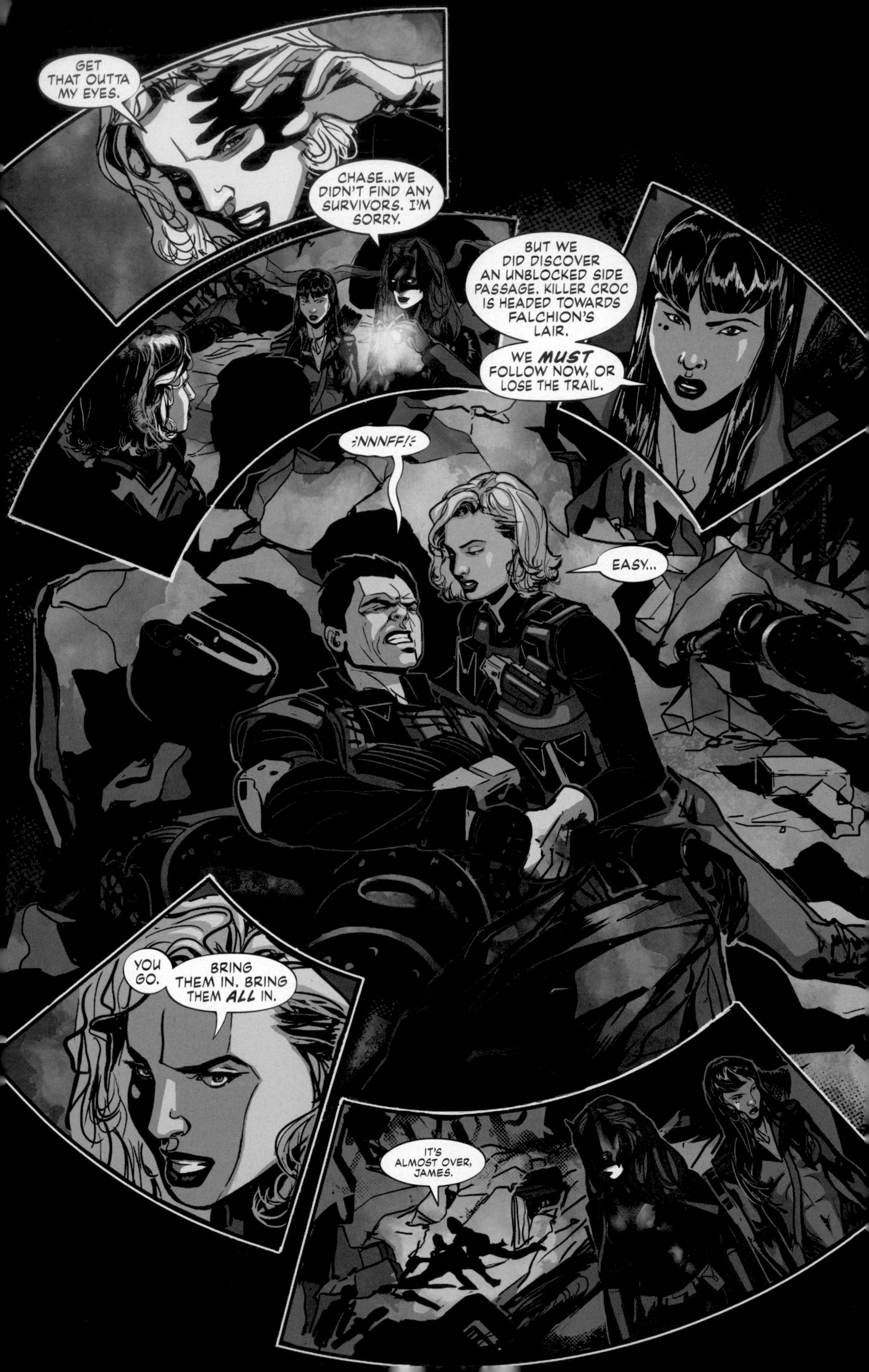
GET THAT OUTTA MY EYES.
CHASE...WE DIDN'T FIND ANY SURVIVORS. I'M SORRY.
BUT WE DID DISCOVER AN UNBLOCKED SIDE PASSAGE. KILLER CROC IS HEADED TOWARDS FALCHION'S LAIR.
WE MUST FOLLOW NOW, OR LOSE THE TRAIL.
NNNFF!
EASY...
YOU GO.
BRING THEM IN. BRING THEM ALL IN.
IT'S ALMOST OVER, JAMES.

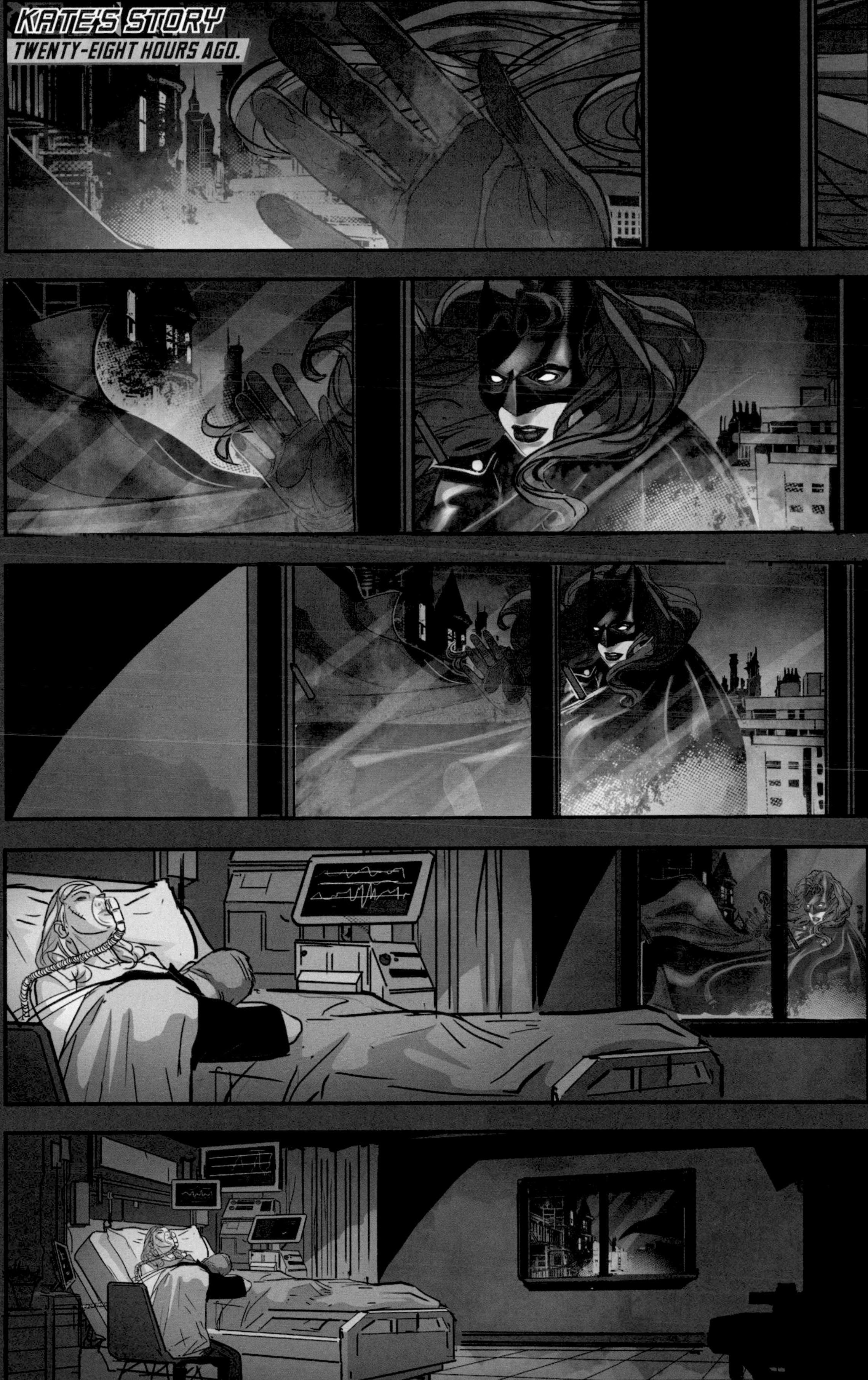
KATE'S STORY
TWENTY-EIGHT HOURS AGO.

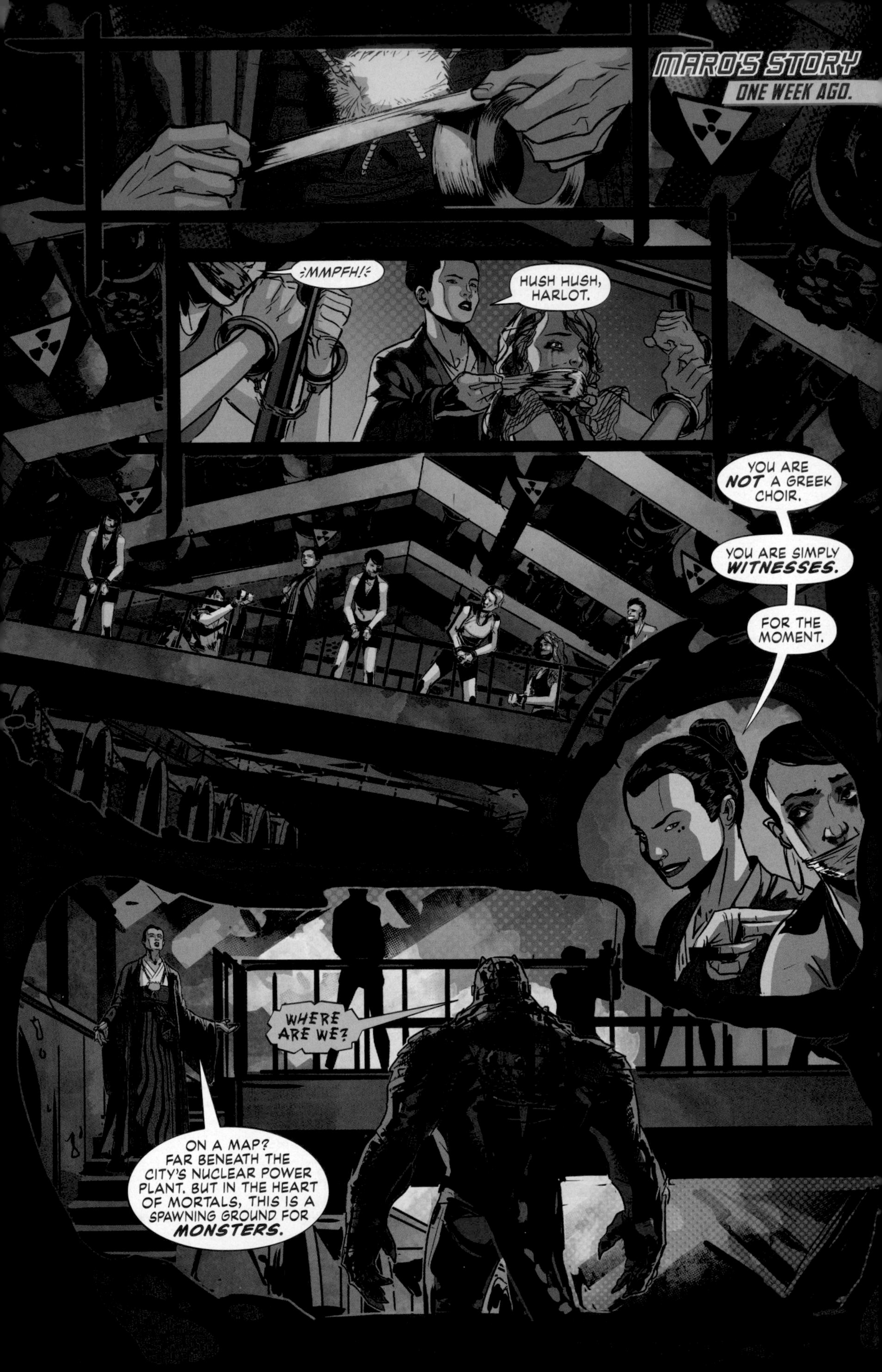
MARO'S STORY
ONE WEEK AGO.
MMPFH!
HUSH HUSH, HARLOT.
YOU ARE NOT A GREEK CHOIR.
YOU ARE SIMPLY WITNESSES.
FOR THE MOMENT.
WHERE ARE WE?
ON A MAP? FAR BENEATH THE CITY'S NUCLEAR POWER PLANT. BUT IN THE HEART OF MORTALS, THIS IS A SPAWNING GROUND FOR MONSTERS.

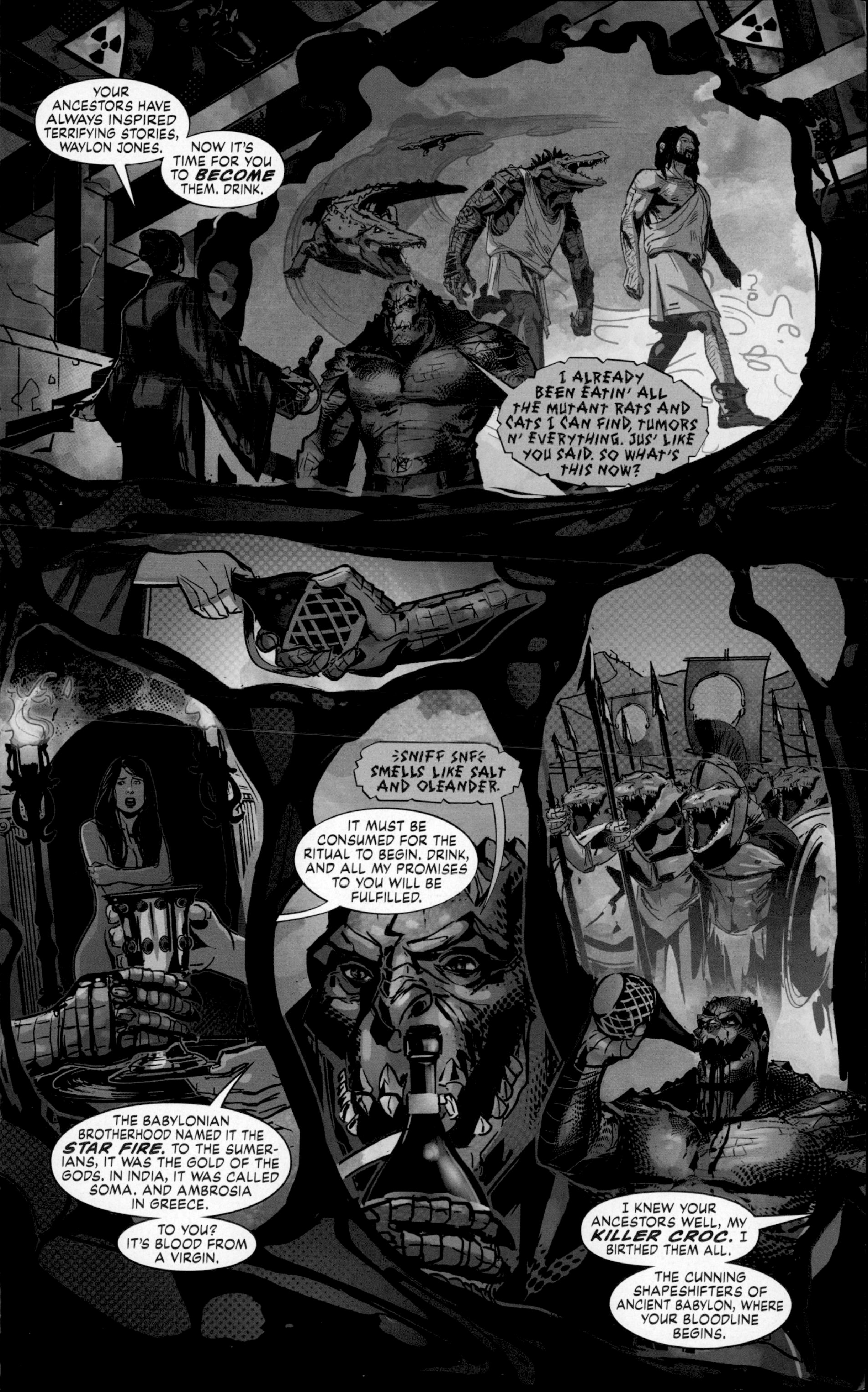

YOUR ANCESTORS HAVE ALWAYS INSPIRED TERRIFYING STORIES, WAYLON JONES.
NOW IT'S TIME FOR YOU TO BECOME THEM. DRINK.
I ALREADY BEEN EATIN' ALL THE MUTANT RATS AND CATS I CAN FIND, TUMORS N' EVERYTHING. JUS' LIKE YOU SAID. SO WHAT'S THIS NOW?
SNIFF SNF SMELLS LIKE SALT AND OLEANDER.
IT MUST BE CONSUMED FOR THE RITUAL TO BEGIN. DRINK, AND ALL MY PROMISES TO YOU WILL BE FULFILLED.
THE BABYLONIAN BROTHERHOOD NAMED IT THE STAR FIRE. TO THE SUMERIANS, IT WAS THE GOLD OF THE GODS. IN INDIA, IT WAS CALLED SOMA. AND AMBROSIA IN GREECE.
TO YOU? IT'S BLOOD FROM A VIRGIN.
I KNEW YOUR ANCESTORS WELL, MY KILLER CROC. I BIRTHED THEM ALL.
THE CUNNING SHAPESHIFTERS OF ANCIENT BABYLON, WHERE YOUR BLOODLINE BEGINS.

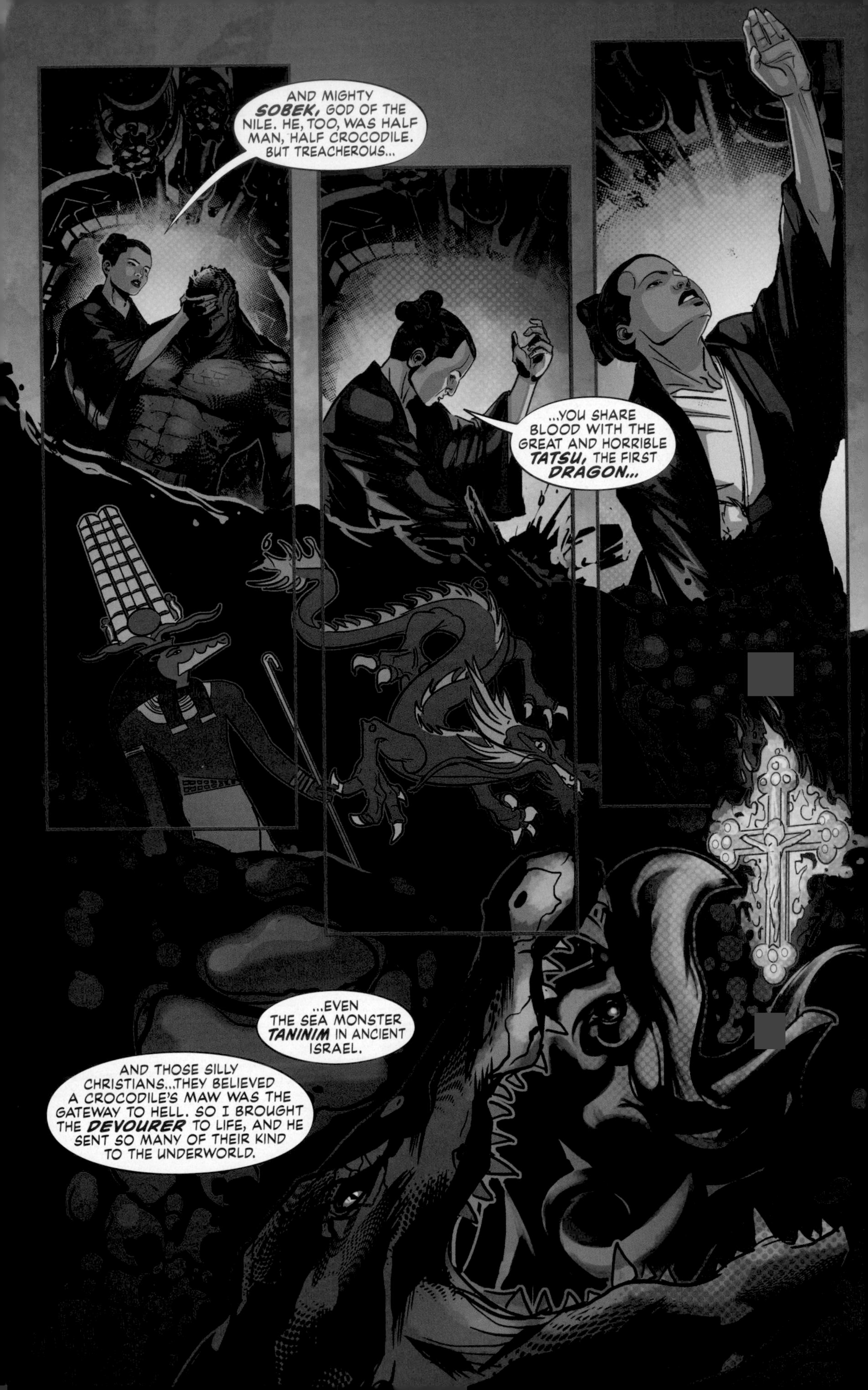
AND MIGHTY SOBEK, GOD OF THE NILE. HE, TOO, WAS HALF MAN, HALF CROCODILE. BUT TREACHEROUS...
...YOU SHARE BLOOD WITH THE GREAT AND HORRIBLE TATSU, THE FIRST DRAGON...
...EVEN THE SEA MONSTER TANINIM IN ANCIENT ISRAEL.
AND THOSE SILLY CHRISTIANS...THEY BELIEVED A CROCODILE'S MAW WAS THE GATEWAY TO HELL. SO I BROUGHT THE DEVOURER TO LIFE, AND HE SENT SO MANY OF THEIR KIND TO THE UNDERWORLD.

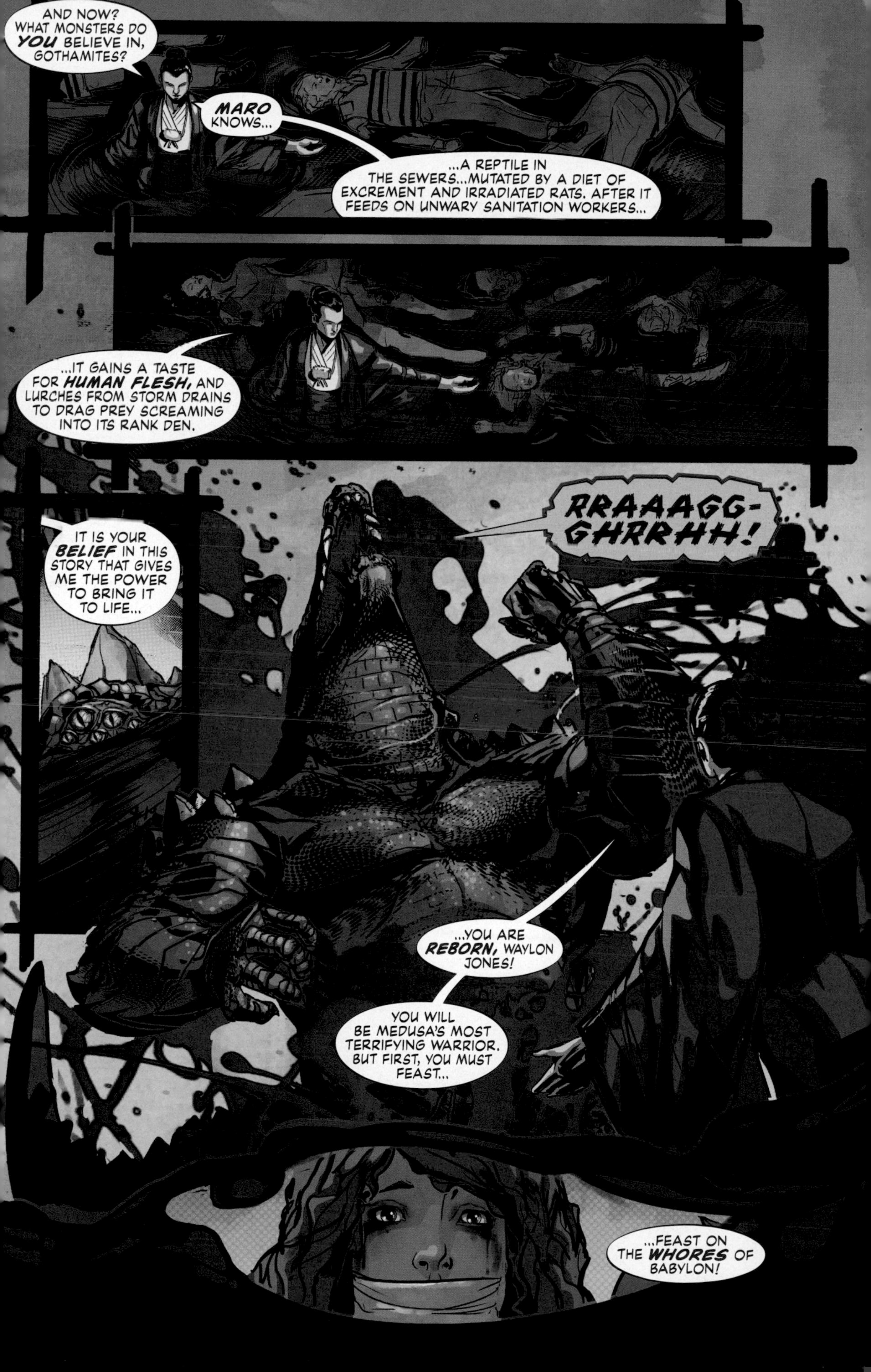
AND NOW? WHAT MONSTERS DO YOU BELIEVE IN, GOTHAMITES?
MARO KNOWS...
...A REPTILE IN THE SEWERS...MUTATED BY A DIET OF EXCREMENT AND IRRADIATED RATS. AFTER IT FEEDS ON UNWARY SANITATION WORKERS...
...IT GAINS A TASTE FOR HUMAN FLESH, AND LURCHES FROM STORM DRAINS TO DRAG PREY SCREAMING INTO ITS RANK DEN.
IT IS YOUR BELIEF IN THIS STORY THAT GIVES ME THE POWER TO BRING IT TO LIFE...
RRAAAGG-GHRRHH!
...YOU ARE REBORN, WAYLON JONES!
YOU WILL BE MEDUSA'S MOST TERRIFYING WARRIOR. BUT FIRST, YOU MUST FEAST...
...FEAST ON THE WHORES OF BABYLON!

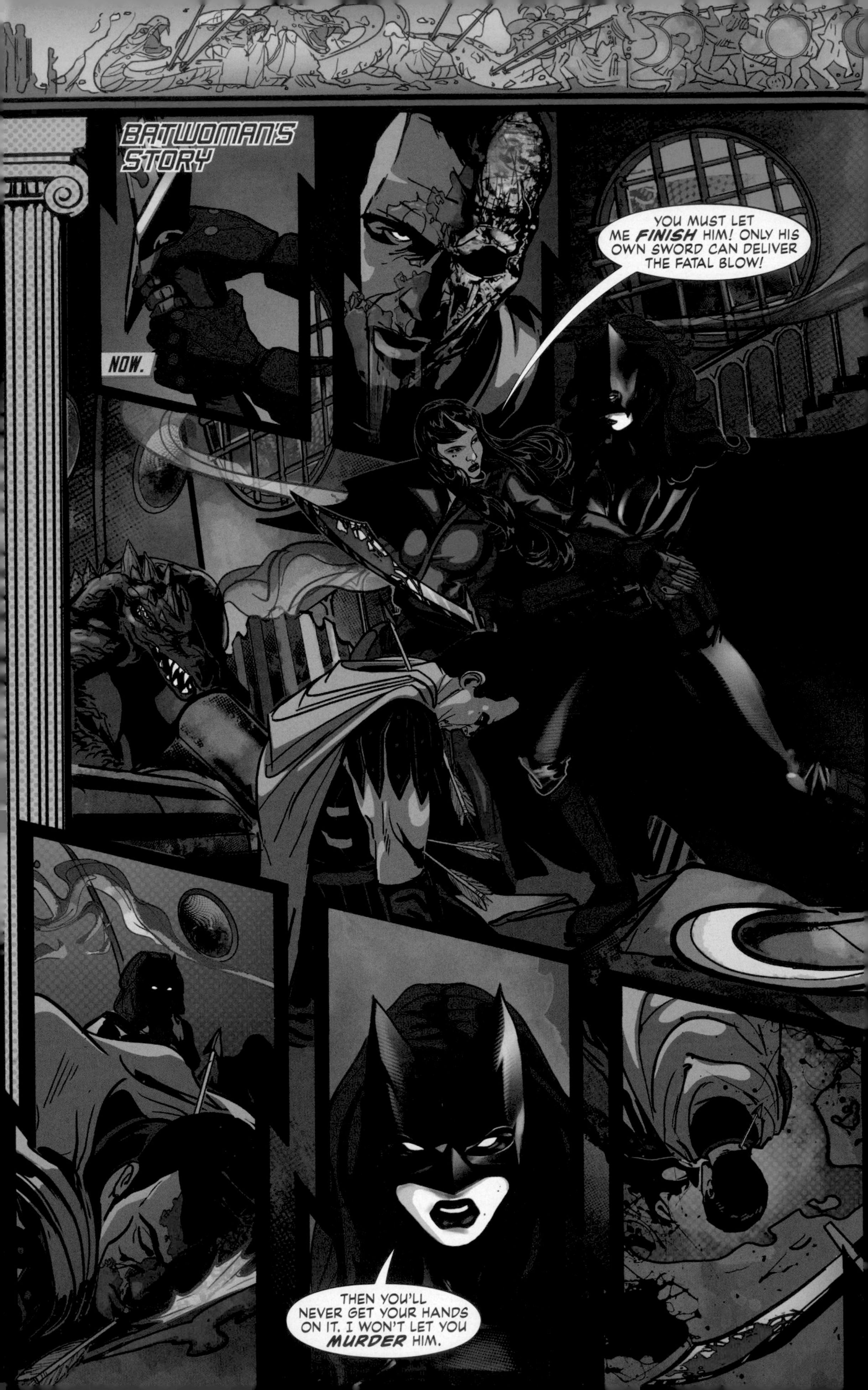
BATWOMAN'S STORY
NOW.
YOU MUST LET ME FINISH HIM! ONLY HIS OWN SWORD CAN DELIVER THE FATAL BLOW!
THEN YOU'LL NEVER GET YOUR HANDS ON IT. I WON'T LET YOU MURDER HIM.

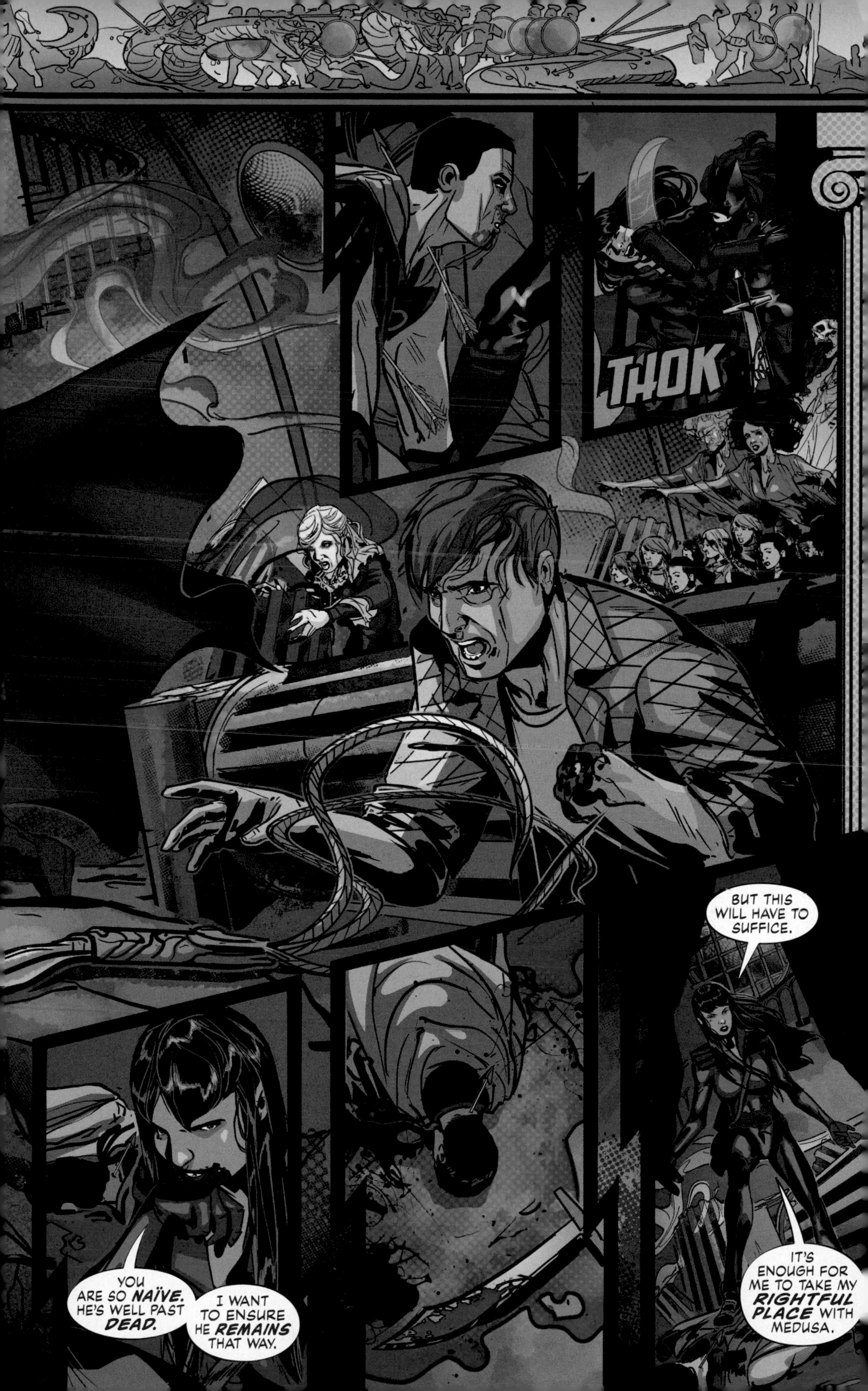
THOK
BUT THIS WILL HAVE TO SUFFICE.
YOU ARE SO NAÏVE. HE'S WELL PAST DEAD.
I WANT TO ENSURE HE REMAINS THAT WAY.
IT'S ENOUGH FOR ME TO TAKE MY RIGHTFUL PLACE WITH MEDUSA.

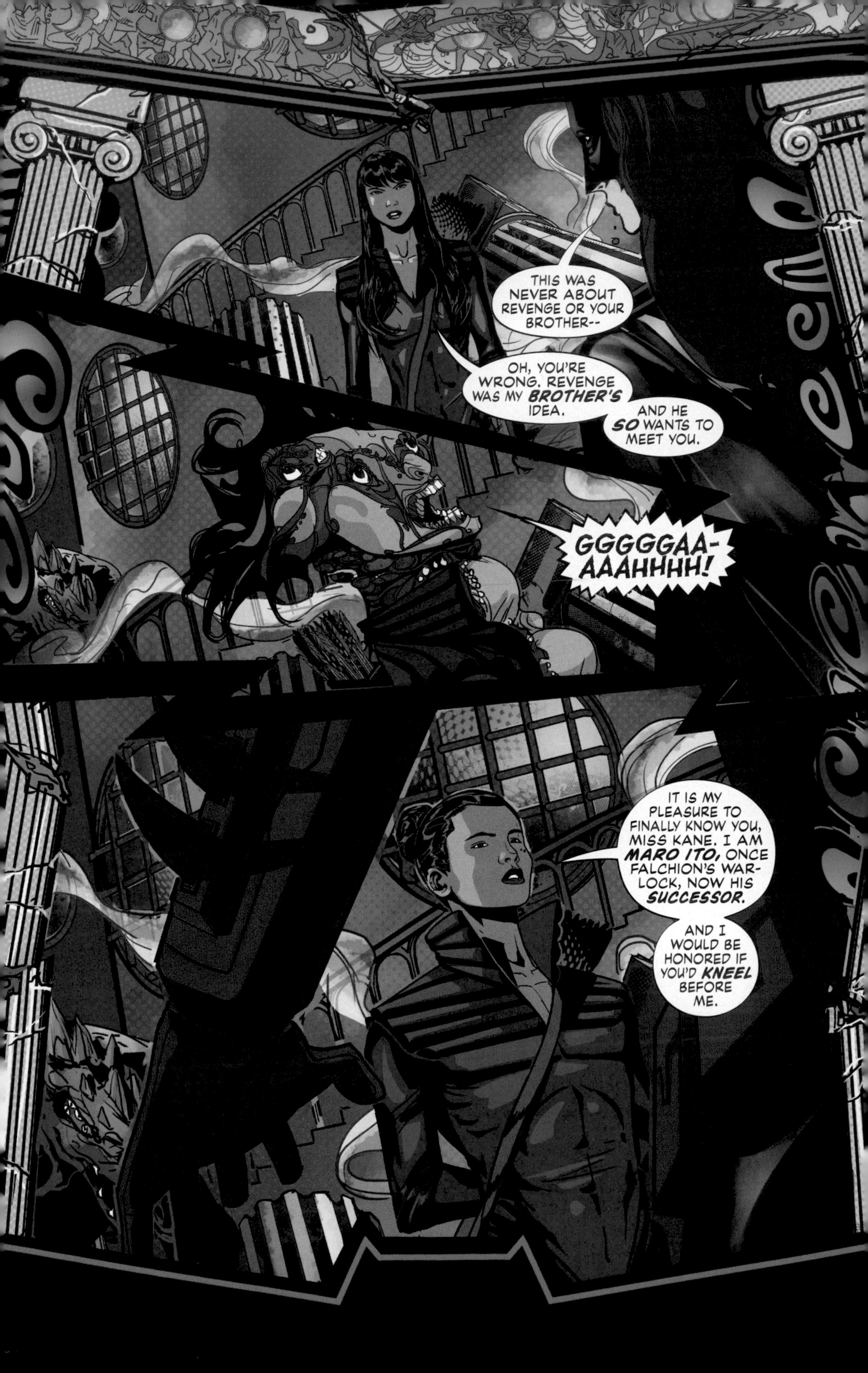
THIS WAS NEVER ABOUT REVENGE OR YOUR BROTHER--
OH, YOU'RE WRONG. REVENGE WAS MY BROTHER'S IDEA.
AND HE SO WANTS TO MEET YOU.
GGGGGAA-AAAHHHH!
IT IS MY PLEASURE TO FINALLY KNOW YOU, MISS KANE. I AM MARO ITO, ONCE FALCHION'S WAR-LOCK, NOW HIS SUCCESSOR.
AND I WOULD BE HONORED IF YOU'D KNEEL BEFORE ME.

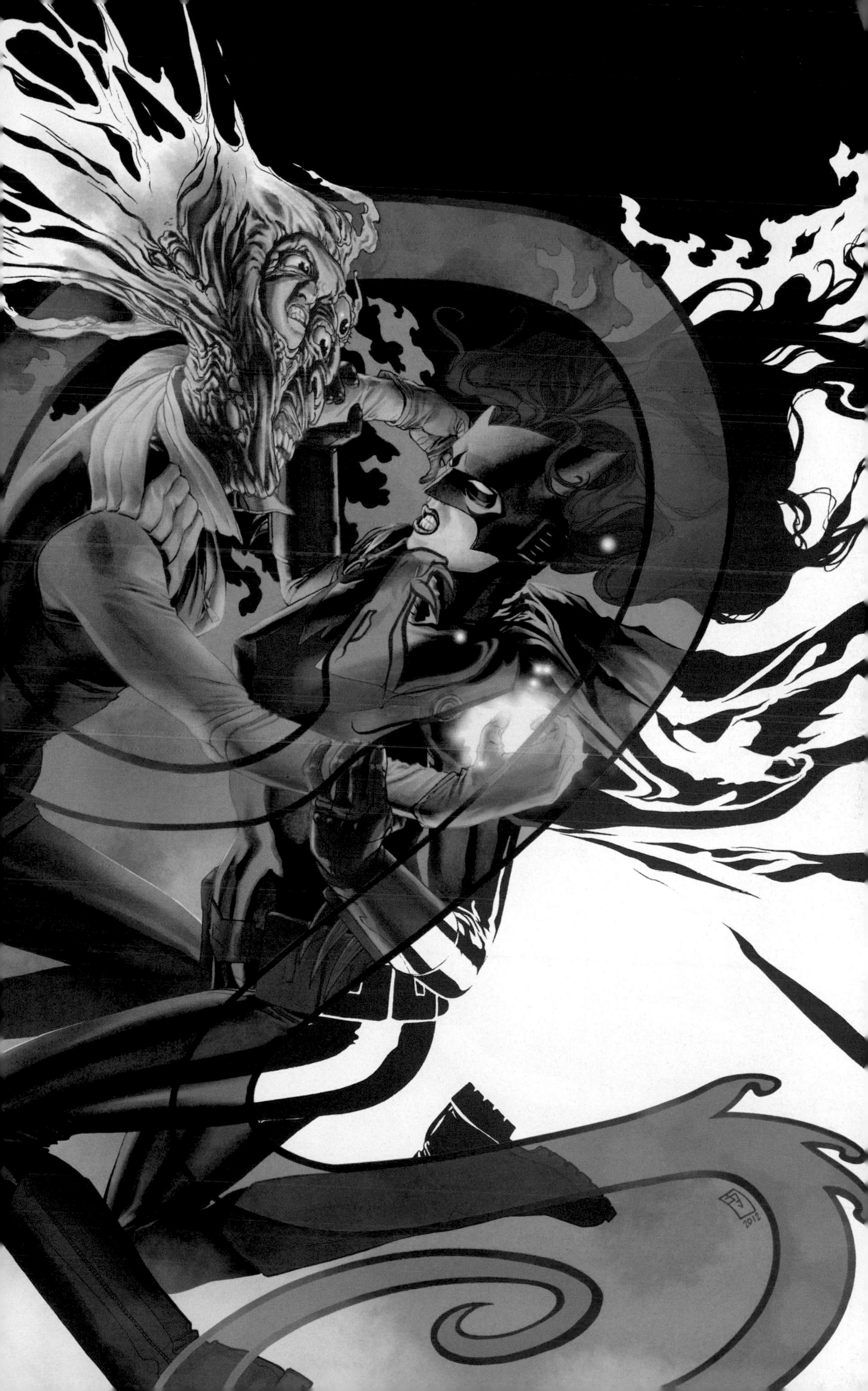
2012

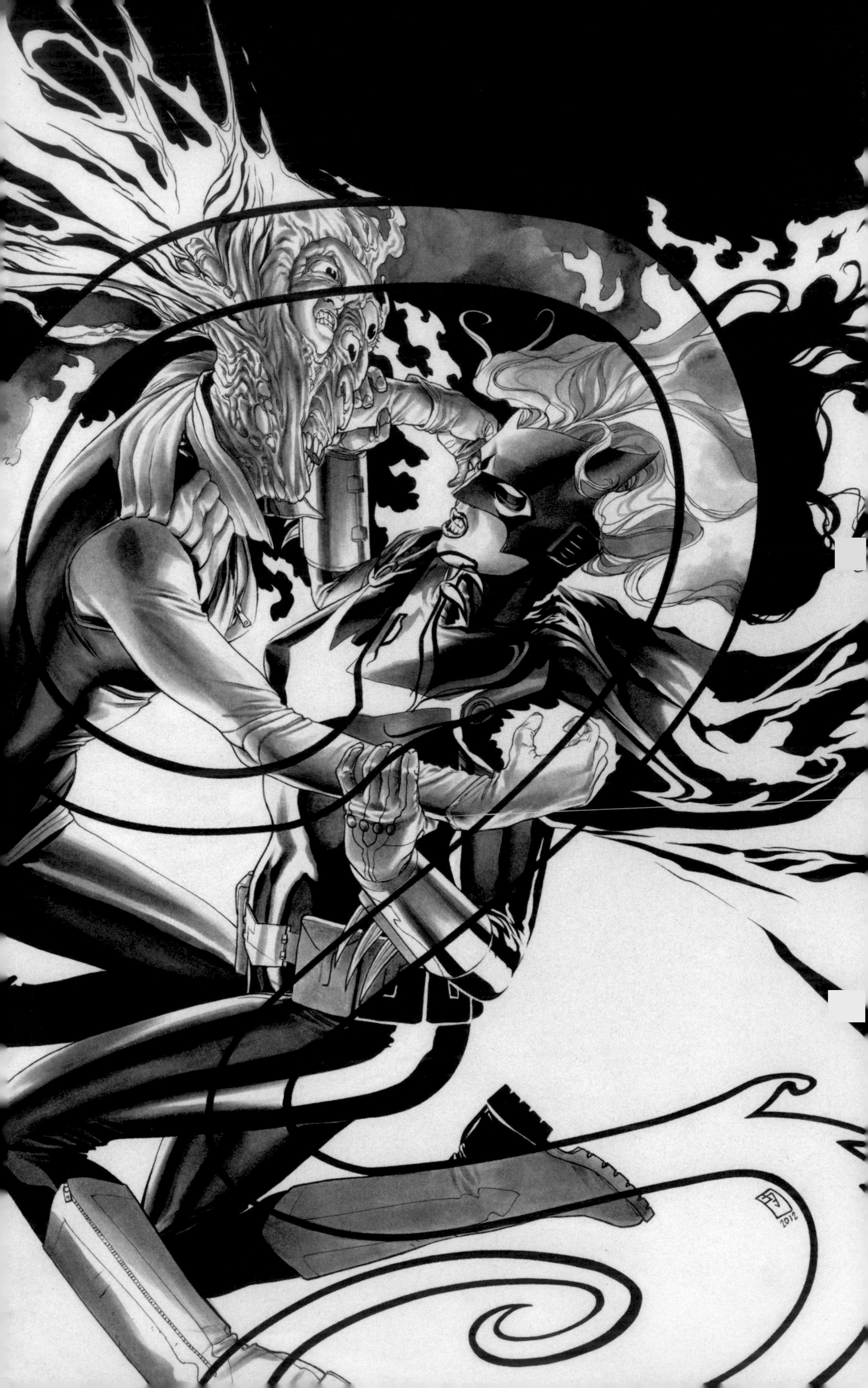
2012

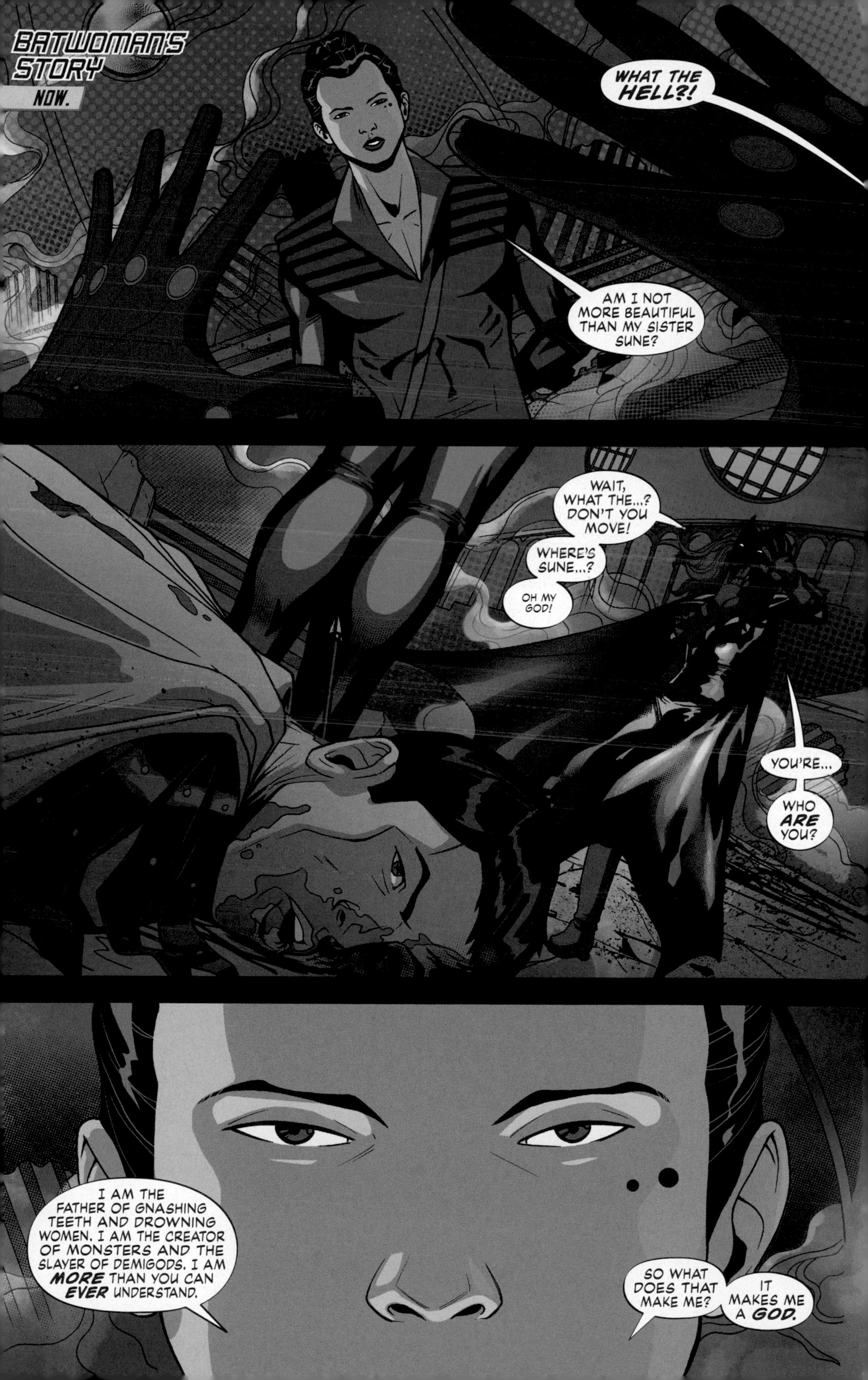
BATWOMAN'S STORY
NOW.
WHAT THE HELL?!
AM I NOT MORE BEAUTIFUL THAN MY SISTER SUNE?
WAIT, WHAT THE...? DON'T YOU MOVE!
WHERE'S SUNE...?
OH MY GOD!
YOU'RE...
WHO ARE YOU?
I AM THE FATHER OF GNASHING TEETH AND DROWNING WOMEN. I AM THE CREATOR OF MONSTERS AND THE SLAYER OF DEMIGODS. I AM MORE THAN YOU CAN EVER UNDERSTAND.
SO WHAT DOES THAT MAKE ME?
IT MAKES ME A GOD.

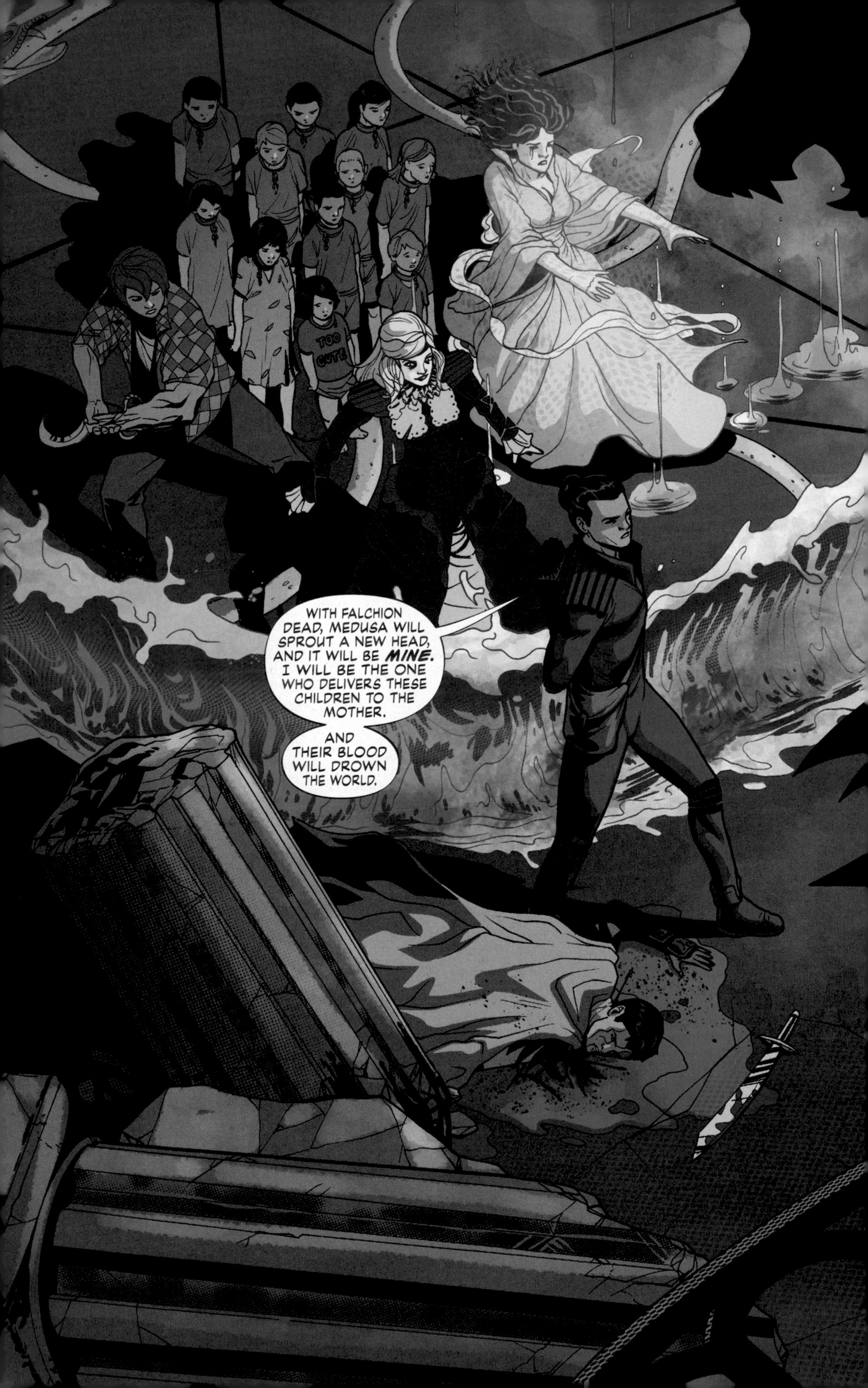
TOO CUTE
WITH FALCHION DEAD, MEDUSA WILL SPROUT A NEW HEAD, AND IT WILL BE ***MINE***. I WILL BE THE ONE WHO DELIVERS THESE CHILDREN TO THE MOTHER.
AND THEIR BLOOD WILL DROWN THE WORLD.

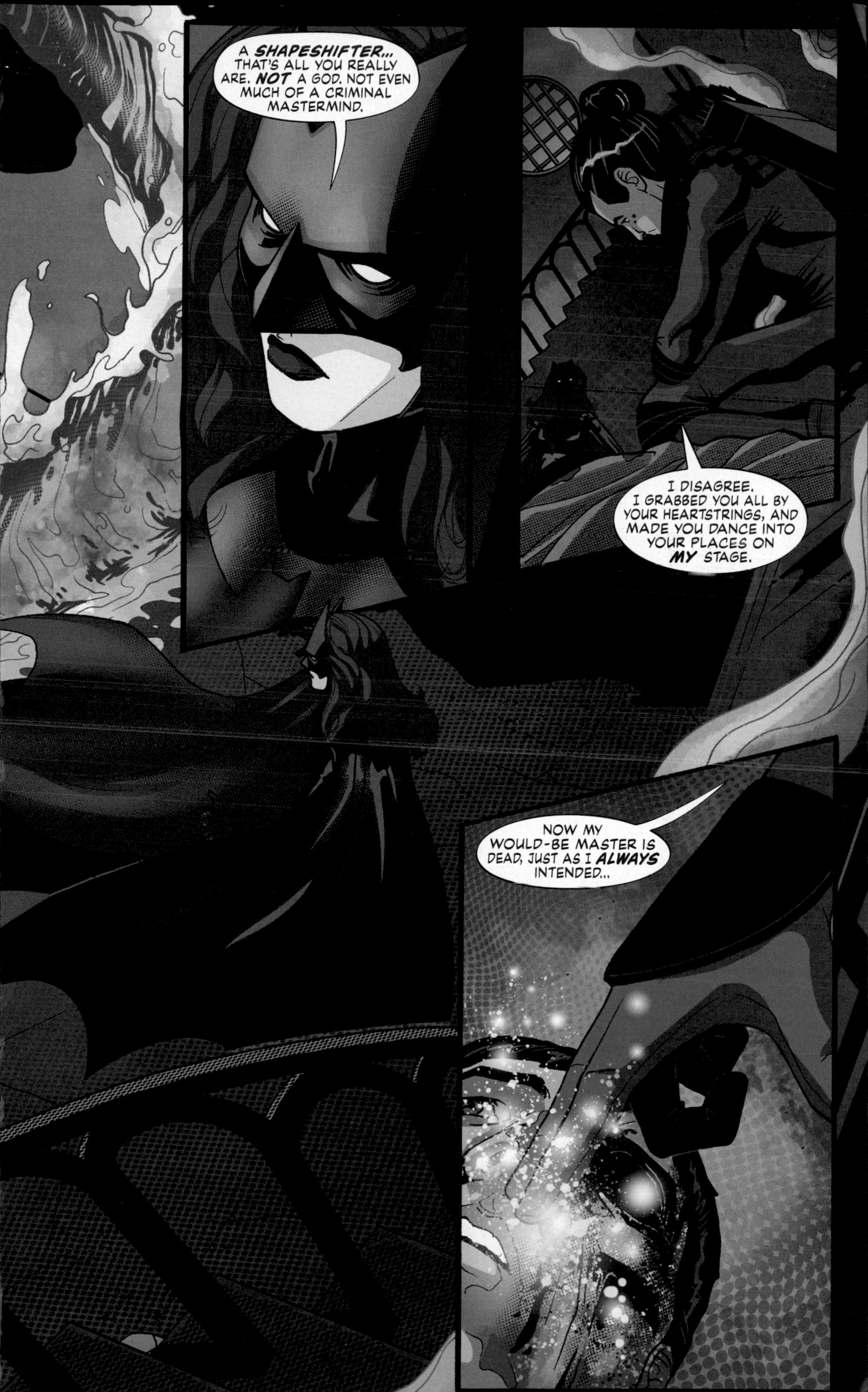
A SHAPESHIFTER... THAT'S ALL YOU REALLY ARE. NOT A GOD. NOT EVEN MUCH OF A CRIMINAL MASTERMIND.
I DISAGREE. I GRABBED YOU ALL BY YOUR HEARTSTRINGS, AND MADE YOU DANCE INTO YOUR PLACES ON MY STAGE.
NOW MY WOULD-BE MASTER IS DEAD, JUST AS I ALWAYS INTENDED...

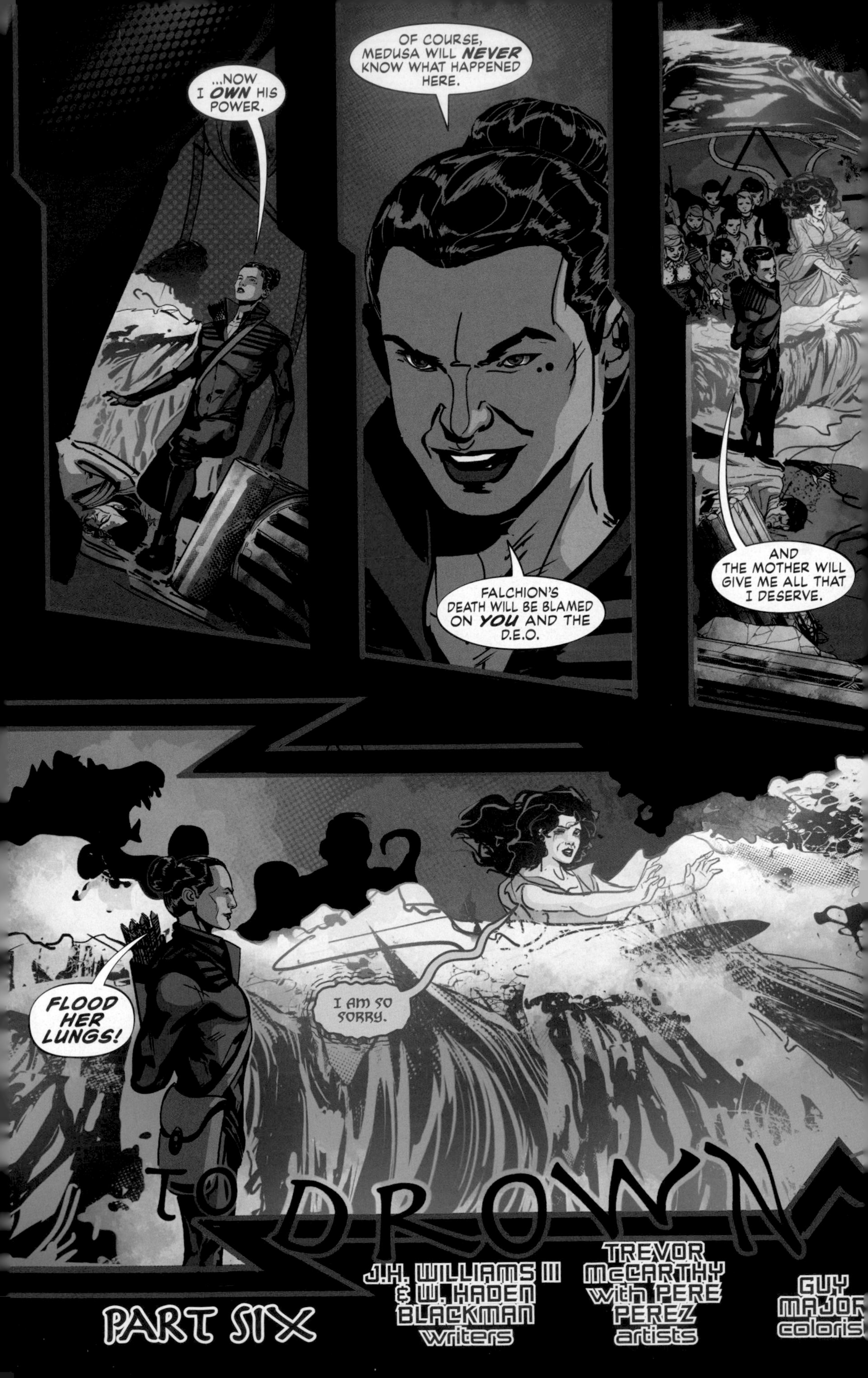
...NOW I OWN HIS POWER.
OF COURSE, MEDUSA WILL NEVER KNOW WHAT HAPPENED HERE.
FALCHION'S DEATH WILL BE BLAMED ON YOU AND THE D.E.O.
AND THE MOTHER WILL GIVE ME ALL THAT I DESERVE.
FLOOD HER LUNGS!
I AM SO SORRY.
TO DROWN
PART SIX
J.H. WILLIAMS III & W. HADEN BLACKMAN writers
TREVOR McCARTHY with PERE PEREZ artists
GUY MAJOR colorist

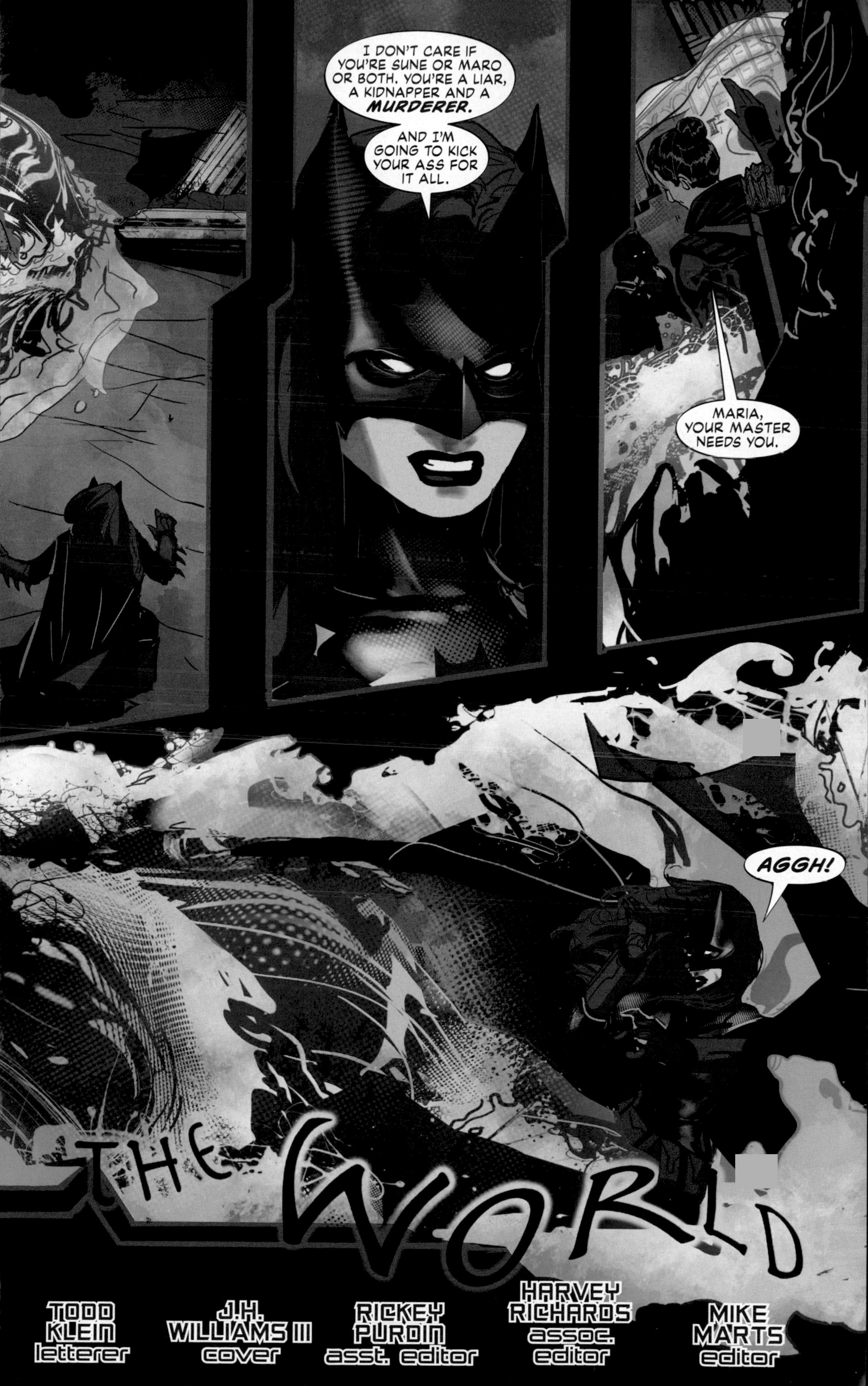
I DON'T CARE IF YOU'RE SUNE OR MARO OR BOTH. YOU'RE A LIAR, A KIDNAPPER AND A **MURDERER.**
AND I'M GOING TO KICK YOUR ASS FOR IT ALL.
MARIA, YOUR MASTER NEEDS YOU.
AGGH!
THE WORLD
TODD KLEIN letterer
J.H. WILLIAMS III cover
RICKEY PURDIN asst. editor
HARVEY RICHARDS assoc. editor
MIKE MARTS editor

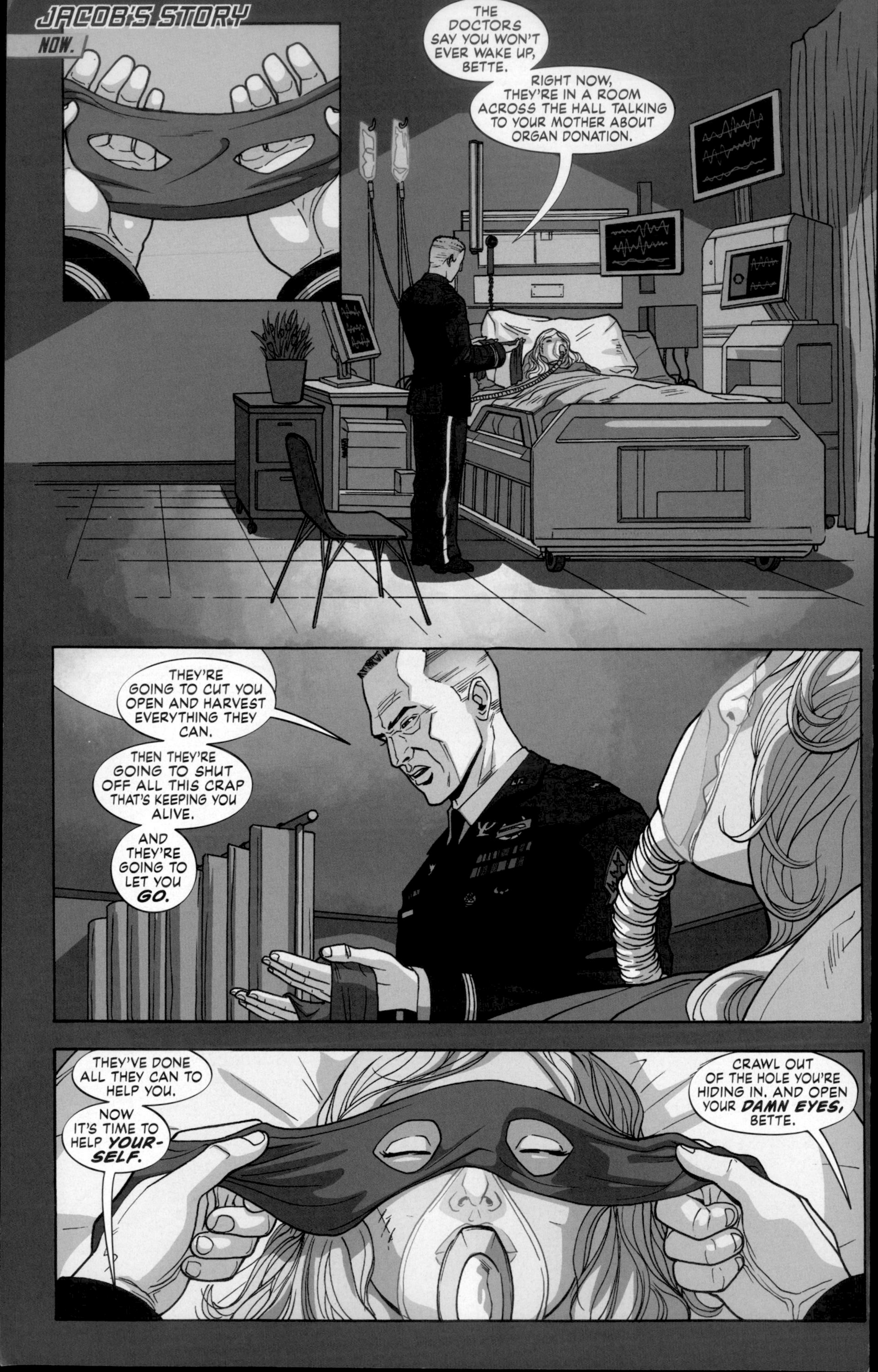
JACOB'S STORY
NOW.
THE DOCTORS SAY YOU WON'T EVER WAKE UP, BETTE.
RIGHT NOW, THEY'RE IN A ROOM ACROSS THE HALL TALKING TO YOUR MOTHER ABOUT ORGAN DONATION.
THEY'RE GOING TO CUT YOU OPEN AND HARVEST EVERYTHING THEY CAN.
THEN THEY'RE GOING TO SHUT OFF ALL THIS CRAP THAT'S KEEPING YOU ALIVE.
AND THEY'RE GOING TO LET YOU GO.
THEY'VE DONE ALL THEY CAN TO HELP YOU.
NOW IT'S TIME TO HELP YOURSELF.
CRAWL OUT OF THE HOLE YOU'RE HIDING IN. AND OPEN YOUR DAMN EYES, BETTE.

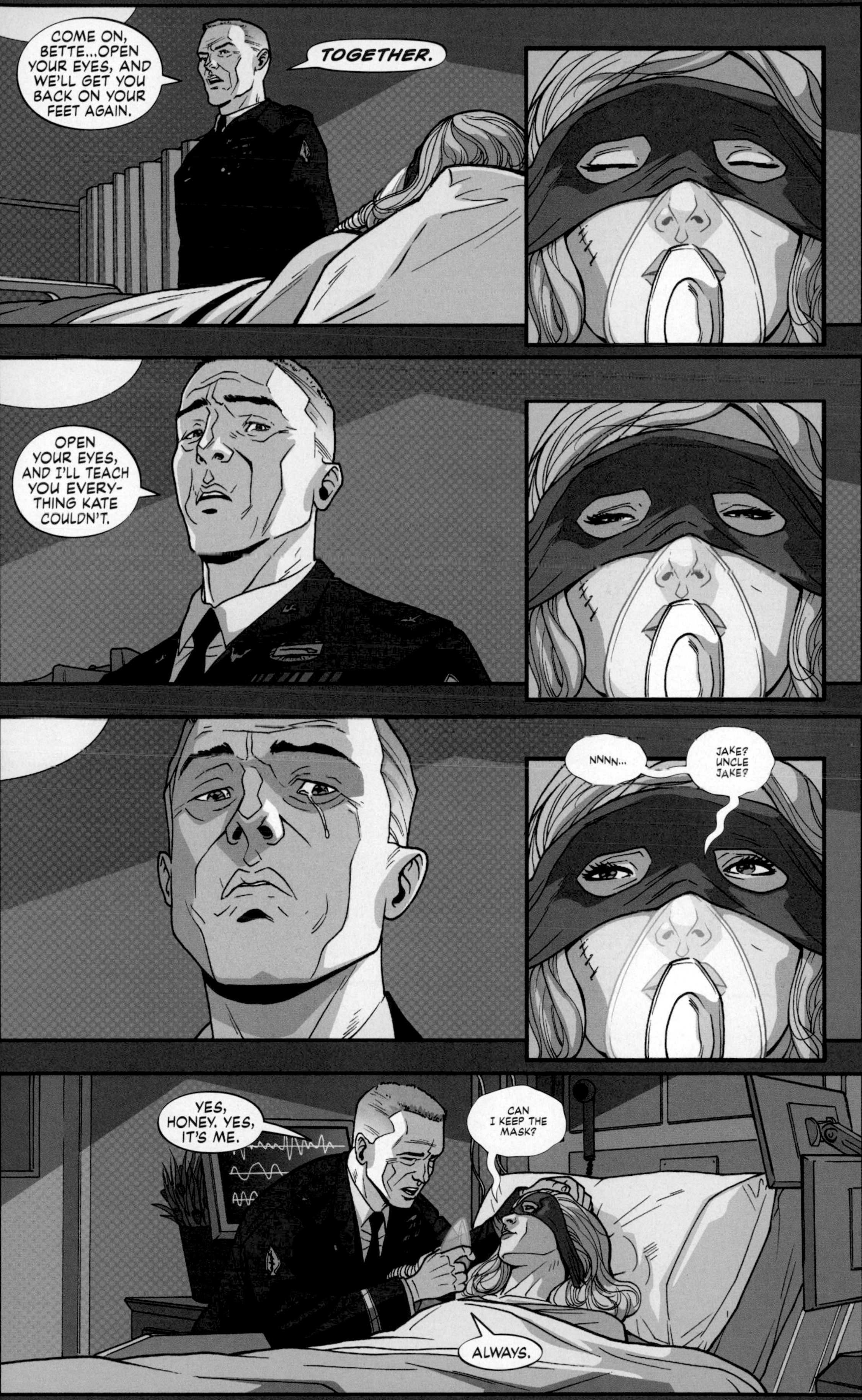
COME ON, BETTE...OPEN YOUR EYES, AND WE'LL GET YOU BACK ON YOUR FEET AGAIN.
TOGETHER.
OPEN YOUR EYES, AND I'LL TEACH YOU EVERY-THING KATE COULDN'T.
NNNN...
JAKE? UNCLE JAKE?
YES, HONEY. YES, IT'S ME.
CAN I KEEP THE MASK?
ALWAYS.

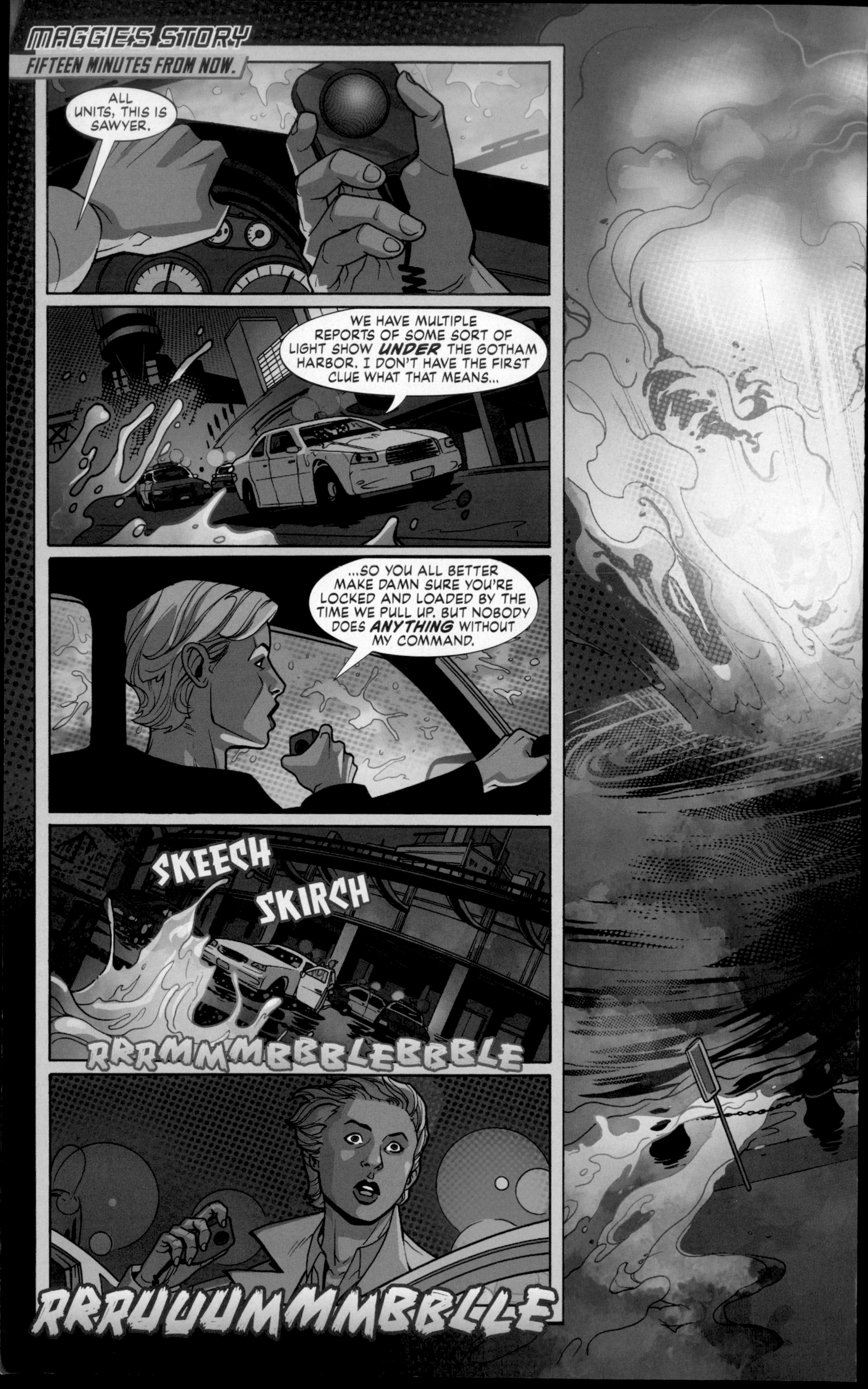
MAGGIE'S STORY
FIFTEEN MINUTES FROM NOW.
ALL UNITS, THIS IS SAWYER.
WE HAVE MULTIPLE REPORTS OF SOME SORT OF LIGHT SHOW UNDER THE GOTHAM HARBOR. I DON'T HAVE THE FIRST CLUE WHAT THAT MEANS...
...SO YOU ALL BETTER MAKE DAMN SURE YOU'RE LOCKED AND LOADED BY THE TIME WE PULL UP. BUT NOBODY DOES ANYTHING WITHOUT MY COMMAND.
SKEECH
SKIRCH
RRRMMMBBBLEBBBLE
RRRUUUMMMBBLLE

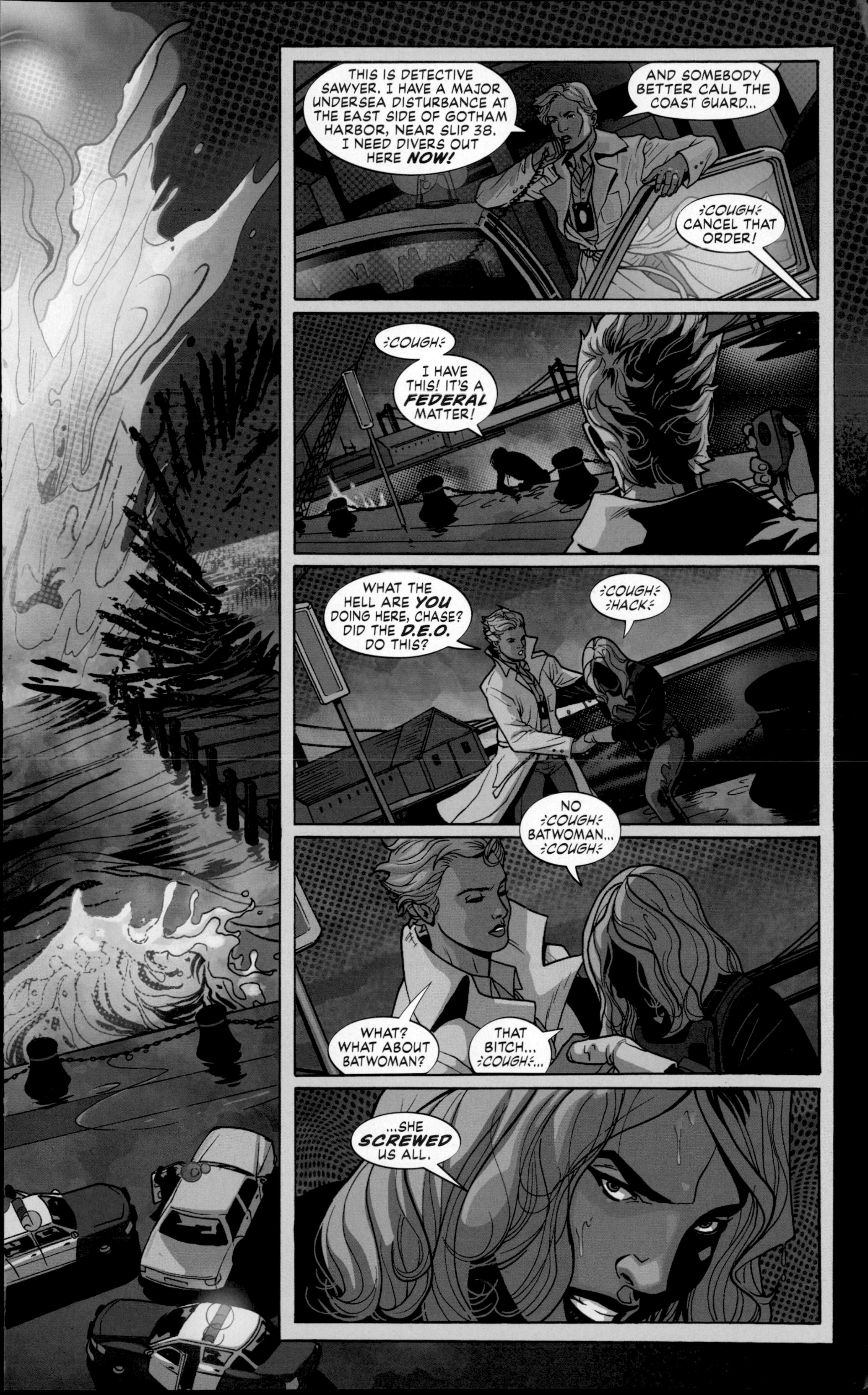
THIS IS DETECTIVE SAWYER. I HAVE A MAJOR UNDERSEA DISTURBANCE AT THE EAST SIDE OF GOTHAM HARBOR, NEAR SLIP 38. I NEED DIVERS OUT HERE NOW!
AND SOMEBODY BETTER CALL THE COAST GUARD...
COUGH CANCEL THAT ORDER!
COUGH
I HAVE THIS! IT'S A FEDERAL MATTER!
WHAT THE HELL ARE YOU DOING HERE, CHASE? DID THE D.E.O. DO THIS?
COUGH HACK
NO COUGH BATWOMAN... COUGH
WHAT? WHAT ABOUT BATWOMAN?
THAT BITCH... COUGH...
...SHE SCREWED US ALL.

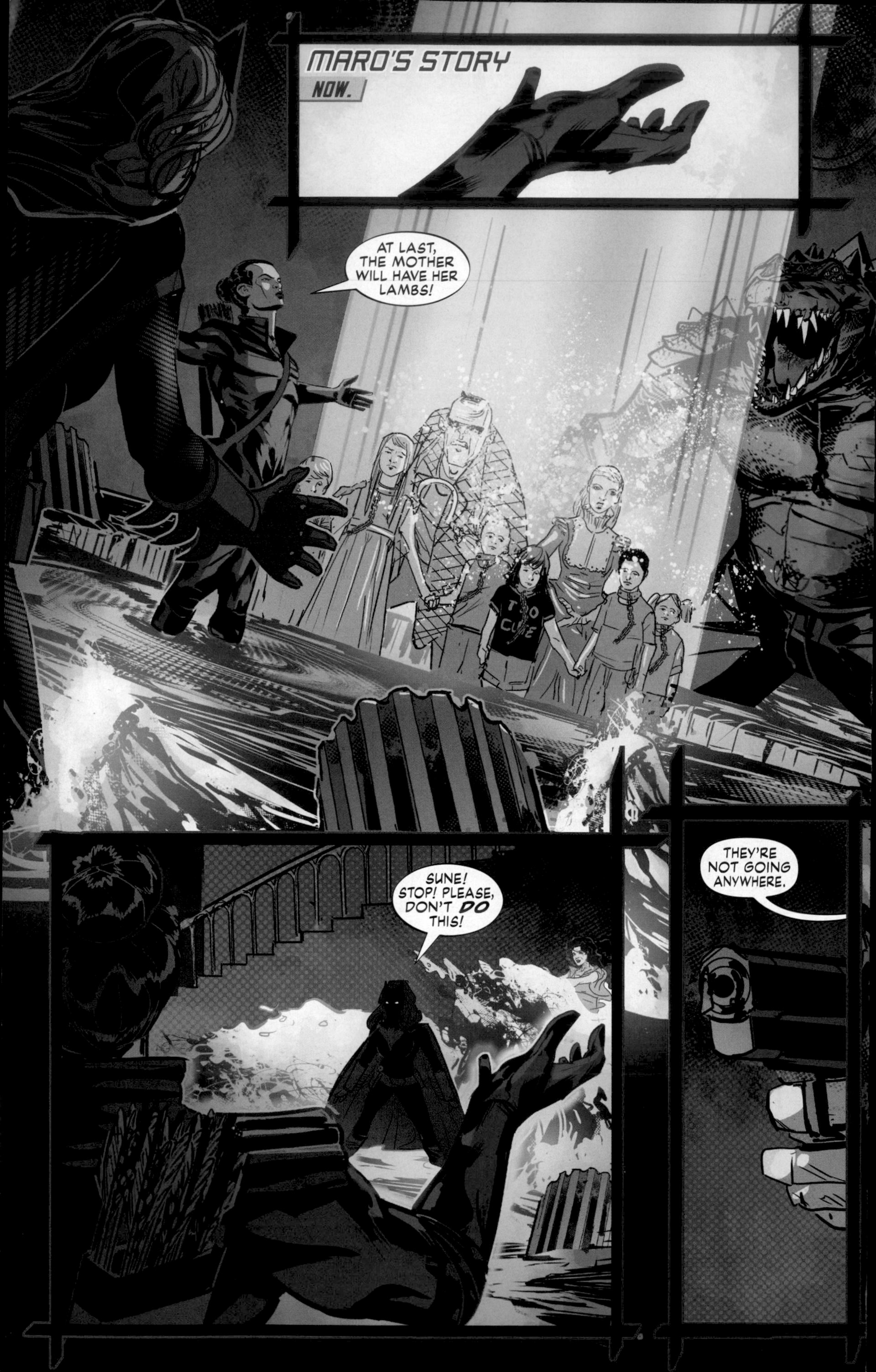
MARO'S STORY
NOW.
AT LAST, THE MOTHER WILL HAVE HER LAMBS!
TOO CUTE
SUNE! STOP! PLEASE, DON'T DO THIS!
THEY'RE NOT GOING ANYWHERE.

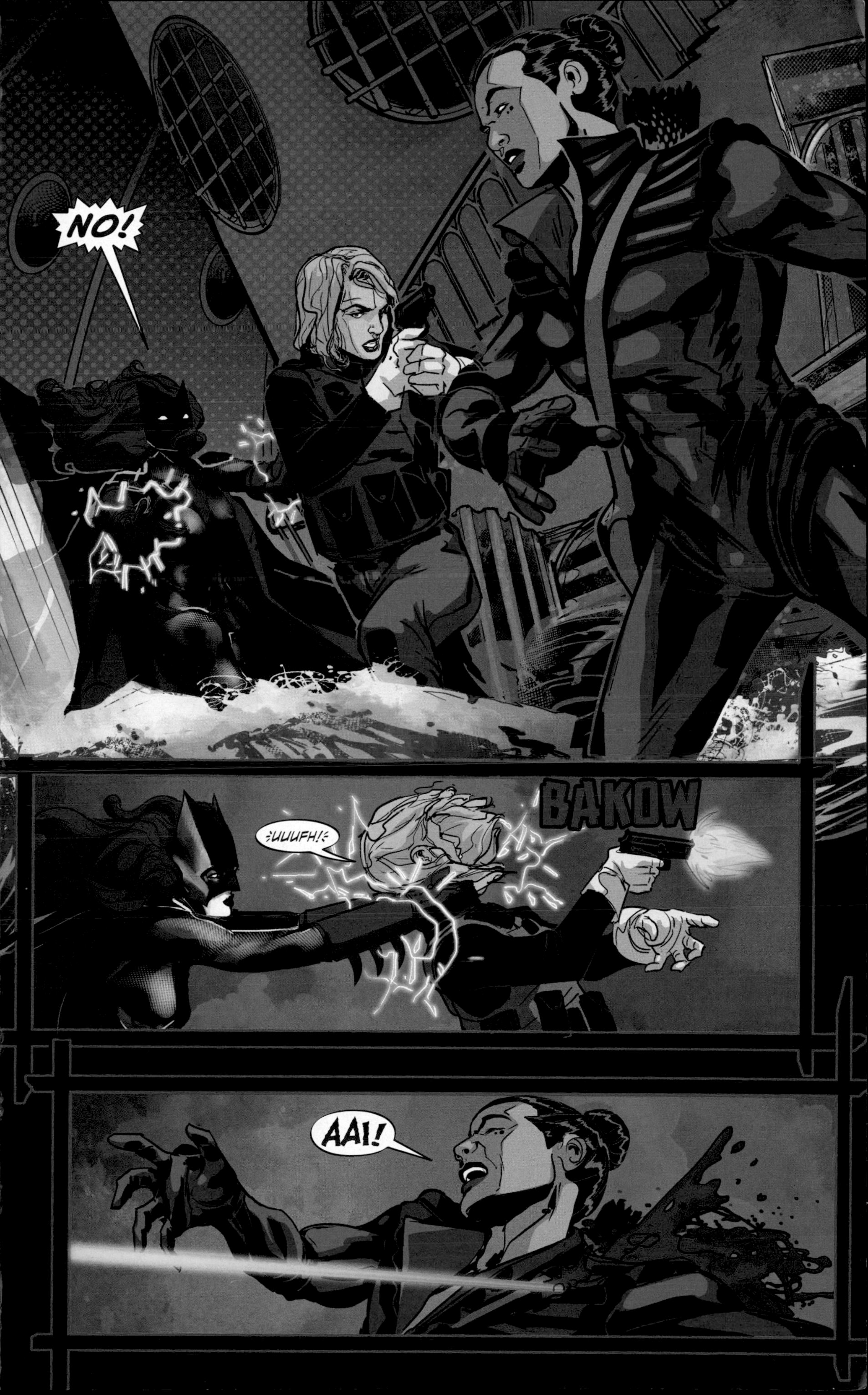
NO!
UUUFH!
BAKOW
AAI!

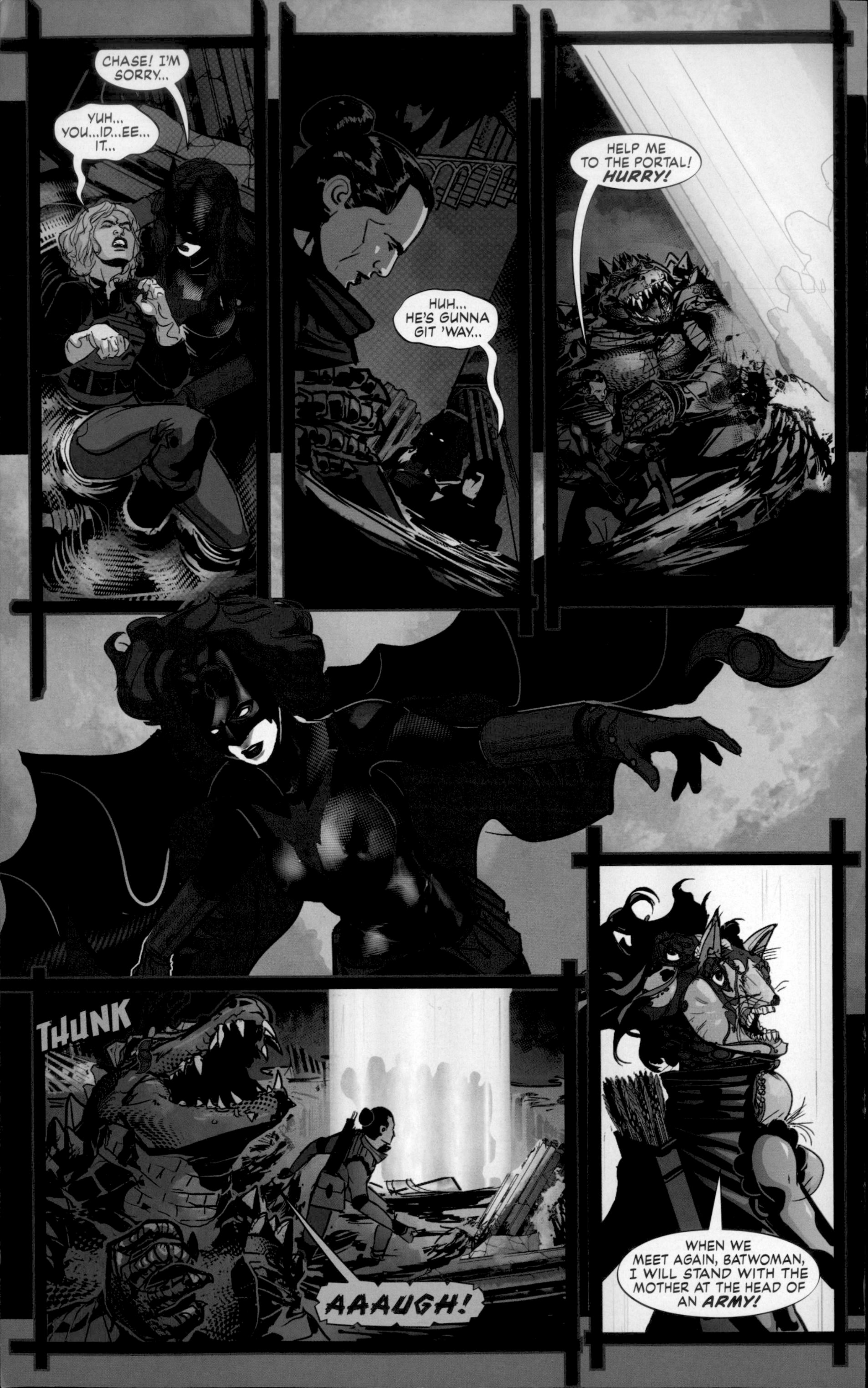
CHASE! I'M SORRY...
YUH... YOU...ID...EE... IT...
HUH... HE'S GUNNA GIT 'WAY...
HELP ME TO THE PORTAL! HURRY!
THUNK
AAAUGH!
WHEN WE MEET AGAIN, BATWOMAN, I WILL STAND WITH THE MOTHER AT THE HEAD OF AN ARMY!

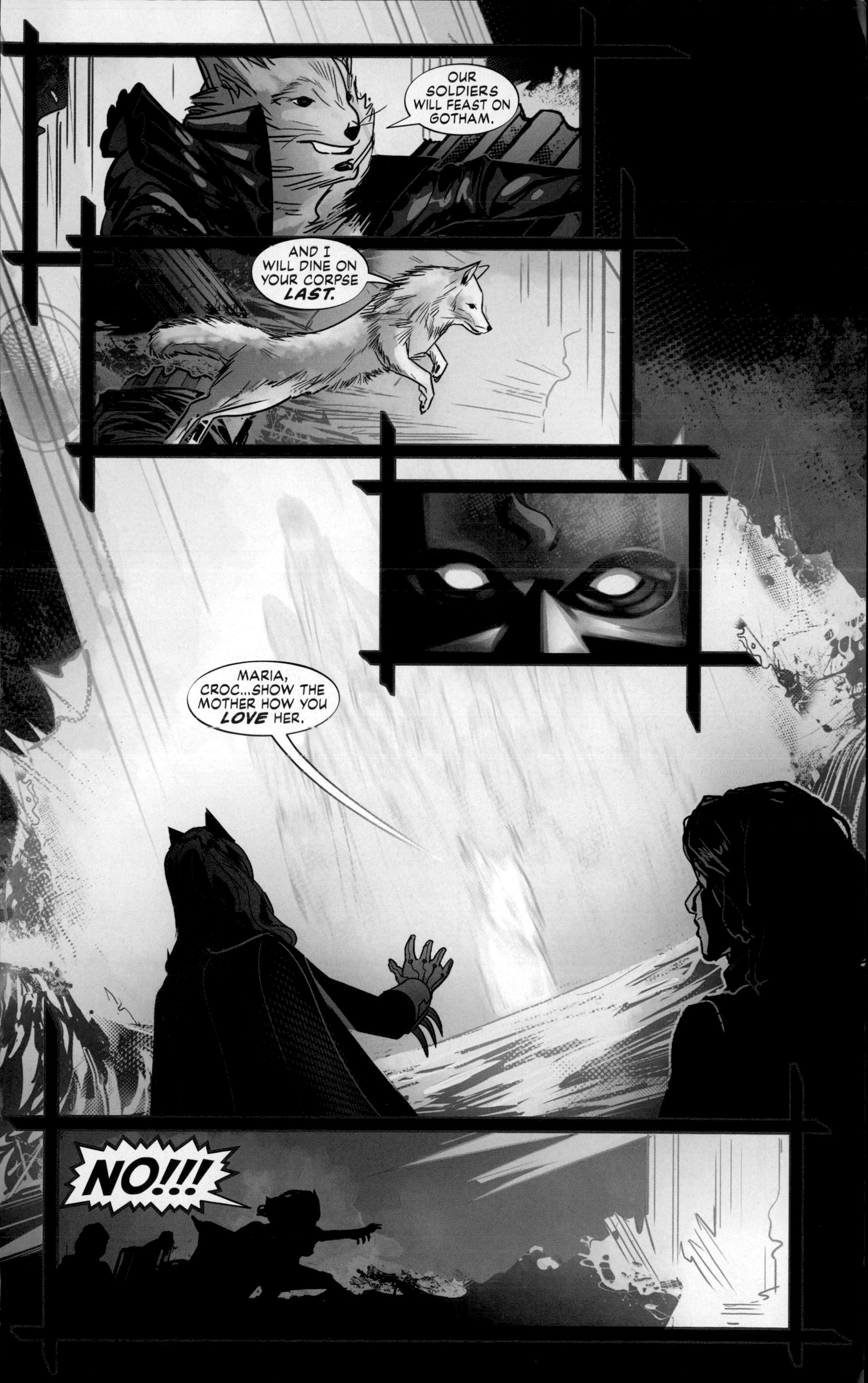
OUR SOLDIERS WILL FEAST ON GOTHAM.
AND I WILL DINE ON YOUR CORPSE *LAST.*
MARIA, CROC...SHOW THE MOTHER HOW YOU *LOVE* HER.
NO!!!

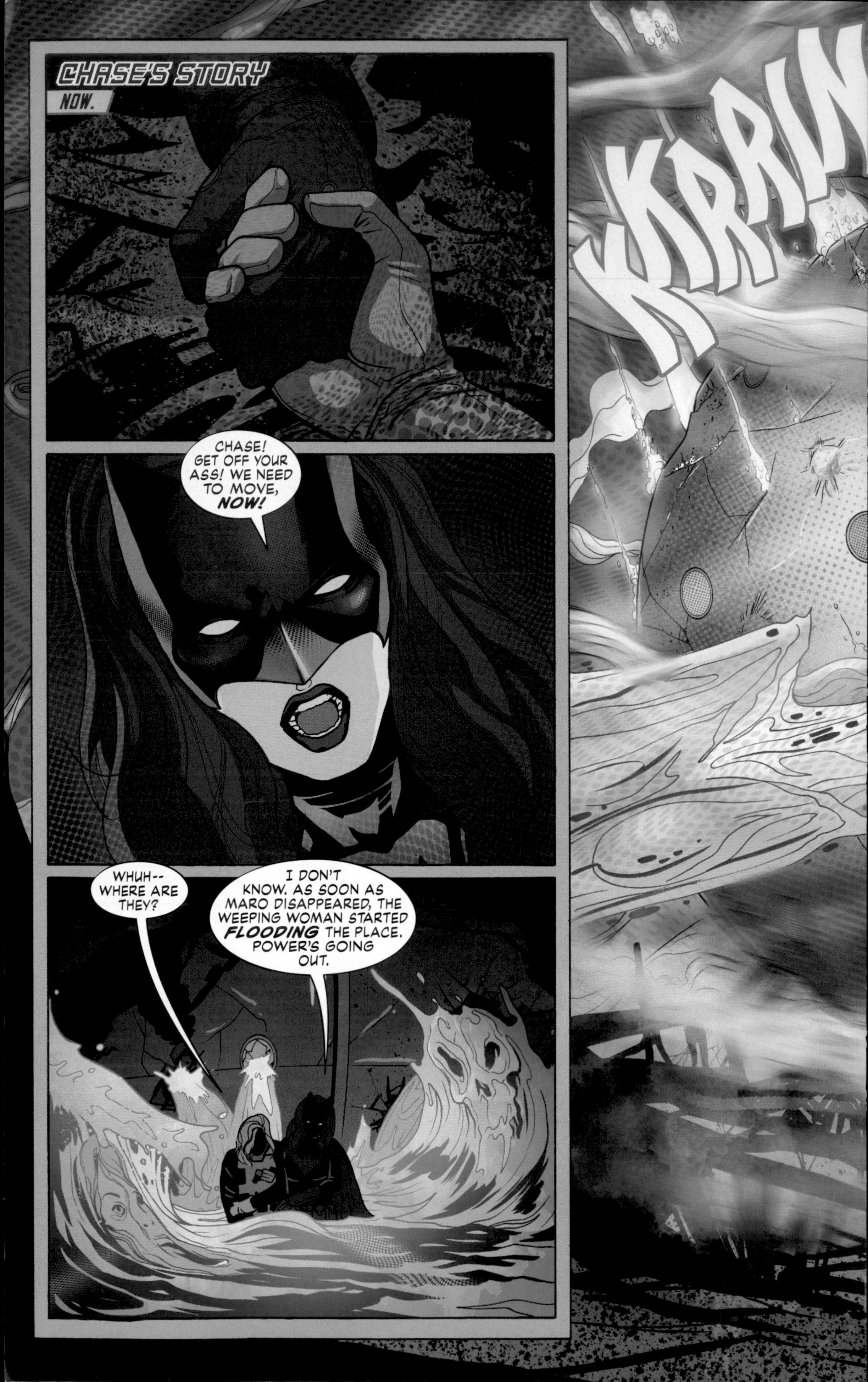
CHASE'S STORY
NOW.
CHASE! GET OFF YOUR ASS! WE NEED TO MOVE, NOW!
WHUH-- WHERE ARE THEY?
I DON'T KNOW. AS SOON AS MARO DISAPPEARED, THE WEEPING WOMAN STARTED FLOODING THE PLACE. POWER'S GOING OUT.
KRRIN

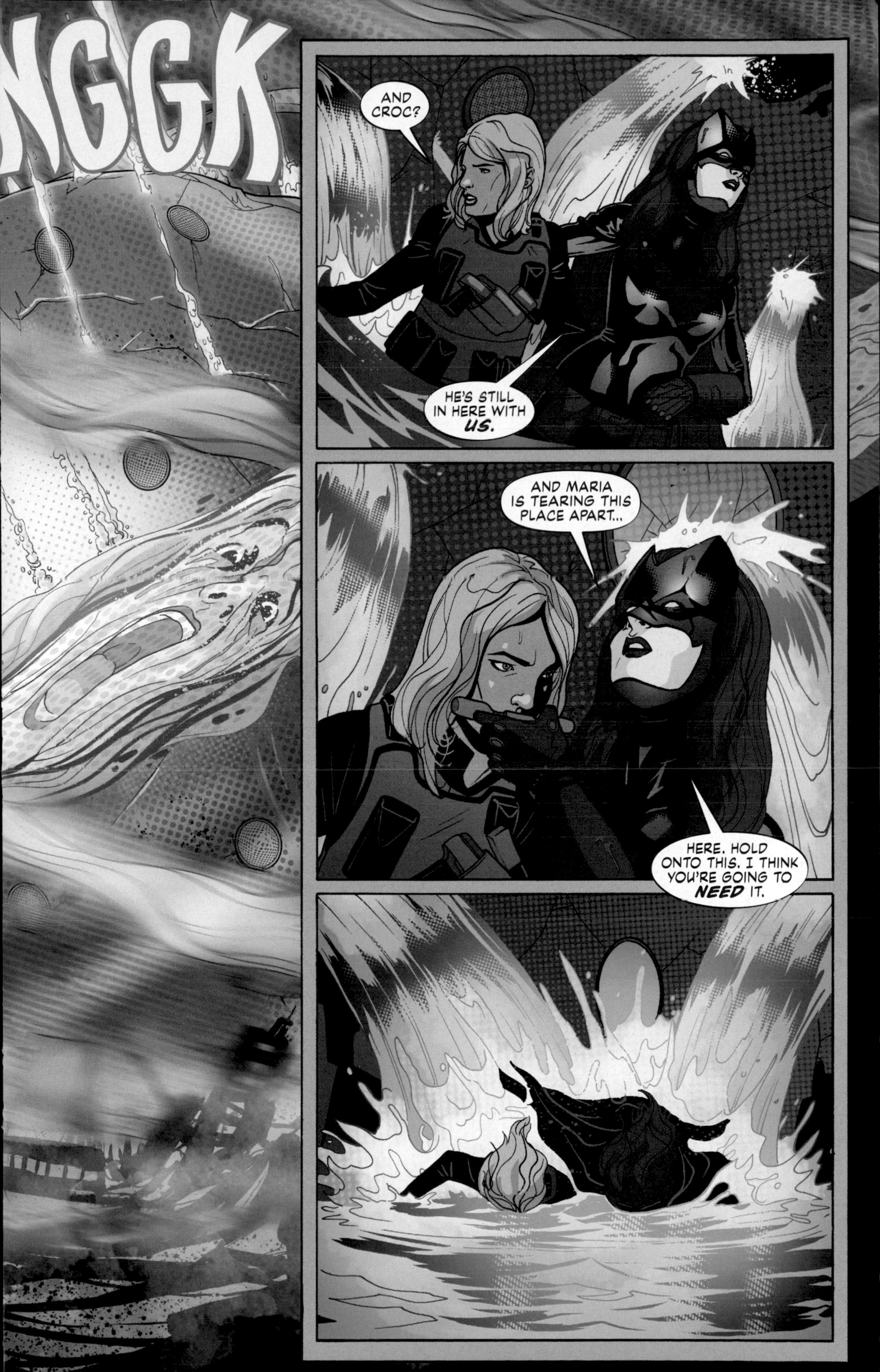
NGGK
AND CROC?
HE'S STILL IN HERE WITH US.
AND MARIA IS TEARING THIS PLACE APART...
HERE. HOLD ONTO THIS. I THINK YOU'RE GOING TO NEED IT.

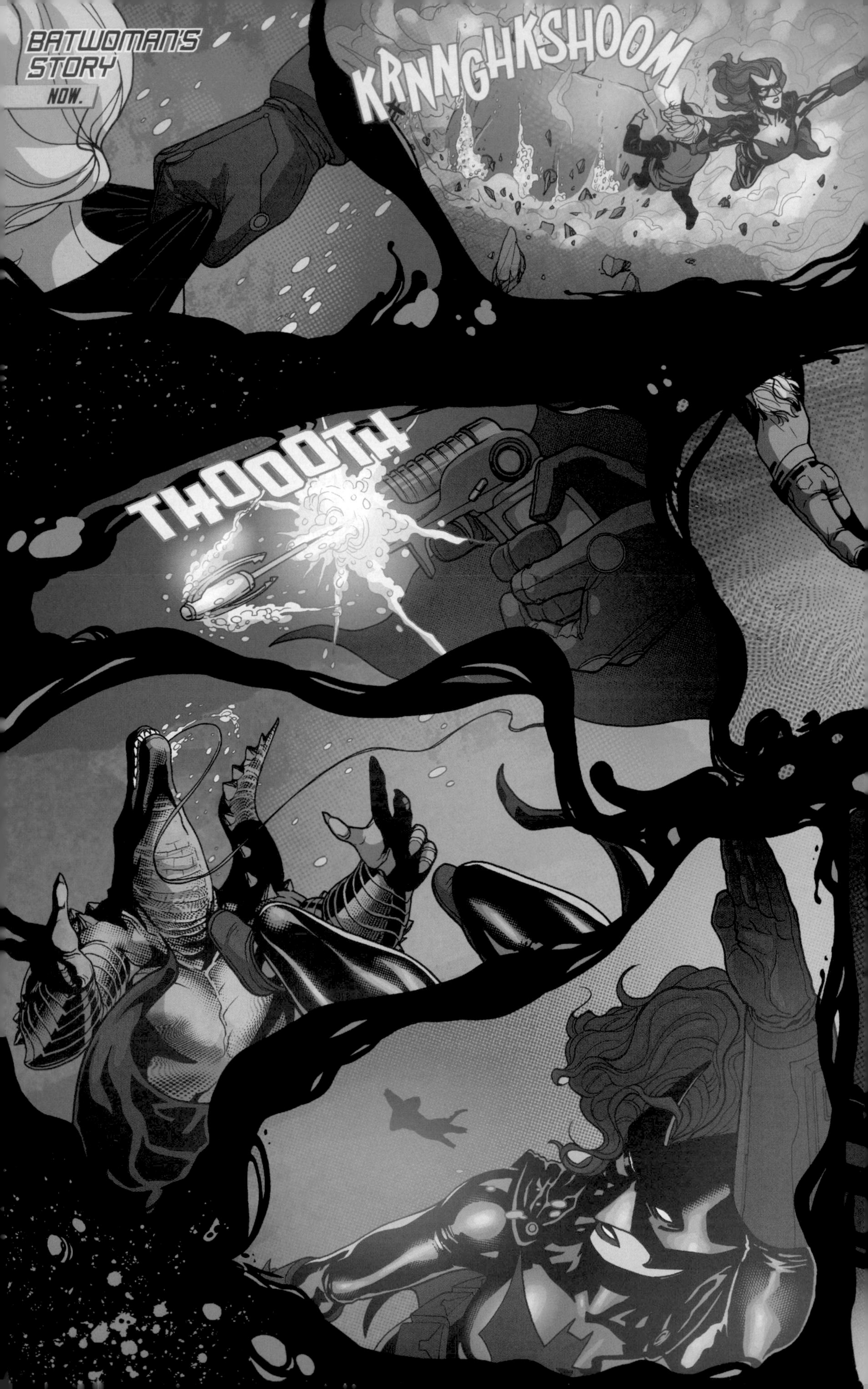
BATWOMAN'S STORY
NOW.
KRNNGHKSHOOM
THOOOTH

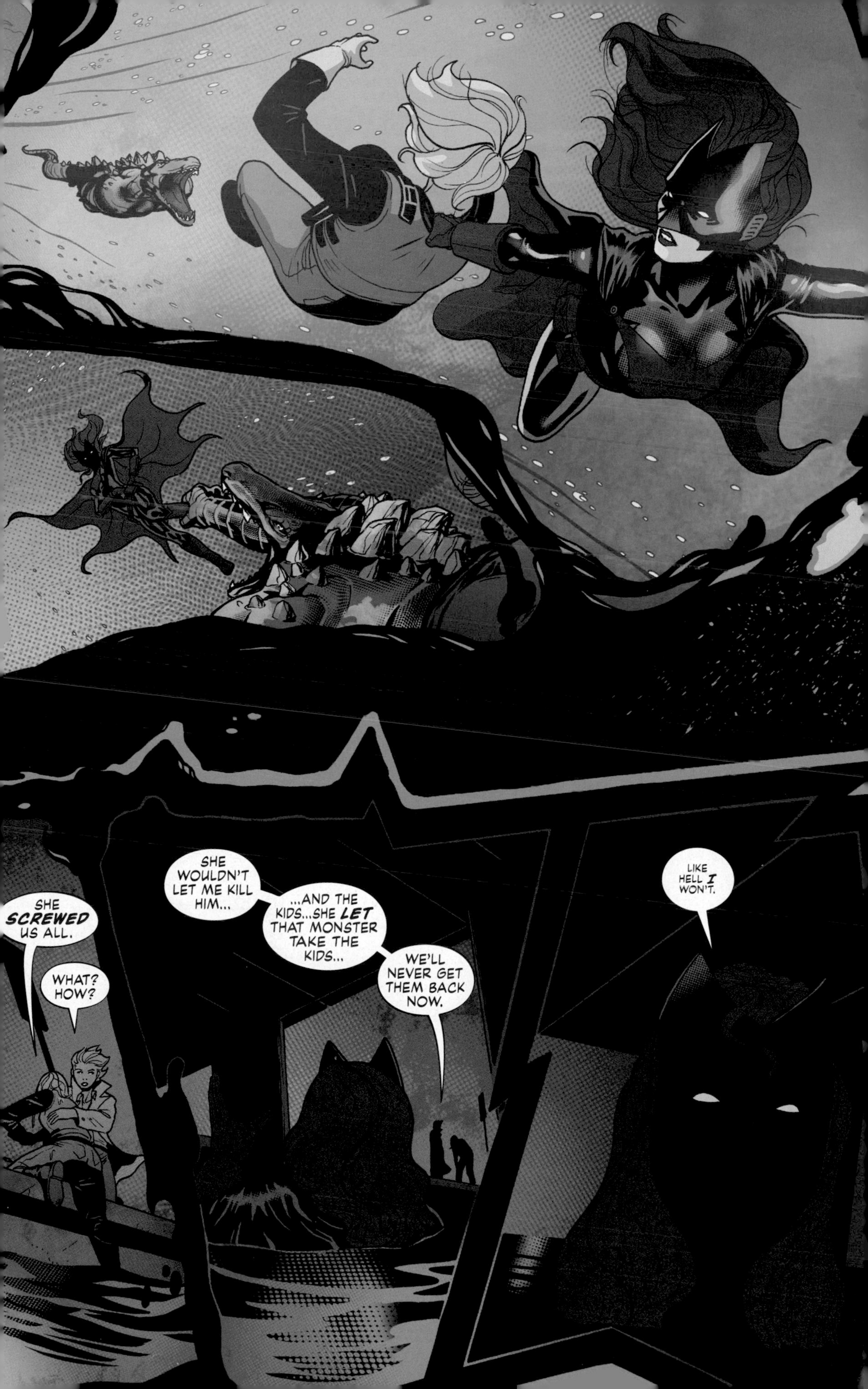
SHE SCREWED US ALL.
WHAT? HOW?
SHE WOULDN'T LET ME KILL HIM...
...AND THE KIDS...SHE LET THAT MONSTER TAKE THE KIDS...
WE'LL NEVER GET THEM BACK NOW.
LIKE HELL I WON'T.

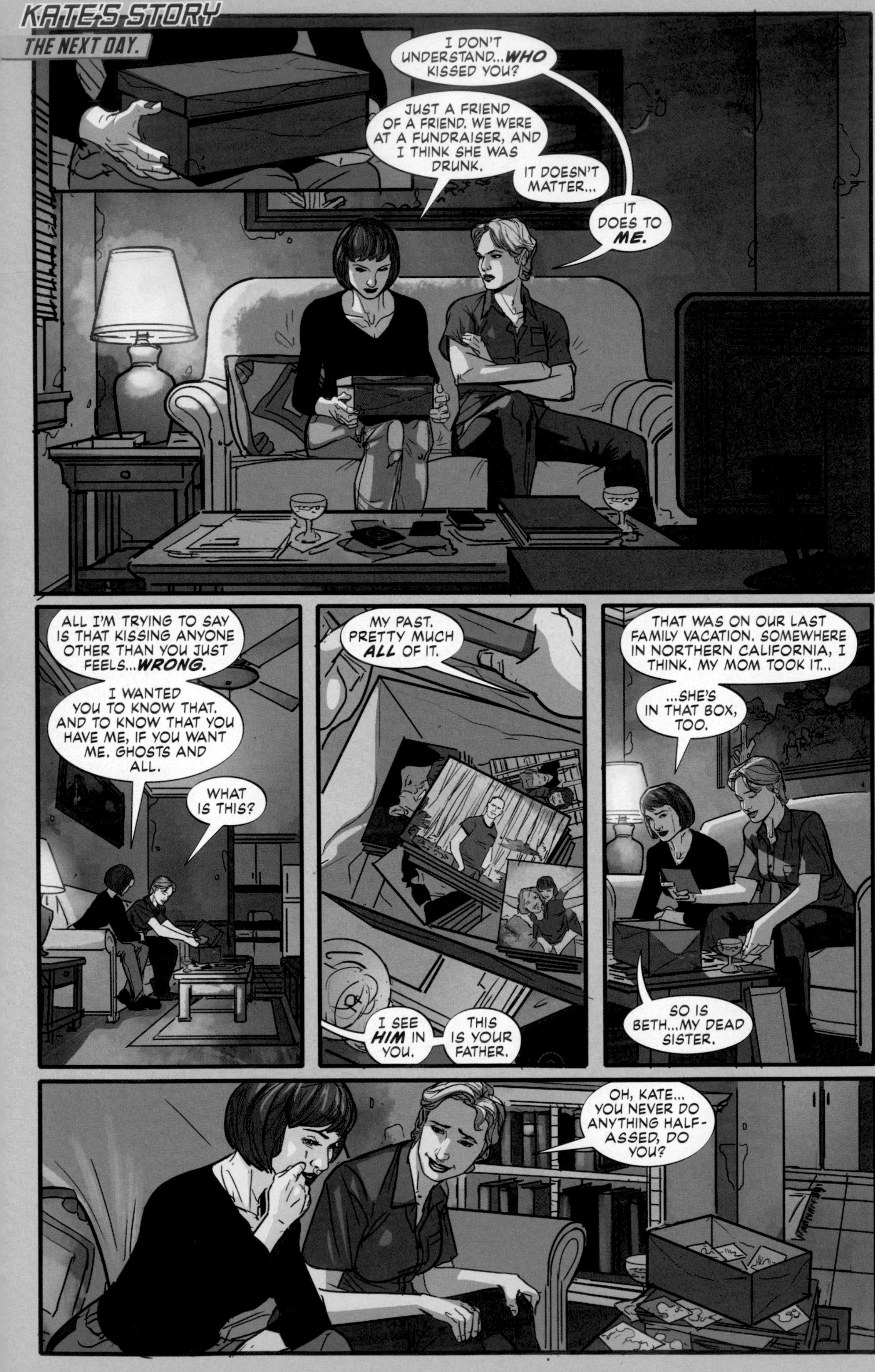
KATE'S STORY
THE NEXT DAY.
I DON'T UNDERSTAND...WHO KISSED YOU?
JUST A FRIEND OF A FRIEND. WE WERE AT A FUNDRAISER, AND I THINK SHE WAS DRUNK.
IT DOESN'T MATTER...
IT DOES TO ME.
ALL I'M TRYING TO SAY IS THAT KISSING ANYONE OTHER THAN YOU JUST FEELS...WRONG.
I WANTED YOU TO KNOW THAT. AND TO KNOW THAT YOU HAVE ME, IF YOU WANT ME. GHOSTS AND ALL.
WHAT IS THIS?
MY PAST. PRETTY MUCH ALL OF IT.
THIS IS YOUR FATHER.
I SEE HIM IN YOU.
THAT WAS ON OUR LAST FAMILY VACATION. SOMEWHERE IN NORTHERN CALIFORNIA, I THINK. MY MOM TOOK IT...
...SHE'S IN THAT BOX, TOO.
SO IS BETH...MY DEAD SISTER.
OH, KATE... YOU NEVER DO ANYTHING HALF-ASSED, DO YOU?

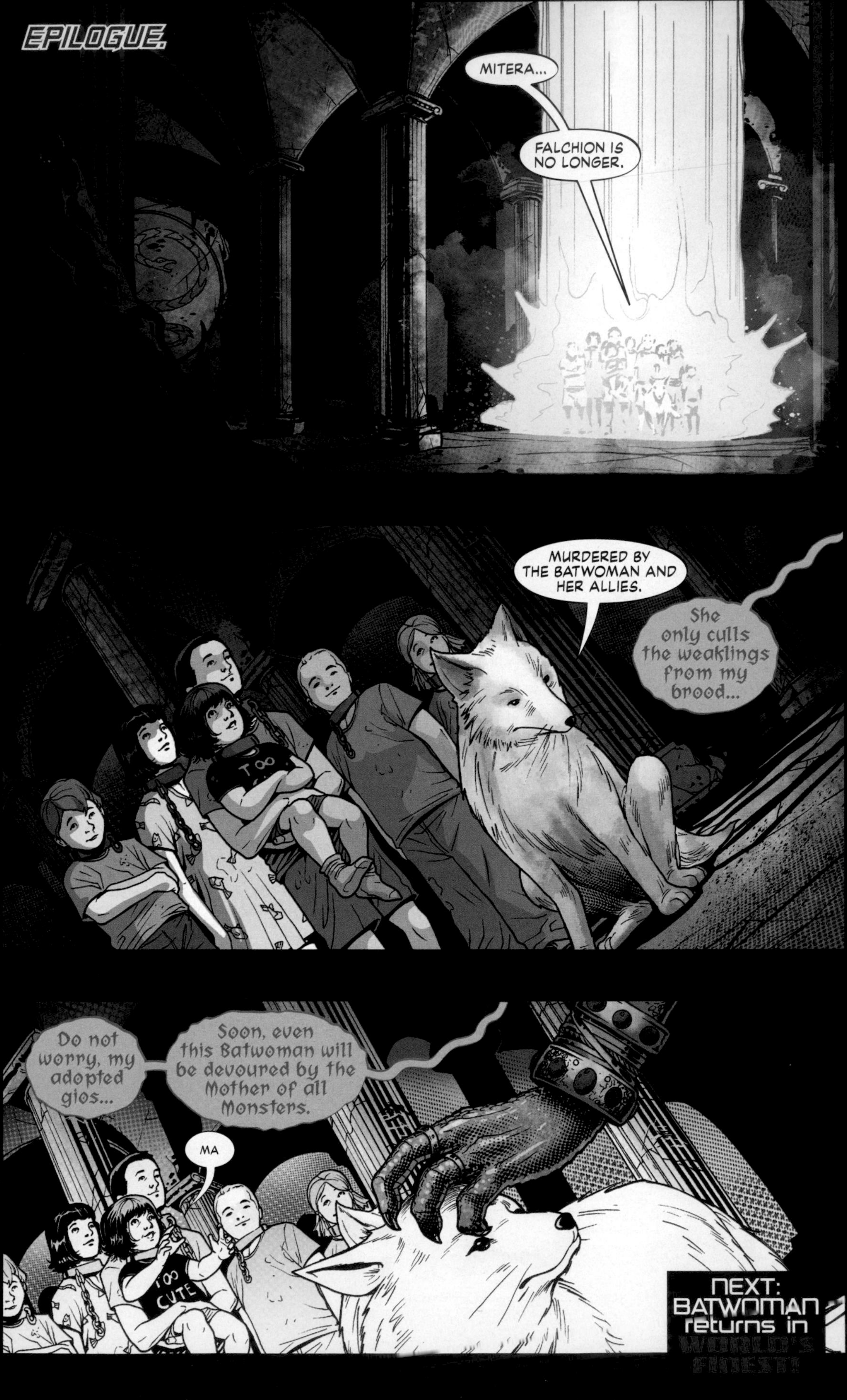
EPILOGUE.
MITERA...
FALCHION IS NO LONGER.
MURDERED BY THE BATWOMAN AND HER ALLIES.
She only culls the weaklings from my brood...
Do not worry, my adopted gios...
Soon, even this Batwoman will be devoured by the Mother of all Monsters.
MA
TOO CUTE
NEXT: BATWOMAN returns in

BATWOMAN

ART BY TREVOR McCARTHY SCRIPT BY J.H. WILLIAMS III & W. HADEN BLACKMAN

Script excerpt from Batwoman #9.

PAGE SIXTEEN (6 Panels)

Panel 1. Kate's hand holding a pair of high-heeled shoes that match her gown. We're now back at the gala that Falchion was holding, the same one from earlier in the issue. But now it's all from Kate's point of view, as we get to see where she was when Maggie was looking for her.

1-CAP:
Kate's story.

2-CAP:
Three nights ago.

3-KATE (OP):
It's not here.

Panel 2. Big panel. We're in Falchion's massive bedroom. There's a big four-poster bed against one wall, with serpents carved into the posts. Kate is standing near a desk with a laptop on it, looking at the screen intently. She looks gorgeous, but is definitely playing the part of the socialite, in the same evening gown with bare shoulders and jewelry as you drew in the ballroom scene earlier in this issue, at the gala on the yacht. She's holding her high heels, and her posture here is all business. Sune is reclining on the bed behind her, not necessarily seductive, but relaxed as she is removing the Golden mask she was wearing in previous panels. She is also dressed as seen before, all in black. There's a big ornately carved chest at the foot of the bed.

4-KATE:
The D.E.O. *data worm* punched through every security protocol and there are no maps, no schematics, no blueprints.

Panel 3. Sune, sitting up, looking around the room, she's setting her mask on the bedding with one hand. And pulling a thin lockpick from her hair with the other. We can see how beautiful she actually is here, as her long black hair falls softly around her shoulders.

5-SUNE:
Perhaps we're searching through the wrong *chest*...

Panel 4. Sune has dropped to a knee in front of the chest and is already working on the lock. Kate has come up behind her.

6-KATE:
Do we have *time* to look through his *luggage?*

7-SUNE:
The guards are of no concern. They believe that five defensive *runes*, two fingerprint access doors and three laser tripwires will do the *job*.

8-KATE:
Right. I still want to know how you *deactivated* those runes.

Panel 5. Sune, both hands on the chest now, stopping for a moment. She is hanging her head, looking away from Kate – the most vulnerable we've seen her, a little like a victim here. If we can see any details of the chest here it of course has snake designs carved into it, and looks very old.

9-SUNE:
Falchion *forced* me to learn many counter spells. Among *other* things.

Panel 6. Kate is kneeling now too, right next to Sune. She has already taken over on the lock.

10-KATE:
Here, let *me* try.

11-KATE:
How did you fall in with Medusa?

PAGE SEVENTEEN (7 Panels)

Most of the panels on this page should be from basically the foot of the bed, looking over the front of the chest at Sune and Kate, kneeling side-by-side in front of the chest.

Panel 1. Sune. She hasn't moved much, but she's looking at Kate next to her, eyes shimmering. Again we can see how beautiful she is, and there seems to be a vulnerable warmth to her gaze here. Nothing outright seductive (yet), but still somehow inviting.

1-SUNE:
My *brother*. He promised me to Falchion, and became his *lieutenant* in exchange.

2-SUNE:
When Falchion realized that I had certain *skills* valuable beyond this room, he sent me into the field.

Panel 2. A small panel inset into the next, larger panel 3. Here, we just see Kate's hands as she fusses with the lock, using the pick here. We can see that the lock is ornate and built into the chest itself – it's not a padlock or anything like that. It has an old-fashioned keyhole.

3-KATE:
Is *that* why you're helping us? *Revenge?*

Panel 3. Kate is still looking at the lock, but Sune is looking at Kate, and has a hand on her shoulder. There is a subtle earnestness from her here, but not overplayed.

4-SUNE:
In part. But I also know that anyone caught in Medusa's *coils* will someday be crushed.

5-KATE (small, sort of to herself):
..damn this lock is squirrely...

6-KATE:
Well, by joining the D.E.O., you're probably just trading in *one* snake for another.

7-SUNE:
I do not want to be allied with that Cameron Chase, *or* her D.E.O.

Panel 4. Sune has hands on both of Kate's shoulders now. It could either be a gesture signifying that they are comrades, or she could be moving in for a kiss... We will never know. Kate is a little taken aback, looking at her. But Sune does seem to have an unspoken ulterior motive beyond the words she is saying, it's intimate enough. Her beauty can't be helped but be noticed by Kate.

8-SUNE:
I want to be allied with *you*.

9-SFX (OP, make sure this falls *after* the above dialogue): KLICK

Panel 5. Almost identical to Panel 4. The two are still looking at each other. Kate hasn't responded, her mouth is still open slightly. Sune is smiling, letting her words sink in.

10-KATE:
I... think I got it.

11-SUNE:
Yes.

Panel 6. The chest is now unlocked and its lid is already open. Make sure we can see the open chest here but not everything in it, so the storytelling is clear. Kate has pulled a large rolled parchment from the chest and has already mostly unrolled it with two hands. The "camera" should be positioned so that we can see her face – she's grinning.

12-KATE:
Huh. How about that? An analog crime lord...

13-SUNE:
That is it!

Panel 7. Looking over their shoulders as they study an intricately hand-drawn blueprint for Falchion's underwater lair, indicating the small travel tube that runs from the bottom of the yacht to the submerged lair/vessel deeper in the waters below. Refer to previous descriptions of this in the artist notes at the beginning of the script, to enhance what you do here for the "blue print" schematic. The ink is rust red, like it's been drawn in blood, there is also a blood red pentagram sort of placed like a water mark off to one corner, and the parchment itself is yellowed and frayed along the edges. Sune has a hand on the small of Kate's back.

14-KATE:
Good. I'll snap a few pictures.

15-KATE:
Then I *need* to get back to the party before I'm missed.

16-SUNE:
Of course.

PAGE EIGHTEEN & NINETEEN (12 Panels)

The design layout for this spread matches the layout concept for the spread on Pages 4 & 5: Blackness and very fine wavy panel borderlines, creating oddly shaped panels that seem organic, unstructured. But here, as the action will be removing the shadow-bomb stuff, the panel shapes slowly morph into standard shaped panels as the spread moves along. The progression of this effect should be in line with the panel descriptions, timing the dissipation of the murky shadow fx so that by the end of the scene, we are completely back to normal square-shaped panels for the last few images of the spread.

Panel 1. Sune and Batwoman are holding hands. The darkness is complete around their hands, the Shadowland bombs still in effect from where we left off earlier.

1-CAP:
Batwoman's Story.

2-CAP:
Now.

3-BATWOMAN (OP) (whisper):
This way.

Panel 2. Pan out to show Sune and Batwoman in darkness. Batwoman is leading Sune over some large rubble in the nearly-destroyed lair. Both are still wearing their funky goggles from the beginning, and the darkness is thick behind them. Batwoman is still holding Sune's hand, but now we can see it's because she's helping her clamber over the chunks of a fallen pillar or statue or machinery or whatever – it's not a romantic stroll. In her free hand, Sune still has her bow. (Based on this, it's key that we see large debris at the opening sequence to this issue.)

NO COPY

Panel 3. They have descended the other side of the rubble. Batwoman is kneeling next to a huge hulking form – the still unconscious Mutant Killer Croc, though only partially visible. He's so large and the darkness is so thick that we can only see his back and shoulders, as Batwoman and Sune are almost on top of him. She is touching him, checking his vital signs.

4-BATWOMAN (whisper):
Killer Croc. Still down.

5-BATWOMAN (whisper):
No sign of the other *freakjobs*. That would *suck* in this blackout...

6-SUNE:
Falchion is *still* here. I can *feel* him.

Panel 4. Falchion bursts from the darkness. His blade is glowing golden light as it becomes a magical tool to fight the fx of the shadow-stuff. He's slashing downward – as he does so, the sword literally cuts through the darkness as if it were cloth, so we can start to see a bit of the backgrounds of the lair behind Falchion as he swings. The Shadowland darkness dissipates when the glowing blade touches it, so we can start to see a bit of the backgrounds of the lair behind Falchion as he swings. He still has arrows sticking out of him everywhere, blue blood running from the punctures -- he looks spattered with the stuff. As he lurches toward us, it's almost frightening, like a startle scene in a suspense thriller.

7-FALCHION (very large):
And I can always see you, slattern!

Panel 5. Falchion is swinging at Sune. Again, the darkness is being rent apart, revealing more the room's details beyond. Batwoman is shoving or pulling Sune out of the way, but the blade still connects with Sune's side.

8-BATWOMAN (large):
Sune!

9-SUNE (large):
Aaagh!

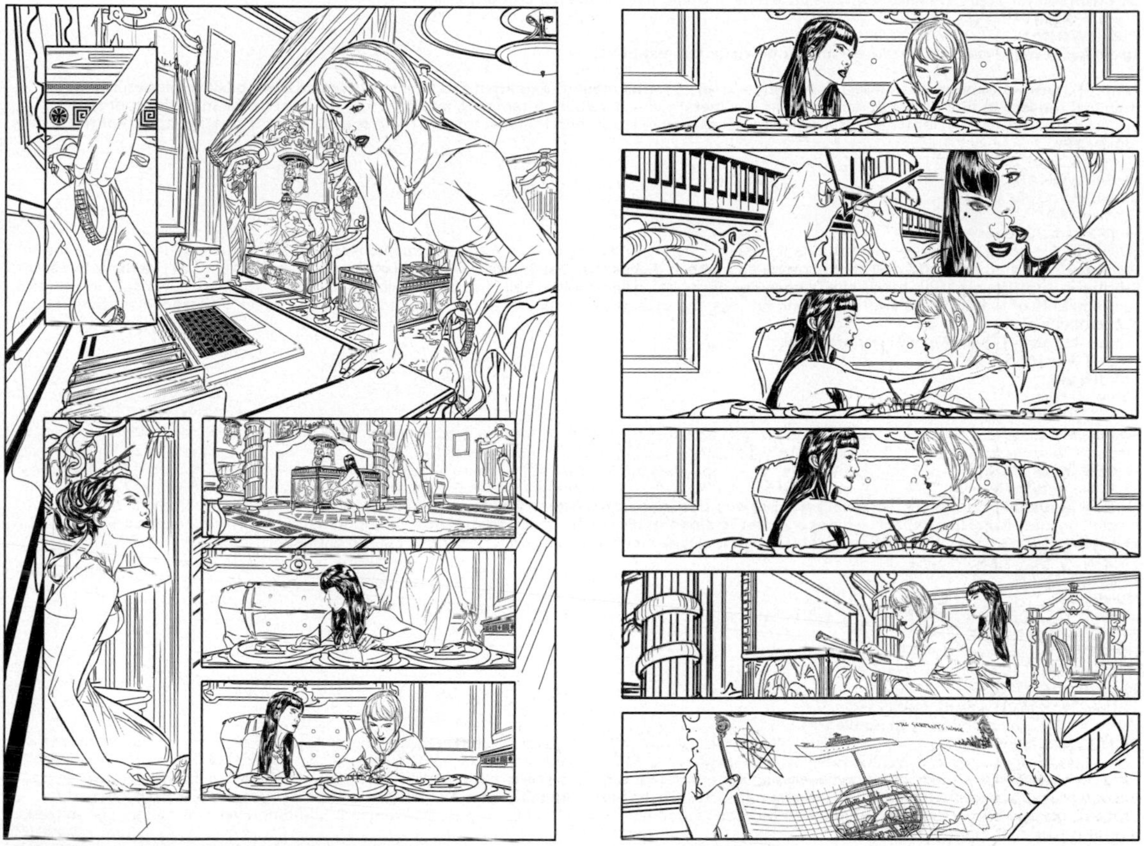
THE SERPENT'S WAKE

Black and white art from Batwoman #9 pages 16-17 (above) and 18-19 (below).

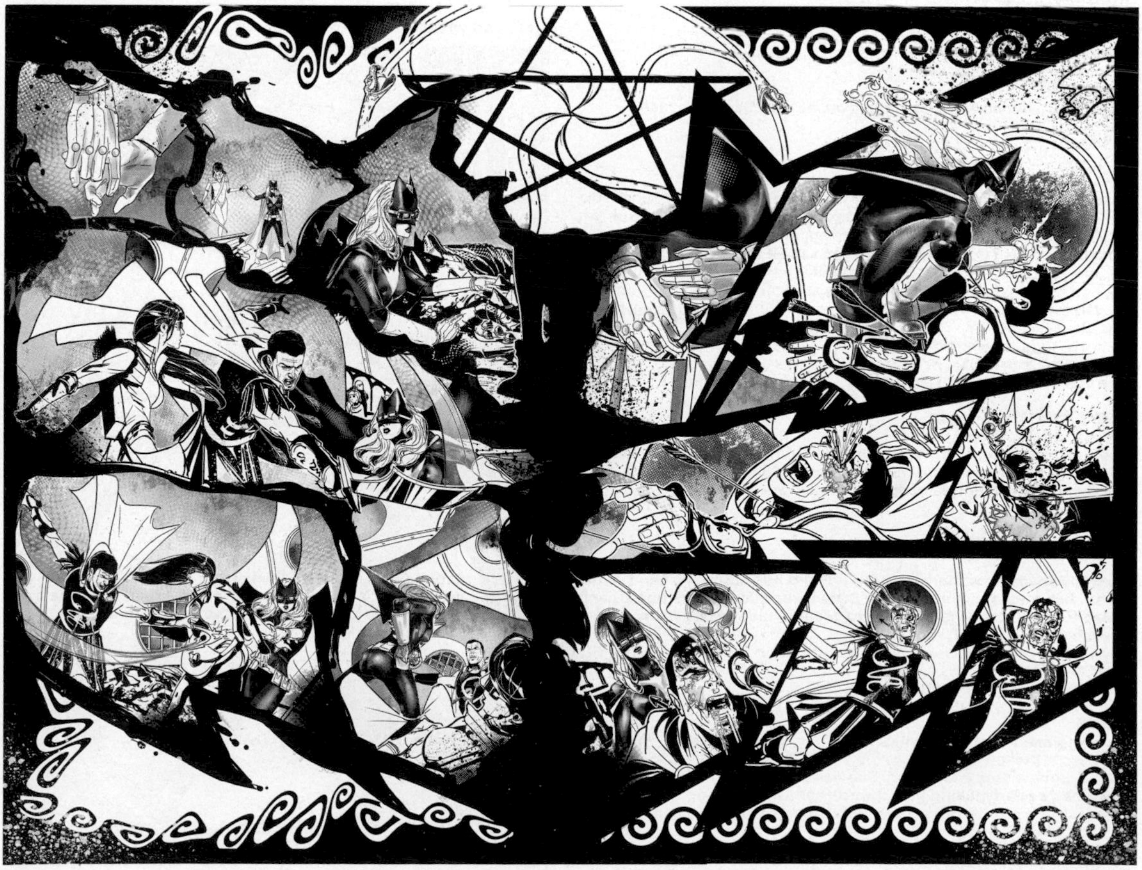

Panel 6. Sune is on the ground, clutching her side. Batwoman is facing Falchion, pissed. She's pulling something out of her belt again. This has to be clear for storytelling here. More of the darkness has been dispelled or is being sliced open by Falchion's blade.

10-FALCHION:
Do not *weep* for Sune. We have *both* misjudged her. I would have made her a *goddess*...

11-BATWOMAN:
You think you're a *god* just because you look down on the rest of us?

Panel 7. Close-up Batwoman's fingertips holding a small, pointed explosive device used for blasting open locks or door hinges. No bigger than half the length of a pen or pencil. One end is a metal spike, suitable for ramming into concrete or other dense material in order to mount the explosive. The other end is a small, round explosive laced with thin electrodes. There is a little tiny activation light that the comes to life here.

12-BATWOMAN:
Because you *use* us?

13-SFX (small): deet

Panel 8. Batwoman has leapt into the air, propelling herself higher than Falchion's head, and is ramming the spike-end of the explosive into Falchion's eye. She has both hands clutched as she drives the device home. Falchion is stumbling backwards, stunned, surprised. We should see remnants of the darkness swirling around his legs, but otherwise it's mostly gone. This shot needs to convey intense violent action on Batwoman's part.

14-BATWOMAN:
Enslave us?

15-FALCHION:
Aaaaaagh!

16-SFX (larger): DEET!

Panel 9. Batwoman is shoving Falchion's head to one side, away from her, as the device explodes. The explosion looks like it is blowing out a small portion of Falchion's face -- his eye socket and part of his cheek. It's clearly doing disfiguring damage to his face, but it's still small enough that Batwoman isn't getting hurt by it, and it clearly won't kill Falchion, just serious painful damage.

17-BATWOMAN:
Murder us?

18-FALCHION (large):
Urk!

19-SFX (larger): DEE---

20-SFX (directly connecting to above sfx):
POMF!

Panel 10. Falchion has dropped to one knee, clutching at his face. Smoke seeps through his fingers, and the area around his eye socket is blackened and scorched. His flesh around this portion of his face is mottled, burned, hamburger. All of his other wounds from the various arrow strikes are still present and seem even more profound here – pouring blue blood. Batwoman is standing over him, tough, committed, a boot on his shoulder.

21-FALCHION:
Nnfff...

22-BATWOMAN:
Try looking *down* on us *now*.

Panel 11. Batwoman kicks Falchion over, he clutches at his face.

23-FALCHION:
Unnngh...

Panel 12. Pull back into an aerial shot, looking down at Falchion on his back. We can see about three-quarters of his body. He looks up at nothing with his one good eye swimming, clutching with his hands or hand at the other eye. Again, we can see all of his wounds here – he looks defeated, broken, arrows still embedded in his body, blood leaking from everywhere. Blue blood is splattered across the floor, on the walls and debris, and pools of blood are forming around his body. He is clearly in agony.

24-FALCHION (small):
Have I failed you Mother?

PAGE TWENTY (3 Panels)

Panel 1. Sune, trying to roll over. She's bleeding badly, holding her side. We can see Batwoman's boots in the frame. Sune has ripped off the goggles, and they dangle in one hand.

1-BATWOMAN:
Sune. Hang on.

Panel 2. Batwoman at her side now, helping her sit up. We can see that she too has removed her goggles. Sune is reaching up, putting a hand on Batwoman's cheek. It's bloody and leaves blood streaks on Batwoman's mask and skin.

2-BATWOMAN:
D.E.O. should be here soon.

3-SUNE:
You saved *me*.

Panel 3. Sune kisses Batwoman. She has one hand on the back of Batwoman's head, pulling her towards her as she lifts up a bit to deliver the kiss. Her eyes are closed, but Batwoman's are wide open.

4-NEXT:
Hidden Faces Revealed

Black and white art from Batwoman #9 page 20.